A Place-Based Guide to Wonder

Matthew Fogarty

ISBN: 978-0-9998661-0-8 (paperback)
ISBN: 978-0-9998661-1-5 (e-book)

This book is intended to be educational and informative. The author and publisher disclaim any responsibility for any liability, loss or risk that may be associated with the application of any of the contents of the book.

Art Credits

Cover Art and Introduction Art: Trillium Swanson
Painting in the beginning of *The Wonder in Wander* chapter: Barbara Hauck

Poetry Credits

Poem "Lead" from *New and Selected Poems* by Mary Oliver, published by Beacon
 Press Boston. Copyright ©2005 by Mary Oliver, reprinted by permission
 of The Charlotte Sheedy Literary Agency Inc.
Poem "The Return" by Geneen Marie Haugen, reprinted by permission
 of the author.

Major Contributors

Josh Lane, *ConsciousNature.net*
Abe Lloyd, *abe@cascadianfood.net* and *cascadianfood.net*
Ben Greené, *www.survivalprayer.com*

Prepress specialist, design and typography: Kathleen R. Weisel, *weiselcreative.com*

Privacy Note

To protect privacy, the names of all clients have been changed and any identifying features obscured.

A Rainbow Crow book

Rainbow Crow

Thanksgiving

No book could possibly be the fruit of one individual mind. The web of connections that craft such a thing spread through space and time in befuddling dimensions. Below is a tiny list of some of those who dedicated so much of their precious living to fertilize this work and tend to our future generations. As you read the names, I encourage you to pay attention to the spaces around them and imagine all the invisible and unnamed people, places, and beings that came together to create the moments that created this work.

To all those unnamed, I first give thanks.

To those people named here: If I could write this easily in a circle, I would. There is no hierarchy, no order to the list. Within your name is embedded a deep spirit-fire of love for you. You are precious to us, and I thank you for your being:

Terrence Healey

Olsen Creek

Jon Young

Claudia Bernal

Matia Zucchini

My family

Naropa University

Wilderness Awareness School

Dinah Grossman

Matia Jones

Chris Byrd

Cody Bebee

Jessica Gifford

The Salish Sea

Aimee Frazier

Mud Bay

Wild Whatcom

Drew Butler

Janet Trinkhaus

Tai Hazard

Cascadia

Joan Lennox

Rick Claffey

Steve Keller

Greg Schayes

David Strich

Mike McKenzie

The Presence Studio Community

Abe Lloyd
Katrina Poppe
Kelley Garrison
Mark Dooley
All the mentoring families
The members of Four Shields
The Racoons on Sehome Hill
The Cascadia Naturalist
Association
Ben Greené
Trillium Swanson
The Nooksack River
All my Mentees and Clients
Tom Dorsett
Price Tsai

Dan Crescenzo
Cam Cameron
Mary Reichert
The Salish Peoples
The Haudenosaunee Confederacy
The many other cultures named in
this book
Odette Scott
Shore Charnoe
Josh Uitoff
Chris Quiseng
Wendy Bailey
Lauren Marziliano
Jenny Macke
Larry Hobbs

Contents

Introduction

This book is a wonder about what happens when we are connected to the Earth. It is an invitation for us to wonder and wander together through storytelling, psychology, memoir, interviews, and practices. What happens in our minds and our bodies when we experience primal competency with the wilderness? How does this process take place? What happens when we identify as Earth?

This book is a meditation on the World as it is now, and the relationship of the World and the human spirit.

This book has more questions than answers, but it is the questioning that crafts the story.

Now, let us craft story together.

Of Place and Wonder

Right now, just outside, a wind travels in a lush, transforming geometry around the houses, through prickles in the hedges, gushing above the treetops, and eddying in the furrows of rocky recesses. In the nearest woods, a black-tailed deer smells the scented air as she pushes her front left hoof into the leaf-littered loam. She carves a shape that, if you read it, will tell you a story of that moment. A moth in the corner of a room dapples the windless wall with the shapes and colors of hemlock bark. A douglas fir branch bends in a gust, causing the eastern grey squirrel upon it to make flash adjustments to his brilliant charge along the thinning strip of brown, moments before his leap fifty feet above the ground to the next bending branch. A human child grabs a dandelion seed pod and blows on it, eyes sparkling joy as she laughs at the great flow of fluff before her. Right now, a mustard seed nestles itself in the cracks of nearby concrete, slumbering darker than any hibernating bear. Waiting and willing with its promise of a future generation.

Listen.

There is a calling right now. In every direction, there is a deep and ancient calling in no human tongue. It is a calling only understood beneath the brain and even the heart—deeply within the bones. A language that is so ever-present that you often forget that it is there, cease to hear it for it always being there. It is a sensation, a tugging, that is becoming you. You know this, even if the bright waking part of your consciousness claims amnesia. You know this.

Listen. A stellars jay lets out her shrill raspy cry. Calls to you to journey. Without leaving the yard or the park or even your place by the window. The cry enters homes, penetrates the hum of electricity and the competing sound waves of machinery. Shrill and demanding. Calling.

The flower of a dead nettle holds a cosmos for you to discover—to nearly lose yourself in.

Tracks of the mink lay like a sentence along a stream bank.

Mold in the shower whispers stories of tiny ecologies—worlds so small you might forget they exist.

A fungus has found its place in the natural world on your very skin.

Fruit in your fridge echoes songs of a summer's journey of sun and wind and water on its great, deeply rooted mother.

This is happening now. Every part of it playing with every other part; playing the grand orchestra of now. Every part, in some way, creating your walls, your breath, your very thoughts. So subtle at times, you may even delude yourself into thinking it is not true, not a part of you or of your now. But it is. It is now. It is calling ever and it will keep calling. Listen.

Outside of the walls of buildings something ridiculous is happening. Some spastic chipmunk with a whacky personality rummages incessantly through the top layer of the forest, obviously harrying his ground-feeding bird companions and sending ludicrous waves of annoyance through the underbrush. He calls you to witness this comedy.

The sky holds patterns that foretell some future hard rain that will call you to ferociously show up. To remember your wild commitment to life.

Mysterious sounds in the bushes await your passing to call you to remember your primal self. Will call your heart to pump faster and your breath to pick up as your eyes dart toward the tangle of green.

Right now a spotted towhee is calling you to remember the living child within you and your birthright of play. Throwing a hide and seek gauntlet before you.

The canopy is calling you to lay down and stare above you. To breathe the fine chemicals that ease your stress and lower your blood pressure, that make your mind a soft thing that can, if only for a moment, forget time and self.

Seed pods are expressing every shape, reminding you of the infinite variation of beauty and of future possibility. Raccoons wander the night, through gardens, over driveways, and in the back yards, exploring a universe of touch with the most sensitive hands in the animal kingdom. A dark mysterious beckoning is rising from the underbrush, beneath salmonberries and fringecup. In this underworld, the small inhuman hands of a deer mouse feverishly grip a recently won hazelnut just as the clever eyes and quick mouth of a weasel approach through the shadows undetected. A mythic meeting of two full individual lives lived with all the gusto and vibrancy possible until some drama of death—jaws or hunger—will end them.

Coyotes are watching you with a keen intelligence that challenges every assumption that your primate intelligence oppresses onto the world.

The skeleton of a glaucous-winged gull at the base of an eagle's nest calls you to contemplate death and to understand without abstraction the dialect of living.

Right now, the child in you is alive and vibrant. Right now, even if all of your life you have been walled and boxed and dirtlessly manicured, a deep part of you is awake and longs for your hands on the low limb of the bigleaf maple. The limb calls to that part of you to grip, to feel its roughness and your rugged touch. Your hands alive with a need to grip and hold yourself. The limb and you teaching you how to have an undomesticated caring for yourself. The bigleaf arm is there now offering to teach you more about what it is to be supported, how to lift yourself up, and how to clearly measure the strength of the object of your dependence.

Right now we are all happening together. We are moving and being moved by one another. Mycelium beneath us shunt nutrients to parts of the forest that need them most—like a vital organ of an even greater organism. Water moves through every living being and carves every scrap of landscape. Children are covering, are creating the entire Earth.

Children wander and wonder with young eyes, curious paws, or untried feather. Sprouts push courageously. Inside worlds of eggs little beings wiggle with all the might they can muster. The future unfolding.

This is Place.

You know, in your deepest being, that right now, you are being called to realize your participation. You are being called to your wholeness, your birthright, and the voices calling are as plentiful as the stars. They are above you, below you, outward in all directions, and calling from inside your living body. Calling you to be conscious of what and who you actively are a part of and from which you can never be removed. You, as the breathing of Place. You, as the thinking of Place. You are Place. Every being around you is Place.

Place.

This book is a field guide of sorts. Not a field guide of the constituent parts of a particular place. Not a list of beings and their habits or a study of the movements of lands and waters. It is a field guide to the wonder within a place. Wonder is what happens when the heart talks to mystery. Wonder is what happens when we forget ourselves enough to behold and be held by the world. Wonder arises when we have enough courage to move through the pain and the overly active intellect and we can love regardless of impermanence. Wonder is allowing ourselves to be in awe and unreservedly in love with the oak tree even as it falls. Wonder loves the tree as it is. And wonder wonders at the living ground that receives the body.

Wonder and Place are something to be remembered and learned and taught. Hence this field guide. We teach them to each other throughout a life time. We practice them especially when things get hard and what we love in this world may very well be lost. We do ourselves a great kindness and remind each other to wonder and to be Place. We come together and nudge each other into courage so that we don't forget the primal art of living. We allow ourselves a togetherness. In this way, the hurt we feel can be held. From this togetherness emerges unfathomable possibilities.

This book carries a naturalist's eye for observation—searching for the truth as it is, not as we would like it to be. As a good naturalist does, this book considers the world from many angles and works to boldly set aside conventions and assumptions in the search for a true telling. You, the reader, are the other half of this book. As it enters the wilderness of your mind it will morph and shift and become a unique landscape with new thoughts. You bring to this book the sum of your experience. You and this book will together create a new world, and you will share this with others in your own unique way. In a sense, a book dies as soon as it is written, and each pair of eyes that relates to the text births a new story.

One of the perspectives used in this book is the scientific perspective. The science used here is as accurate as I could find at the time that I wrote it. Yet science is always changing and is always contentious. That is the nature of good science. So I suggest investigating any shifts in knowledge that have occurred since the writing, then asking yourself how this shifts the big story. It is also worth noting that we are working with general scientific concepts that have arisen from concentrated observation of specific and very detailed processes. If you are curious about a piece of research or theory in this book, I suggest digging deeply into it and learning more specifically how it works and how it fits. This is not a book of explanations. It is a constellation of experience and thoughts that are meant to inspire you and others to ask questions and to engage more deeply with Place and wonder. The job is wonder and the focus is on us with Place. If you learn more and want to share, write about it or teach it or create art around it. Try ways of *becoming* what you have learned and share those experiences as well.

This book is like a good wander; it roams through many different landscapes. The unexpected pops up and we linger with it for a while before we stroll onward. It is written to you and to us as a whole. It is a conversation and it will flow as such. Sometimes personal reflections. Sometimes delving into the world of psychology. Sometimes words that seek a poetry and teachings older than the loam. Sometimes suggestions and practices. Sometimes a simple guide. Sometimes just a good story to help fertilize the soil of our beings. Sometimes questions for all of us to hold. It is a book for you, for us, to hold near our hearts and to feel in our feet. This book is a song calling us into thinking, expressing, and being our mad aliveness and courageous awareness as we propel our generations forward. Questions for all of us to hold and to share and to boldly say *yes* to.

The Practice of Place

Time with plants reveals a truth: in order to grow up, you have to grow down. No root means no stalk, no leaf, no seed. For people, growing down means practicing Place. Which begs a question: how does one practice where one is? The question is not about where so much as how and who.

So, let's start with a story of fear and mayhem.

Before working as a counselor, I spent years mentoring cohorts of youth through outdoor explorations in local parks. Each group had its own identity woven by the personalities of the members, their shared experiences, and their unique relationship with Place. Over time, a pinnacle moment would often serve to unite the group under the banner of a newly chosen group name. One such group had been together for about three years and still had the name that the mentors had arbitrarily given them when they first formed. Many times, a name had been proposed but it just didn't sit right with all the members. So they remained in name limbo.

This is not the story of how they got their name.

However, it leads in that direction.

On a hot and sunny summer day in the dry season of the Pacific Northwest, we had gathered for a summer outing. The mentors had heard stories of a "secret trail" that lead up a gentle mountainside toward a much-loved community lake. Our job, as a group, was to use the paltry directions we got from a directionally challenged friend and find this little-known cutoff. This was a typical outing. We rarely did anything straightforward, and the mentors were just as interested in trying something new as the kids were. So, we put our tracking skills to the test and started checking out any game trail that looked like it might have human traffic. After a few false leads, we found our quarry and started triumphantly marching along the thin trail, admiring the balmy canopy and the gentle summer buzz of insects.

I would estimate that we went two hundred yards. Maybe two hundred and fifty. The screaming began. Then the running and screaming. I distinctly remember seeing boys running full speed up the trail, swatting the air. One finally shouted a word, "bees!" (To be fair to the wasps, they weren't bees, but the sting felt just as bad if not worse.) The boy who was in the front was tearing up a suddenly steep section. Others had eddied in an opening behind a bigleaf maple and were scanning the air around them frantically. I was stuck with four people on the other end of the now visible swarm of wasps. The other mentors and I called out for the boys to gather on the trail a safe distance from the wasps. The ones with me were to follow as I walked a trail through the brush that gave a wide berth to that swarm of angry insects.

We were successful at that point. Our group of bushwhackers made it unstung to our companions and I got a chance to assess the situation fully. One of the mentors was treating a boy who had been stung four times. He was crying but showed no signs of a severe reaction. Another boy got stung once and was proudly displaying his war wound to anyone who wanted to see. A third boy had not been stung at all but had gone completely pale with a thin layer of sweat on his face. His hands clutched the rock he was sitting on. He looked terrible. I checked in with him to make sure he hadn't been stung. He could barely look at me. His breath was rapid. All he could say was, "I have a phobia of bees."

Then the other thing happened. It was wasps. Again. (Not bees—I kept telling these guys the difference but in the heat of the moment it's always "bees.") Someone shouted, "Bees!!!" I looked up the trail and again saw the same kid who had already been stung four times running further down the trail with a mentor running right behind him. He was flailing his arms in the air, shouting, "Bees!"

There is a moment, even in the most extreme situations, where time seems to pause. When the whole situation seems so stupidly improbable that the mind just pauses everything for a second as if to say, *really?* to life.

"Really?" I said as I watched them run down the trail and the rest of the group spin into panic. Lo and behold another nest had been kicked up and wasps were swarming the trail. And again, we were divided.

I shouted directions to the boys in front of me, guiding them to cut off the side of the trail and head toward the others, keeping a safe distance from this second swarm of wasps. I looked down in front of me and saw Evan turn eggshell white while white-knuckling his rock. He was so stiff that if I pushed him over I bet he would have tumbled down the hill with his body locked in that seated position. I heard some shouting from up above as kids started to meet with the other group. "Evan," I said as I got down to his eye level, "I know this is scary, but I need you to move right now. I want to get us together with the rest of the group in a safe place. Can you move for me, Evan?" Evan's eyes darted toward me, then shifted right back to stare at the ground. "No," he whispered. His body shook. "No," he said again.

"Evan. Evan. Can you look at me?" I got his eyes. "I know you have a fear of bees…"

At this point Evan exploded. His eyes got huge in their sockets and he shouted as loudly as his fear-constricted throat would let him, "it's not a fear! It's a PHOBIA!" Considerations of the suggestive power of diagnosis paired with psyhcoeducation aside, Evan was very attached to the distinction between a fear and a phobia. And all gest aside, it was important to accept this and work with it in the moment.

"Okay Evan, I know you have a phobia of bees, and I know this is very scary for you right now. I need us to move toward a safer place. I need you to help. Can you stand up and walk with me in this direction?" I pointed away from the wasps and toward where the others now were.

At this point Evan really shut down. He started shaking his head back and forth and only said, "no. no. no."

I tried talking. I tried coaching his breath. But Evan was stuck.

Another kid came scrambling over via the new side route and relayed a message: the kid who had been stung four times had now been stung six but was doing fine. The rest of the group was calming down. He asked if we need anything. I simply said, "time."

I may never forget turning back and attending to Evan in that moment. The only way I can describe it is that he had become utterly inward. Like he wasn't even present and he was lost somewhere in some dark scary corner of his own agitated mind. I could sense him spiraling into this reinforcing pattern of retreating further and further into the fear. It's a cliché, but it truly was like that same force that draws a moth to a flame. If you can bust through the cliché and actually see that, you will know what I mean.

I got down in front of him and positioned myself so he had to see my eyes. He was so inward that he didn't even seem to register my presence. He was rocking back and forth a little and saying, "no. no. no."

"Evan," I said, with a directive voice. "Evan. Look at me." His eyes came into focus and we saw each other. It was like looking at a boy who had fallen down into a well. He was distant, and the walls of fear surrounded him, but we could still see each other. There was still light. I did not know what to say, so I opened my mouth and let inspiration do the rest.

"*Where are you?*" He tried to move his eyes away from me. "no," he said.

"Evan, I need you to look at me." He met me. "*Where are you?*"

He shook his head.

"Evan. Where are you?" He gritted his teeth and then said, "I'm here."

I kept a firm gaze, holding him. "Yes."

"But I don't want to be."

"But you are. You are here."

"Yea," he said and his whole body seemed to soften. "I'm here."

Evan and I got up and walked to the others.

Later that day, we actually kicked up one more swarm of wasps—the most encounters I have ever had in a single day. Evan worked, with the support of mentors and the group, to move past that swarm and to stay "here" the whole time. He did.

Since that outing, I find myself so curious about those moments with Evan and that question. I don't know what exactly compelled me to ask it, but I do suspect it was *the* question that was needed in that moment. *Here* is the only place where we have power. With Evan, we found where we were.

Then it became a journey of how and who.

From that day onward, this group seemed doomed. Profiled by any wasp that laid eyes on them. Over the years, they got more yellowjacket and bald-faced hornet stings than all the other groups combined.

Nearly two years later, the same group had gathered for an outing in a place that the locals call the Hundred Aker Woods. As mentors, we had decided that the groups needed a regular spot to visit every season so that we could get to know that one spot very well. Much like Winnie-the-Pooh's Hundred Aker Woods, we would build knowledge of the place through the stories we won there.

On that day, we were all in an adventurous mood, so we played a few games and then ended up exploring a fascinating tangle of vegetation hidden among walls of downed douglas firs. The whole group was crawling around on their hands and knees, ducking under logs and climbing on the remains of those great trees. By that time, these kids had a good idea of the plants and animals in their area, and had an especially good eye for wasps, bees, and hornets. We had spent a decent amount of time discussing these insects over the years and how to distinguish one from another. In recollection, it should not have even come as a surprise when I heard the all-too-familiar cry of "bees!" Wasps again. All around us.

At this point, the group moved with the efficiency of a well-trained sports team. I am still in awe of how quickly we got out of that particularly constricted and tangled area and made it to a clearing. These wasps were particularly tenacious and even managed to pursue us into the clearing, which made for some interesting maneuvers in the group.

I will save the play-by-play of our emergency response. Needless to say, we handled it quite well and when we were finally in the clear, we were left with one very unhappy member with about a dozen stings. The boys, at this point, knew what to do. They formed teams and ran down the trail looking for plantain. Plantain, either the broad leaf or the narrow leaf, is a wonderful little medicinal plant that often gets slandered as a "weed" and is well-acquainted with the lawnmower blade. It is grace incarnate when dealing with stings and burns in the field. Something magical happens when this little plant is chewed up and mixed with human saliva. The tissue regenerative properties in saliva mix with the medicinal properties of plantain and make a super poultice. The kids all knew this well.

Knowledge mixed with compassion and a call to action forms its own super-medicine. The kids knew the land well enough to know what to do. They were together throughout the years through the many wonders and challenges that the undomesticated world presented them. They had practiced compassion. They knew that they depended on each other.

So, we all sat around and embalmed our young friend in spitty green and watched as the welts subsided before our eyes. You may be skeptical of this detail, but I remember being struck by it. I could see the welts go down as the poultice was applied. When our friend was ready for it, we exited the woods and gathered on the park lawn at the edge so we could process the event and make some meaning out of it.

We formed a circle, had a little snack, and opened up conversation. Our first topic: the cougar and the deer.

A teacher of mine, who has dedicated his life to mentoring deep nature connection, talks about how the deer has the cougar's medicine. First, it is important to think of medicine in a very broad sense here—as something that promotes health and empowerment. With that in mind, the next question might be, how does a predator promote the health and empowerment of its prey? For an answer to that, we have to stretch our culturally trained fixation on individuality and think of each deer as an expression of a long lineage of being. So, too, with the cougar. Every deer that lives inherits the genetic expression of its ancestors. The story with all the choices and responses to the environment that each individual made is condensed into this embodied expression of "deer." Current genetic research yields some fascinating insights on how this works, but that is a side trail for you, reader, to wander if you wish. For now, we can simply think of the deer evolving over time. The cougar growing alongside. As the deer grows, it needs to evade the cougar so it may live long enough to raise young and continue the story. As the cougar grows, it must eat so it may live long enough to raise young and continue the story. As the cougar grows muscles and bones for quick bursts of running, the deer develops larger ears that can hear the quietest sounds. The cougar develops great muscles that control its foot enough to soften each step. The deer's ears grow larger, her sense of smell increases, she develops behaviors that pay attention to the birds and the other beings in the forest who may alert her to the cougar's presence. The cougar grows the ability to be still and unseen. The two back and forth in a constant dance of becoming. D.T. Suzuki would say that the mind and the body are not two; they are not one. So, too, with the cougar and the deer. The two grow into, around, and through one another. It is unfathomable to try to separate the deer from the cougar. Each pushing and pulling one another to greater ability so that each may survive and pass on the story to the next generation. It is a strange dance, this dance of medicine.

So, with this wonderful batch of young people, we considered this truth of being. After some time, someone spoke up and said, "I think it is time for a name." They looked up wasps in a field guide and found the Latin name: *Vespula*. Someone suggested "the Vespula Veterans." It was unanimous. They became the Vespula Veterans: humans with the wasp's medicine.

Strangely enough, after taking on this name, the group didn't seem to have many problems with wasps, bees, or hornets. The universe is a strange place and it is made mostly of dark matter—mystery incarnate. Who fully knows what is connected and how?

You will notice that time and again there was real danger for this group. Anyone trained in wilderness medicine knows that a life threatening allergic reaction to stings, anaphylaxis, is one of the biggest concerns we have in the field—especially in a culture where allergies have become highly prevalent. That danger was a necessary ingredient for these youth to grow. It was necessary enough that every parent signed their child back up, knowing exactly what had happened.

Practicing Place will always be a dangerous business. I am afraid, as I write this, that practicing Place might be considered an option only for those who wish to brave it. That is not the case. Place is *who* we are and every single human not only has the bravery to face danger, we need it. It is an essential ingredient for growth. No danger: no wonder, no appreciation, no power, no Place.

There are some deeper dangers that are specific to our dominant industrial culture. After these years of personally practicing and mentoring so many others, I have noticed two Great Dangers to the practice of Place: 1) you will slow down pace and 2) develop a stronger orientation toward your own deep happiness. The danger is that you will have to deal with all of the changes to your life that come with it. They will be changes for the better, so "danger" deserves to be in quotes here, but they will also be uncomfortable at times.

Slowing down and orienting to your deep happiness will often feel like remembering who you are, As that happens, you will find yourself questioning behaviors and values that you have been holding: ones that really are not serving you or what you love; ones that are making you smaller than you really are. You will shift over time, and that means deep change. Deep change comes with some resistance, some challenges. On the other end of those challenges is wonder and a greater experience of living.

So, to practice Place, we need to start by orienting to the truth. No creature on this planet can survive if they don't work with the truth of what is right before them. No metaphysical proposition or intellectual abstraction can trump the workings of gravity on our bodies. One truth to start with is very simple. We all know it to be true: we are all connected. We all know and, if we let ourselves, we wonder at the interconnectedness of all things. On this planet, we share breath and body, the waters pass through each of us and cycle again and again. We actually know that each one of us is, on some level, the planet. What else could we be?

So, here's a wondering: why is it a struggle to act that way? Why do we commit actions that seem to be based on the premise that we are not connected and dependent upon each other?

That is a big question for me, and I suppose for many of us. This book is riddled with some ideas around that, but, more so, this book is focused on the practice of embodying the positive response to the question. I suspect, and maybe you do too, that just coming up with the ideas does not really lead to a depth understanding. The intellect is wonderful, but I suspect we are missing something when we have all of the intellectual knowledge of our connectedness and our participation in our only biospheric home, and we still struggle to act in a way that reflects this identity.

Maybe we are not the first people to have this problem. Maybe it has to do with our little human minds, our fantastically diverse egoic senses of self, and our busy apish hands. There are a lot of maybes we could throw out here. But the point is that it seems that part of a human culture is having practices for people to remember their connectedness. We have to practice. If we look at some existing wisdom traditions of cultures who have retained their identity as part of the natural world, we find constant and elaborate practice. Practice does not mean getting ready to live; practice is a concentrated effort of living. Practicing means becoming even more alive. It is not a means to an end. It is a way.

The Haudenosaunee Confederacy holds the core value of the Seventh Generation. In its public literature, the confederacy states, "in their decision making, Chiefs consider how present-day decisions will impact their descendants. Nations are taught to respect the world in which they live as they are borrowing it from future generations." All deliberations are to consider how the actions will impact those seven generations from now. Why would a people include this teaching in a great law and binding principle? What caused this? For the Haudenosaunee, this particular teaching came at the end of great wars and miseries. The great law of that confederacy was birthed to end some very real suffering. Perhaps so many of our teachings are hard won lessons. Not to be thrown away. A deep and vital calling from our ancestors to remind us of what they learned. Perhaps we, as humans, have learned again and again that we must take care of our home and tend to the future lives of all beings who will help to create a healthy planet. We have learned this because we have been the children of war. We have been the children of destruction. We have all, at some point in our lineage, been pushed out of our home—which was a part of our very identity—by other people or by disasters. We have walked that suffering and we have learned that we must practice to re-member. We must practice.

The practice, it turns out, often does not have to be heavy. It can and will be filled with wonder and meaning.

Growing up too fast is a cliché indicating a malady. So, let's pause growing up and grow down for a while. Let's get grounded. Let's do this together right now as we participate in this book. Let's practice.

Right now, pause and take a good breath. Wherever you are.

With the wonder of a child, take a look around and ask yourself this: *what have I not been noticing until just now?* Savor this. Really let yourself slow down for a moment. What are you not noticing?

Listen. Listen in front of you. What is the quietest sound?

What is the quietest sound to your right; behind you; to your left?

What is alive in your surroundings right now? What other living experiences are happening right now around you?

Give yourself another breath.

Did you have resistance to that? If so, why? Did you find any value in this experience? I suggest being truly curious about it.

When I was growing up, I had a Catholic priest in my parish who was much loved by many. He had that vibration of being a truly loving and wise person. He once stood in front of the parish and gave a homily that got him kicked out of the church for a hot minute. Many loved him even more after this. The gist of the homily was this: all the religions of the world are boats. And all of the boats are heading to the same shore. And all of the boats leak. You just have to pick the boat that leaks the least for you.

So too with the practices of Place. There are so many ways to reconnect ourselves to Place. This book will offer many angles. No set order. What works now might be different from what works later in life. But practice. It may be sloppy and weird. But practice. Practice is a way of stepping outside of comfort, outside of the realm of perceived possibility, to experience and be something new. To truly and deeply grow.

Right now, however, let's switch our focus to a very important topic: wonder, cats, and perceptual narrowing.

Cats. Let it be known that our scientific heritage has, at times, justified some excessive abuse of other life forms. With some time and patience, perhaps we will fully change this behavior. For now, we can use some of this history and its insights to help us toward a more contemplative and happy course. One ethically questionable experiment involved cats. From birth, these kittens spent their waking lives in pens. Half of the cats lived their lives in pens that only had vertical stripes, the other half in pens with horizontal.

As those kittens grew up and their worlds only produced a certain type of visual stimulus, their little brains started making decisions on what to grow and what to prune. The "vertical cats" had no need to be aware of horizontal lines. Whether the ability to see the absent lines was pruned by the cats' nervous system or simply never cultivated, the situation on the ground was real for those felines. When the cats were grown enough, scientists put them in an environment with horizontal lines. The cats *could not perceive* the horizontal lines. They did not see them. It was only with persistent strong stimuli (like bumping into horizontal bars) that, slowly, the cats began to regrow those long-gone abilities and, little by little, the horizontal world became visible to them for the first time.

From the scientific perspective, humans show similar patterns. When humans are born, they display a broad preference for speech and seem to have the ability to perceive every possible linguistic sound. According to some research, human babies up until three months old have speech preference that is so broad that we are as responsive to rhesus monkey calls as we are to general human speech. We do, as newborns, show a stronger preference for our mother tongue. As babies grow and they experience a consistent linguistic environment, it seems that we begin to grow our perceptive abilities around the languages we are exposed to. We prune our ability to distinguish sounds that we don't hear in our environment. By nine to ten months old, we begin to prune enough that our abilities to distinguish those absent sounds begin to wither and, as we grow, our perception narrows. Just like with the cats, however, it seems that the plasticity—the ability of the brain to grow new pathways—never completely dies. Though it seems more difficult the older you get, there always seems to be some ability to regrow perception if there is enough stimulus.

Some socially-minded researchers conducted experiments with human babies around facial perceptions. It turns out that babies have a similar pattern with their visual perceptions. At six months old, human babies reacted with as much perceptive stimulation to a rhesus monkey's face as they did to a human face. In a way, each face was just as new and nuanced. At nine months old, babies continued to grow discrimination for human faces, but pruned away their ability to show as much discrimination for a monkey's face. Other studies indicated that this held true for racial groups as well. Babies who were shown faces of people outside of a racial group that they were consistently exposed to began to prune away their perceptive abilities and generalize faces that were outside of their racial group.

Compassionately speaking, these studies seem to reveal a general way in which our minds grow up. We prune what our minds don't practice, and even very full and important things, like some wonderful person's face, can be generalized and dulled. If you have ever lived in another culture for an extended period of time, you might have directly experienced the plasticity of your perception. The language and people around you become more nuanced and full over time. Most likely, this happens with smells and tastes as well. Literally, your mind expands and your world becomes richer. This might be a reason why peacebuilding often includes sitting down with others and having a sustained awareness practice of paying attention to them and what they say. To see them directly, at the same table.

Perceptual adjustments seem to be happening in subtler ways all the time. We are exceedingly perceptually attuned to the nuances of our romantic partner's face. Over time, in a job, we become increasingly aware of the finer details of who and what we are working with.

Jon Young, a naturalist and teacher to whom I am quite indebted, speaks about his experiences mentoring people in his work with deep nature connection. Over many years, he noticed patterns. One was the "wall of green." Many people, when asked why they were resistant to learning about the natural world, shared the experience of looking at a patch of woods and just seeing a wall of green. Basically, there were so many unknown plants in that mix that it became an impenetrable wall of ignorance. It was difficult to even know where to start. Having experienced this myself, I can still feel those sensations. What I suspect now is that the mind actually does perceptually generalize this diverse world of wonder into a wall of whatever. It takes some effort and, usually, the guidance of another person to start to see that wall differently. The mind starts to make distinctions and, over time, it learns. After enough effort, it is impossible to look at the edge of that same forest and experience it as a generalized mass. Perception itself has changed.

So, it seems that humans and cats and probably many more of our world companions are pruners. Our living world and our choices narrow our perceptions so drastically that we become able to sense some things very clearly and some are pruned all the way to oblivion.

Any good arborist would ask, what are we pruning right now and is it a good idea?

Luckily, with the mind, if we can identify what we've pruned, we can usually grow it back.

Back to Cats.

My friend, Josh Lane, offers the world a wonderful array of gifts. Among them is his capacity to be both gentle and curious. This has led him into a lifetime of paying attention. One day, Josh came to visit my home in the Pacific Northwest for the first time. We went for a walk in the morning and, just outside my back door, we heard a loud bird alarm call. We both, stopped, and Josh looked over to me. With big, curious eyes, he asked, "do you think it's a wren." "No." I said instantly. I was thinking of a winter wren and I knew what they sounded like. I was not, at the time, remotely aware of the presence of another type of wren that lived in my backyard. It was that wren. I'm sure Josh knew it. His eyes got wider and his bushy eyebrows raised, "Oh," he said, nodding. We heard it again. "Do you think it's a cat?" Josh asked. Now, this might seem like a strange question, but I knew what he meant. He wasn't talking about the bird, he was talking about what *the bird* was talking about. I shrugged, knowing Josh's great skill in this area. "Let's check it out.," I said. So we did. Slowly and quietly, we crept across the street to the neighbor's yard, where we heard the wren and another bird alarming. We crept around the bushes, peered over a fence, and sitting there on the concrete was fluffy cat with a twitchy tail.

Which would lead any sane person to the next topic: consciousness.

How was Josh conscious of that? I know that Josh did not grow up with that knowledge. I know that he spent a large portion of his lifetime studying and listening and refining his awareness until he was able to go to a foreign environment and instantly translate that bird's call. This might be called "learning," but I suggest that we also look at it another way: perceptual widening. Every one of our deep ancestors and many people still alive today have that ability from a very early age. We are all born with the capacity to hear and translate the nuances of those particular birdy tones. What if, as we grow, we prune that awareness because we are not using it? What if, after some time, we literally do not hear the nuances? This voices in the natural landscape undergo the same narrowing into generalization that happened in the previously named experiments. Josh's learning could be looked at as a reclamation of a vital natural relationship. Josh is a cat that can see both vertical *and* horizontal lines.

Even more cats.

I have friends, colleagues, and teachers who have spent time tracking with the San Bushmen. Interestingly enough, this wonderful culture uses a "click" language and the people have a name that includes sounds that have been pruned out of most of our perceptual awareness. No keys on this keyboard will make that sound pop up in your mind. It's not there. But it could be. So, I beg pardon as we refer to this vibrant culture as "the San Bushmen."

For many of these folks, awareness of their natural surroundings is as important as it has ever been. As they hunt and gather essential wild foods, tracking animals is important for understanding what has been happening in the world around them. Like reading a newspaper, the small fissures and pressure releases of each little track on each trail tell a story of who was going where and what they were doing. From what I have heard, the conversations around a trail can get quite elaborate—each person sharing what he or she sees and sometimes getting in debate over the smallest aspect. I have heard that it is not uncommon for a person to find a quiet space in their mind, to sit with some lion tracks, and then to get a vision in their head of where the animal currently is.

I have heard from other trackers in the States, that they have known people who experience the same phenomenon. They sit next to some tracks and get a vision of where the animal is in the present. I have even heard of folks putting this to a kind of test with groups of people and being surprised at how statistically accurate a group was in determining the current location and behavior of the mountain lion who authored the set of tracks.

There are entire human cultures where this is not impossible. Even ones where it is not strange at all. Perhaps something has not been pruned from their consciousness.

Which leads us to considering the corpus collosum, consciousness, and the readiness wave.

A somatics teacher of mine often cites some interesting experiments done with people who had their corpus collosum severed. If you happen to have learned a little bit about our bilateral brains, you'll know that the left and right hemispheres seem to generally serve some very different functions. There is a very famous TED talk by Jill Bolte Taylor that is worth looking up where she shares a story of having a stroke and thinking almost wholly with the right side of her brain as a result. But in this book, let's focus on one very interesting set of experiments. It turns out that the corpus collossum, a structure running midline between the hemispheres seems largely responsible for communication between the two halves of the brain. If the corpus collossum is severed, as sometimes happens with particular surgeries, then the two sides of the brain have a tremendous amount of difficulty talking to one another. In such cases, inquiring minds have the ability to directly communicate with one side of the brain without the other side knowing about it. One curious experiment was relatively simple. Experimenters knew that if they talked only in one ear, then their speech would only be processed in that corresponding hemisphere. So, through an audio channel in the left ear, a researcher asked the person to start waving her hand. The left brain heard it, and the person waved her hand. Then, the researcher got onto the audio channel that was in her right ear and asked her, "why are you waving your hand?" The right brain considered the situation. The person responded, "Oh, because I thought I saw somebody I know." Curious. Another example: in one channel the person was asked to start laughing. In the other channel they were asked, "why are you laughing?" The person responded, "because you're so funny!"

The side of the brain that was asked the question did not know the actual reason for the action. So, the brain did what brains do best: it made up its best guess at a viable answer and went with that. That viable answer was lived as direct experience for the person. The science around optical and auditory illusions provides a boatload of other examples of a similar process. The evidence seems pretty clear. Our perceptions are dependent on a lot of educated guesses.

Another interesting set of experiments: the readiness wave. The readiness wave is electrical activity on the surface of the brain that seems to indicate a preparation for voluntary muscular action. It seems to be the first event in a chain of events that leads to action. There are some very interesting studies that seem to indicate that, when a person chooses to do something, the readiness wave actually happens *before* the person is conscious of choosing to do the action. I've found that the more I think about that one, the stranger it gets. If the readiness wave happens before the consciousness, then what is the role of consciousness? The choice has already been made and the order began, and *after that* the person is conscious of having decided. One way to look at these experiments is to say that our conscious reality is not where the action takes place at all. It is not where we decide or have any will or agency. One way to interpret these wonder-filled findings is to say that the role of consciousness is simply to explain what has already happened in a way that seems most probable and best fits our perceptually narrowed past experiences. Our entire conscious world is a kind of best guess using whatever stuff we happen to have not pruned.

What that also says it that there is a lot happening right here and right now that is well beyond our awareness or is simply being interpreted into something more probable by our minds. Plenty of room for wonder.

The first part of wonder is to let the doors blow open and accept possibility. The here and now of Place, the taproot of real awareness will ground you. Don't worry. Just let the doors open while you read this book. Trust that there is a rugged practicality to Earth and that no matter how much you accept as possible, you will need shelter, water, fire, and food. You will need to take care of your loved ones and of your own health. These are non-negotiables. So let the doors of possibility open wide and accept that you are only perceiving a thin sliver of an explanation of what is.

Travel now through some other slivers of perception that work quite practically for so many people. That have meant survival and thriving through so many millennia of some hard and harsh history.

I heard a story once about a teacher in North America who was hiring a new tracker for his school. He subjected the applicants to a grueling series of tests, the least of which was this:

The teacher had a fifty-five gallon barrel filled with pebbles. He gathered all of the applicants around and grabbed a handful of pebbles. Keep in mind that this teacher is kind of famous for his photographic memory and his eye for detail. So, he walked around to each applicant and placed a pebble in each of their hands. He then told them that they had five minutes to get to know their pebble. This was a group of brilliant minds, so they each went about their own highly skilled way of knowing their pebble. At the end of five minutes, the teacher instructed them to throw their pebble back in the drum. He then, unceremoniously pushed the drum over. The pebbles spilled out and covered the ground. The teacher said, "find your pebble."

People dropped to their hands and knees and started scouring the rocky multitude. All but one. One person stayed still and very quiet. While all the others were scrabbling and scrambling, this one person seemed concentrated and poised. After about five minutes, the man turned his head and looked at a particular spot in the pile. He slowly, as if being guided, made his way down closer, knelt, and gently began moving pebbles from the surface. With a concentrated gentleness, he separated pebbles until he came to the one. He placed it in his hand, stood up, walked over to the teacher, and gave it to him.

The teacher looked at the pebble, then looked at the man. "This is your pebble," he said.

The man nodded.

"How did you find it?"

The man answered by telling the teacher that he spent many years in Australia. While he was there he spent a lot of time out in the bush and was mentored by some of the native folks who lived there. He said that they taught him to hear the songs that the rocks sing. He said that, when he was given his pebble, he listened to its song. When the drum was spilled, he just had to clear his mind and listen for the song that his pebble was singing.

On a very similar note, Wade Davis, in one of his TED talks, tells a story of traveling to spend time with a people of the northwest Amazon. He is a wonderful storyteller, so I recommend looking this up. For now, we'll enjoy a brief summary of a piece of his talk. He said he was researching a combination of sacred plants that these folks use for ceremonies. They consistently identify seventeen different varieties of one of these plants. However, Wade Davis, a trained botanist, could not distinguish any notable difference in the varieties. They all looked like the same plant. So, he asked them how they told them apart. They said, as if it was obvious, that they lay them out on a full moon night and listen to the songs that each plant sings.

Over the years, I have met a notable amount of people in my culture who live very normal unassuming lives and who have confessed to me, with some aire of secrecy, that they talk to rocks and rocks talk back to them.

Rocks speak. Plants sing. The world before us is a narrowed sliver of known in a sea of happening. Our practical consciousness provides the best *is* that works—the boat that leaks the least for us. Maybe there is no absolute truth where rocks speak or they don't. Maybe there is no baseline where Newton is wholly right or wrong.

The subjective is inextricable. Consciousness is explaining in as many modes as there are species, in as many languages as there are cultures, in as many texts as there are individuals. There is Truth, but it is always bigger than the perceiver's scope of consciousness. So, in order to get a little more wholeness, more grounding, we pay attention. We wiggle our consciousness by attending to other people, other beings, by stretching our senses and our patterns

So, let's step into wonder, allow our imaginations wiggle room with the constrictive bounds of our chosen reality, and see what happens. There is a lot that *could be*, and some of it is really important for our health and wholeness. We'll embrace potential and new ways of thinking and being. But fear not, we will be steadfast in grounding ourselves in some very earthy concerns and at the end of the day we'll make sure that the most sacred and mysterious edges of our explorations can find their way to the tough, rocky sphere of the mundane. Ordinary Magic.

The Wonder in Wander

When I was a child, my mother made a painting of the Winnie the Pooh map of the 100 Aker Wood. When my brother outgrew it, it hung in my bedroom and I would often let my imagination roam that simple and sweet representation of a place. The world is so strange and the shape of events is a seriously confusing consideration. It is suspicious to me that so many years later in my adult life I would live in a place that had a dearly loved "100 Aker Wood" of its own. It is suspicious that the world whittled me into a place-connection mentor for hundreds of youth and, for many of them, the 100 Aker Wood has been our home base.

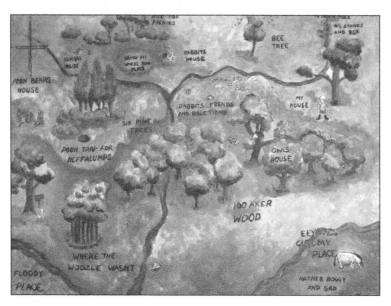

Our own 100 Aker Wood map would be luscious. The aforementioned Deadtree Tower of Waspliness would surely make the map. So would the Brackenly Bog, the Secret Lummi Sacred House, the Deadtree Wastes, the Olde Road, The Bathtub Rushes, The Buck's Back Path, The Elder Tree, Twin Standing Bow Alders, The Nettle Spring, The Oyster Farm (think mushrooms), The Birch Bumps, Sit Spot Slide, and Hawthorn Path. Those are some poignant memories that clearly enter my mind's eye as I write this. Those places within the Place are associated with deeply formative memories for myself and many others. They only encompass an area of about fifteen acres. There is much more that I left out. There is much more map that could be drawn beyond those fifteen acres. Each named Place is a world in and of itself. To add to that map, we could include all the wild food we know to be there, the tools, the shelter, the fire, the water. We hold a map in our minds and hearts that tells us where to go if it is raining and we need fire: to the paper birches, then to the stand of hemlock, then to the windsheltered hollow. If we need rope, we go to where we know the nettles are. We know this little spot of land because we and the land have become together. The land is an extension of us and we an extension of the land. Our wonder-filled 100 Aker Wood is a city park a few blocks away from a public school. Not at all a remote and unattainable wilderness.

How did we learn and become all of this? That boy that I was when I stared at Winnie the Pooh's map was not graced with some magical nature connection mentor in my life. The wild world was a wall of green until my mid-twenties. The young girls and boys who our own 100 Aker Wood alongside me had the grand array of family stories you might expect from a slice of this part of America. No special "nature" genes. They were not unschooled paleo-kids (well, maybe there was one or two—but that's part of our culture too.) How did we bypass the psychological monolith of Minecraft (or whatever video game is dominant at the time you read this) and access the joy and wonder of a redcedar tree?

Here's one way: we got lost!

We got honestly, really lost. We got kind of lost. We pretended we were lost. We lost track of time. We lost each other. We lost our senses of selves. We lost our favorite sticks. We lost knives and bandanas and our lunches. We lost our fears. We lost the trails of deer. We lost our minds at times. We just kept consistently getting lost. It was a rigid protocol of *strategic lostery*. We were lostigicians. Unparalleled.

Getting lost, it turns out, is the only way to get found.

If you have ever been truly lost, you know what a rush it is. I have a distinct memory of a mentee who was on a trip with a group of us in a very remote section of wilderness in the North Cascades. This was not the easily accessible 100 Aker Wood. This was days out from civilization. We split up to do various tasks and this person was out looking for firewood. Ten minutes later we heard gut-wrenching panicked screams for help in the distance. I was in the middle of bear-proofing our camp with another pair of young people. The three of us went wide-eyed and ran as fast as we could toward the screams. I will never forget arriving and looking around for blood or Bigfoot gone aggressive and brandishing a small tree as a club. Instead, it was this young person with impossibly large eyes and his panicked breath stuck in his throat. "Oh, thank God!" he said and hugged us. He was not a regular hugger. "I thought I was lost."

He thought he was lost. So he *was* lost. Lost is a state of being. Lost is what happens when the mind ceases to find reference points and no longer can determine where you are in relation to where you are familiar. I imagine we have all been embarrassingly lost. Even if it's just a memory of yourself as a kid in a department store. You get lost and then you panic. And then you start walking through very familiar places, but for some reason your perspective has shifted enough that you are no longer seeing the familiar even when you look at it. Your perception becomes terribly narrowed. You become lost in "being lost" and then you are *really* lost. Most of these stories end with that weird sensation of relief of being found coupled with the mind doing something very interesting. If you can put yourself in the experience, I bet you'll know what I'm talking about. In that moment of being found, the world of your perception kind of twists and shifts in front of you. You see a familiar safe zone or a safe person and the mind wraps itself around that anchor. Then you look around and suddenly so much of your immediate environment becomes familiar. I suspect that this is us experiencing a bunch of neural networks connecting to the memories of what just happened. We'll get a little more into the relationship of neural networks and Place later on in this book. For now, let's just consider neural networks to be familiar pathways that the brain likes to travel. The brain, in that instant is taking an experience and making a map of it so that it connects to the familiar stuff. Like in the studies mentioned in the last chapter, the brain is providing us with a viable explanation for what has already happened. We can call this orienting. It's essential for being good little critters on our planet.

Bluntly, we all know that the experience of being truly lost sucks. So then why in world would we do it on purpose? We could flippantly answer that it sucks to exercise at first, but after some time you can love and crave it because it is good for you. But let's try to unpack this a little more elegantly.

We'll start with kung fu, balance, and lostery.

I apprenticed under a kung fu teacher who used the arts as something very similar to physical therapy. Like most of the kung fu teachers I've known, he was eccentric, probably had more than a few screws loose, and was a fascinating human being to spend time with and learn from. He was very curious about the nervous system when it came to exercising, and much of his health and healing-based exercise was focused on getting more nerve signal to happen when a person's posture wasn't habitually getting in their own way. He found over time that the shape-habits of our body had a tremendous attractive force (as neural networks do) and the nervous system sometimes has to be tricked into doing something new. One of the ways he did this was to introduce a balance challenge to exercises.

I can think of numerous times when he was working with me and had me in a very unfamiliar shape with a stretchy band or a five pound weight or maybe he was telling me to reach out in a very particular direction. I could feel my body resisting and he would consistently give me minute corrections like "drive your left hip back and down while you're reaching toward the corner of the room with the fingertips of your right hand." Then, he would ask me to hold that same shape while balancing on the balls of my feet. I was already working hard, and my body was already being asked to do things that it never does. When I went up on the balls of my feet, and my body suddenly had to struggle for balance as well, it was often a moment of disorientation.

The strange thing was, as I was disoriented and struggling for balance, my mind would be so tasked that it would forget to tell my muscles to hold to their habitual patterns. I would stop getting in my own way and my body would open up. I could hold an unfamiliar shape posture easily. My body learned something new when it stopped allocating energy to tell my muscles what their habits are—what they *don't* do.

Either that or I would wobble too much, lose the shape entirely, and fall on my butt. In those cases, my system went into overwhelm:

meaning that I panicked. I got consumed by the task of trying to balance and my body forgot that it was doing anything else. My mind fixated on trying not to fall. I lost my force and all my other stability. And I fell.

Another thing that teacher would often say was, "the best way to balance is not to think about balance. Give your mind another task." I guarantee that the way he learned this was to experience that balance panic over and over again and to precisely figure out ways in his own experience where he could bypass that panic. When the panic went away, he found a vibrant field of learning in the imbalanced place.

When we are lost, it is like a balance challenge for the mind. We are disoriented and the mind suddenly allocates full forces toward the task of re-orienting. If we panic, the mind forgets everything else it was doing or could do and focuses on trying not to be in the state it is already in. If we learn, over time, how to handle our lostness and meet it with curiosity and the excitement of growing our ability to orient, we find that the being lost piece isn't even a stressor any more.

Being lost becomes the exact place of magic. The world loses its known-ness and becomes a shimmerful cascade of wonder. We lose our need for control, and that may be one of the kindest gifts the undomesticated world can bestow upon us. The hard world of the known and the predictable, the world of transactions and expectations and schedules and invasive marketing muddles our sense of mystery and leaves us in the quagmirey falsehoods of what will be. It's such a grace of the human mind that we can predict and plan. It's such a brilliance that we can use our thinky internal experience to simulate actions and outcomes. And that same graceful brilliance comes hand in hand with a deepest need of *resting* in the unknown. The wild world offers space and discovery. It offers a break from control. Offers something around each corner that you have never seen and no legislation can dominate.

In lostness, secrets wait only for you: the secret moss-gilded hollows with their fantasy microscapes of lichen and curious bugs; the bleached bones of the old bear who laid down one day there and released his final breath into the Earth; the clandestine orchid who lays in secret amongst the split boulders on the crumbling hillside; the great mother tree who stands regal above all others—some mysterious force having blessed her with salvage from the chainsaws; the winking flutter of a song sparrow returning to her hidden nest in the snowberry thicket; The magnificent orange blush of edible mushrooms coating the loam. The world just past the known is filled with prizes that are utterly personal—memories that will lay in the banks of your living mind like ever-warm stones; every time you hold these memories they will warm your hands and beckon you to lay them against your chest and they will give a gentle heat to your heart's center. Getting lost means finding these gifts, the warm ones that last to your deathbed. The ones that will smile you whether you want it or not. The ones that will help you to remember that you have been a part of this strange world, and she has unfolded special moments in special places just for you.

Getting lost can be the palanquin of Wonder. It transports Wonder to your very place and moment and this regal state of being imbues all that you perceive. You become very curious and this changes how you think. This changes who you are.

Strategic Lostery—Tips and Tricks

All that is to say that I use strategic lostery with all of my clients, and consistently with myself. It is a foundational practice because, like the balance challenge, it helps us to learn and grow efficiently. It also opens us up more to being available to the natural world's influences instead of getting stuck so much in the human dialogue routine. Talking is great, but that's not a nutrient we lack in this culture. Emersion in something outside of the human-centered experience is something we might be starving for.

Sometimes, getting lost simply means exploring in a place that is hard to navigate. The 100 Aker Wood has about a hundred trails in it. I'm not sure if that number is remotely accurate, but it does at least give the accurate impression that it is a bit of a maze. It's also heavily forested. It is also in the Pacific Northwest where for about eight months out of the year it counts as a "sunny day" when sunshine has managed to momentarily penetrate the blanket of clouds and has graced the ground with its passing balm of warming light.

This is a perfect recipe for getting disoriented, which leads to being lost. It's also a safe place for this to happen because it's completely surrounded by roads. If you walk in any one direction for long enough, you're bound to find a road and get oriented. It's pretty amazing to me, given that situation, how lost I've gotten. Quite a few times, I've been running down trails with a mentee trying to figure out where we were and how to get back in time. In those moments, being lost is real. We both get a certain spark in our eyes, and the young person I am with usually drops the formalities that come with addressing a person in a teaching role. We work together to reason out our location, and it usually takes a combined effort to do so. This is a wonderful teaching.

As a professional guide and mentor, it's kind of expected that I don't get lost. It would be very tempting to write in this book that every time I do get lost it is because I am creating a learning environment for myself and others. But the word humble is derived from the word *humus*, which means "Earth." Being a wilderness guide is an innately humbling experience. The bigness and raw power of nature is unremitting. Emersion in this uncontrolled world acts upon the ego in the same way waves and sand act upon beach rocks. Wave by wave the burs of egoic resistance get pounded out and chipped away. I have always wanted to claim that I have a good sense of direction, but let it be known that I am naturally pretty bad at navigating. It takes a lot of work for me to get to figure out where I am. I have learned to always ask others and double check my theories. I am better at it now... and I still get lost.

And that has become a great gift.

That said, it is highly impractical to get actually lost every time you go out in the natural landscape. If things got really bad in the 100 Aker wood, there is a solid final strategy: use a compass and walk in one direction till you hit the road. There is also cell service. There are also occasional joggers or hikers. You can get actually lost without having it be truly dangerous. High perceived risk in the moment, but low actual.

So, there are other ways to practice. S*trategic lostery* has many facets, far more than I'll cover in this book. But you will get the gist and then your creative mind will do the rest of the work.

Here are a few techniques that can be wonderful:

Internal Compass Wander

This is essentially doing the thing that gets the kids in trouble in fairy tales. On purpose. Those fairy tales point out that we need a little trouble in order to grow up and find our gifts in the world. So, we drop the responsible logical mind. We tune in to that deep compass within us, and then we follow the "tugs" of where we feel like we should go next. Yes, it's that simple. And, having a little simple intentionality with it is helpful. The practice that I use personally and with clients of every age is to really pause and open up the senses, then feel, then follow. It's amazing what happens when we give ourselves the permission to feel and follow. There's trust in there for sure. There's also the permission to live the part of you that's not so cognitive.

This practice can be a great balancer for our heavily scheduled, expectation-rich culture. It can also teach a growing trust in the deeper aspects of one's being.

And it's fun. It's really really fun. And there is something so great about knowing that there is *no wrong answer* and *no destination*. It kind of tricks us into being in the moment after a while. We become those "foolish" illogical kids in the fairy tale and the strange path of our curiosity mixed with the gentle callings of the living world yields a mythic journey into accidental mindfulness.

Blind Practices

Many years ago, Josh Lane, who was mentioned in the previous chapter, and I decided to blindfold ourselves for three days straight. We were living in the same apartment. Those three days were nothing short of profound. And they yielded some amazing comedy. But this book is not about our antics. It *is* about stretching the edges of our experience in order to learn some of our deeper connections. Blindfolds are a great tool in this capacity.

I have many fond memories surrounding the combination of people, blindfolds, and the natural landscape. It really gives one an appreciation for the diversity of human expression. I've seen everything from the stalwart "hell no" response to the triad of teenage girls who put the blindfolds on before I was done talking and ran full speed into the thickest patch of woods screaming. We are strange animals, indeed.

Between those two extremes lies the majority of human responses to being presented a blindfold. Most people are cautious at first, to varying degrees. They put their hands out and take very tentative first steps. They build confidence fairly quickly. And then the smile comes on their face, and often a giggle. It doesn't matter what age they are. Blindfolds pull out the kid in all of us. They are adventurous by nature. It is exceedingly fun to get a group of adults to put on blindfolds and walk through the woods. I absolutely guarantee that it will supply an experience that will be worthy of multiple reminiscences. Kids love blindfolds. High schoolers love blindfolds. Really, if a person agrees to give it a try, it's almost always a positive experience.

Why?

This book has some real questions that I would like to remain as questions for all of us to pursue. So, first and foremost, this question is open and unresolved. I will share a few things I've noticed that may help: blindfolds cause us to slow down and open up non-dominant senses. This creates an instant vulnerability, which co-arises with a high degree of alertness. It's a very efficient learning state. Our bodies switch from vision-centered balance to internal balance, which is more from the core, so it's very physically healthy. We have to map our area spatially when we are blind, and this brings online a much more pronounced three-dimensional awareness. We notice the feels and smells and the contours of the land in ways we actually never would without some corresponding sensory deprivation. There is an amazement and sense of deep accomplishment when a person realizes that she or he can sense the trees even though they are blind. It's a very real, non-mystical sensation. And I've seen it happen with just about everyone over time.

There are deeper psychological aspects, of course. Being blind brings up trust in the land and oneself. It gets very frustrating if you try to navigate for over a few minutes. And that frustration can become a very deep teacher. No one needs to coach you through it. You just learn. And then a part of you relaxes into the blindness, and eventually each person realizes that flowing through the landscape has to be more like graceful partner dancing than bulldozing. You can't bulldoze with a blindfold. With some awareness, this can be a great teacher for relationships.

So, there are many possibilities for blindfold activities, and you can look them up or think them up. Having people move toward a drum beating in the distance is a powerful experience. Getting to know trees or plants with blindfolds on will build a relationship with those living beings that sight can never accomplish. I've played games of blindfold capture the flag, which were absurdly fun and so deeply educational. A friend of mine took a class with a tracker on the east coast, and they were blindfolded for a whole day, given a knife and some cordage and told to figure out how to start a fire. Again, there are many possibilities. Start simple.

You can probably envision what you'll need in order to do it relatively safely, but you will have to invite risk into your life to do this. I have learned from blindfolds that people are much more resilient than we give them credit for. We are amazing animals.

Quarry

As I write this section, I'm realizing just how mythically charged these practices are. A quarry leads you deep into adventure. Like the quest for the grail or the golden fleece, having something that you are searching for begets an entire journey of internal and external discovery. The reason I am writing this book is so that we can remind each other that we can actually do these things. We actually need to do such things in order to find our wholeness and our deep power. Again, the myths speak to our deepest humanity.

So the practice of having a quarry is simple. Choose something that you want to find and begin courting it. Learn about the common yellowthroat. Become enraptured with its song, a knight templar chasing the divine beauty. Learn from field guides and your local birders. Learn what the yellowthroat eats and how the bird mates and who builds the nest and where. Draw pictures like a kid. And all the while, have that one quarry pull you into the living wild world. Have it draw you into places you've never been, listening to ancient songs you never thought you would begin to understand.

Follow that...

And then there is the myth of the magical bird or the white stag or the little faerie lights that just had to be followed. And the hunter or the maiden or the child just went deeper and deeper until the lostery was complete. Here's the secret. That thing that you follow is never something that you end up obtaining. It's just the vehicle for the true path, the true quest. The thing that you follow does you the deepest life's service of getting you lost. It performs for you a sacred, loving duty of letting you lose your place so that you can find your Self. Now, in our wonder-ful mundane world, we can practice this myth as well. I have had very powerful experiences working with people who can't figure out their next steps. Whose typical environment is very controlled but something is calling them from within. So, we practice following. And we practice from without. Something so powerful happens when you simply choose something to follow. Be it a flock of chickadees or deciding to follow a type of tree along the landscape. As a naturalist, it reveals patterns that you would never have seen otherwise. Also, as a human soul, it reveals patterns that you would never have sensed otherwise.

Maps!

Strangely, a map can be a great part of strategic lostery. I was taught by my mentors to wander maps. I have made it a practice to make sure that I wander and wonder at a map every day if I can. The way this connects to lostery is the curiosity that maps inspire. Pull out a map of your local area and really start to wander it with your eyes and your imagination. You will find yourself making connections about your land that you never made before, and then you'll stumble upon something that is curious to you. You will see a stream that you didn't know was there or a hill or a pond or a road. If you listen to the calling within you, you'll hear that the object of your curiosity is begging you to check it out. You will take the long way home just to find that little spot, and guaranteed there will be at least some moments of lostness entangled into your journey.

It is also good to note that getting that map in your mind's eye and becoming more oriented to your immediate landscape builds a certain primal confidence. We see it in our day-to-day interactions. People feel a sense of pride and even competition when displaying their knowledge of the landscape. I'm sure each one of us has been in or witnessed an argument over which road is the best one to take. Being curious about the deeper drives for such behavior, it seems that this is connected to being a skillful animal in our environment. We are made to feel a pulse of positivity in our biochemistry when we know where the watering holes are, the best trails to take, or the hazards to avoid. Getting to the sushi bar efficiently while avoiding construction may be simply a recapitulation of this primal design. Developing some skill here may have some deep positive effects on our psyches.

Get Small and Get Lost

Every one of us has the art of microwandering deep in our bones. Watch little kids and you will know what I mean. Little kids love to wander the microlandscape and make it big and meaningful with their imaginations. A tuft of grass becomes a faerie kingdom and the carnivorous ground beetles become armored monsters. Hours of adventure can be found in a few feet of lawn. Why do kids do this? This is a consistent behavior across cultures. There must be a deep evolutionary value. Human development seems to include microwandering, which indicates that it provides some essential life skills. One thing that I notice is that microwandering is a method for looking closely with suspended attention at fine details of the earth. We grew up, in an evolutionary sense, as trackers. Tracking tells us where the prey is, where the predators are, who has been passing by, who is eating who, and more. Tracking means learning that every single mark in the landscape has a cause. It is a grand doorway to ecofluency. Microwandering allows us to be transfixed with these little details, and our biochemistries encourage this with positive pulses of fascination and wonder. We also learn so much about the smaller plants, the bugs, the fungus. All of which hold to potential for medicine, food, and tools as well as teach us some very creative and skillful ways to live a life on our planet.

So, in practice, microwandering could be something as simple as a hundred inch hike. You could choose a three foot circle of grass and not leave it for thirty minutes. Crawling instead of walking is a great option. For adults, it may take some conscious commitment to let yourself use your imagination and wonder in the way you did when you were a kid. You will find that it is there, waiting for you, and it has the same positive benefits it always did. It would be curious to see what kind of antidepressant and anti-anxiety properties this practice might have on our beings. I have no doubt the findings would be clear.

Songline

Finally, a songline is a lostery skill that helps one not to get lost. It's as old as dirt and I'll bet there is some version of it in the lineage of every culture. I have heard quite a few stories of people using songlines to navigate some of the most confusing environments. The technique is simple: wander into the wild landscape, and as you do, consistently tell yourself a story about some clear features that you notice along the way. For instance, you might notice a very large redcedar with an unusually long chunk of bark peeling off. Using your imagination in your own quirky way, like telling the story of the redcedar who shed his skin. Wander further to another clear feature that is in sight of that last and connect the story.

Songlines get us to see the land differently and to notice new elements. They help us to engage creatively with our world, and that makes our journey more personally valuable. It is also a very important practical skill to know. Stories sit in human memory far better than lists of details. This technique works with the best of our memory. It can be used in any environment and it is one type of navigation that can be taught to very small children.

As we engage in strategic lostery, the mind becomes sharper. We discover new places and learn new ways to see. We start to see more trails, more possibilities. Perceptions widens. The natural landscape changes before our eyes. It starts with noticing bigger game trails. If we keep getting lost and we stay curious, the mind sharpens to even subtler trails. Worlds of movement open up. The once imperceptible becomes barely perceived and, by and by, as our perception recovers, we clearly see the wild "lost" world as a canvas being painted with a multitude of life journeys.

Trails arise. And absolutely correlate with that is what is happening in our own minds. More neural pathways are being forged. We are deeply learning and growing, and our minds are networking. Literally, our interior and exterior are mirrors for one another. More trails in our wild world mean more pathways in our neurology. More pathways in our neurology open up our perception and allow us to see even more trails. The two co-arise, support, and grow one another. The brain and the landscape are not one, are not two.

The inadequacy of words to communicate inflection and emotion makes me wish for the power to literally burst through the pages or the screen and, as a real, embodied human being to *say* and *feel* that last sentence with you. A moment of real relationship where we can both recognize that something powerful is before us. This truth about the trail and the mind deserves such a fantastic superpower. It deserves to be said and felt. So, in dearth of human to human contact, I ask that you, right now, simply pause.

Take a breath and look around. Do you hear a bird call? Be curious about what you do hear. Which direction is the air flowing against your skin? Look at your surroundings with some curiosity. If you close your eyes, can you picture the details of your surroundings?

Not One, Not Two

The brain organ and the landscape are not one, not two. Trails are external realities carved by many beings. *And* they are your own private neural pathways. *And* they are cultural pathways of experience and perception. So, let's think about different trails. On the external, a trail is a pathway trodden repeatedly by living beings. The more it is trodden, the wider, smoother, and less obstructed it becomes. The more beings that trod it, the more it becomes prominent to our perception and the more improvements are made to streamline travel upon it. From a rugged barely used game trail to a footpath, to a gravel path, to a sidewalk, to a road, to a highway.

Notice this the next time you are out walking around. Take a very familiar route on a well-traveled path, like a drive to the grocery store. Then take a walk that you take about once a week. Take a walk in the woods with a friend down a very well made and clearly marked path. Take a walk down a clear trail that less people use. Take a walk down a less used trail that you haven't been on before. Take a walk on a rarely used trail or a major game trail. Step off the trail and walk fifty steps in one direction.

Notice what happens to your attention. Notice what thoughts you have while you go through this process. With different levels of familiarity, do you notice a different tendency in your thought patterns while you walk? Where does your attention go as you walk on increasingly unfamiliar paths. Do you start to notice more of your surroundings? Do you find that you don't have as much time and energy to allocate to looping thought patterns? I've paid more attention to this over the years while exploring by myself and while working with groups of people. On a major gravel trail, the conversation is lively and almost without fail oriented toward everyday life. Generally, kids talk about school or games or tell stories about their personal lives. Adults talk about their personal lives or have intellectually driven conversations. As the paths get less familiar, the conversations do shift naturally, without any conscious decision-making. Conversations tend to shift more into the surroundings: into the here and now. People pause more and look around or get curious about a plant or a big tree in the distance. If the trail gets unfamiliar enough, there are bouts of silence.

Familiarity can be considered, quite literally, the experience of taking paths of strong neural networks. On a sidewalk, there are so many entrenched networks associated with it that a lot of novelty-seeking awareness can go offline. The mind does something very interesting. It makes a bunch of assumptions about its surroundings and fills in the gaps in awareness. We retain just enough situational awareness to walk effectively, navigate, and notice major changes to the environment. The rest of the energy can go into thoughts that are not associated with the environment. Of course, nothing is absolute, and we are oscillating all the time. But generally speaking, we tend to "be in our heads" more on a sidewalk than we are on a game trail.

I've heard that there is an Akamba saying, "to walk the same path twice means death." If we consider the role of the mind here, that saying takes on an interesting depth of meaning. Most animals walk the "same" trail more than once in their lives. But it is the job of awareness to perceive how the trail is different every single time. That awareness is what detects the predator that is hiding in the bushes. Literally, death. But for industrial growth civilizations in a relatively safe section of a town, that death might simply mean the death of awareness. The death of awareness means the death of connection to the here and now. That causes real problems for us. We tend to rely on and "live" in looping patterns of thought and this is a recipe for all kinds of suffering.

As an everyday practice, one of my teachers taught a remedy for this, simply making a habit of intentionally taking different paths in everyday life. Driving a slightly different route or walking on the other side of the street changes habit, and with that change in habit, the mind turns on awareness. We are really into will power and individualism as a culture, and there seems to be a pervasive assumption that you should be able to control your thoughts by using your inner personal strength. But, honestly, how many people do you know who actually have consistent control of their minds?

Mindfulness is a practice of being in the moment, and we're becoming very aware, as a culture, of just how important that is for our well-being. In order to experience this, we need a skillful means to get us there. The term *skillful means* comes from the teachings of Zen Buddhism. One of the first things a Zen student learns is that Zen is based on a transmission beyond the texts. So, one of the first questions many students ask is, "why do we have texts?" The Zen answer is often this: because the texts are a *skillful means* to help you get to the experience. Skillful means is akin to the "ship that leaks the least for you" that my beloved priest talked about. We need practices that do a skillful job to get us to a truly new way of being; ones that encourage our minds to take new neural pathways. To take new neural pathways, we can increase our situational awareness and physically put ourselves on new paths of experience. So, we change our landscape to change our brains.

In the art of lostery, we follow curiosities instead of following a known path to a destination. We are also graced with the wonder of connection. We drop the isolated human project and rest in the grace of being a part of a much larger and beautifully diverse life community. The call of the chickadees plays our nervous systems like instruments, and tiny tracks of the shrew whisper us into remembering the grand mystical drama that happens without us being there. We get to experience some primal thinking that our entire species grew up with and into. And we don't feel like we're the center of the universe. That is such a gift to remember at times.

But, delving deeper, the work gets even stranger. Minds become more like an ecosystem than a set of individual pieces in a machine. When we follow a sidewalk, we're following values and destinations that carved that trail. We are following *a way* of being, a way wrought by the particular culture of the human species that made it. But when we follow a deer path, we are following a very different creator. In trailmaking, the deer weave the human—literally structuring our consciousness. We follow the decisions of hoof, land, vantage, and foliage. Our neurology is actively begotten as we walk these undomesticated more-than-human paths. How long have we co-evolved with these hooved grazers? Deer write neurology. Step by step, millennia by millennia leaving mossy indentations in our human essence. This is true. Can we stop and sit with this as not just a pretty thought? The feeling of prettiness is that tapping of the deep wellspring of truth. Now, as we really sit with it, let us drink.

Neurology is ecological by nature. Our minds are grown by our relationships. The trails we follow dictate *who* we are. Who we are dictates what we are capable of perceiving. Our spectrum of perception acts as the bounds within which we are capable of conscious action. What is the difference in our relationships when we stop following the deer and accept for straight lines? What paths are we reinforcing? What are we pruning? Is it a good idea? Does living a life only walking human paths with so many straight lines and so little physical and biological variation affect our ability to laterally think when we are faced with large systemic problems? How can we really think beyond the sidewalk when the other options are largely pruned from our experience?

What about stepping off the trail completely? What could that teach us on deep levels, below the cognition, about other ways to be? About our impact in the world? About who we are and how we can act?

Einstein's famous quote about not being able to solve problems with same mindset that created them seems to ring even more true when we consider how perception and networks seem to work.

The beautiful truth is that we are ecological: we are the force of bios. It does not take much time or effort observing the natural world to appreciate the amazing capacity for resiliency and responsiveness. Our ecological neurology sings the same vibrant song as the seed that survived the glacier, the fish that scaled the waterfall, the fungus that penetrated the deepest cave, the strange bacterium that floats in the deepest anaerobic vents near the bottom of the ocean. We are resiliency.

The main motto of the long term, outdoor youth mentoring program that was co-created by myself and many other wonderful people, is *stretch your edge.* I am sure that one of those wonderful people will someday write an entire book on what *stretching your edge* means. I look forward to reading it. Here and now, in this Place-Based Guide to Wonder, we can simply say that in stretching your edge, you stretch *who* you are. You stretch your perception of all that you are connected to, all that creates you. You leave the well-known trails and adventure into the unknown.

It has been such a gift to stretch my edge and to help mentees stretch theirs by working with our natural communities. It is a gift to work with adults, counseling outdoors, and to watch the edge-stretching capacity of a person as they connect with the vibrant, biodiverse wildness of their own being. We do this most often by wandering and wondering. We wander up hillsides and through backyards, to little known creeks and bold mountaintops. We stretch the edges of our geography and find that, in perfect synchrony, we are wandering and wondering through the discovery of our own personal psyches.

If there is one take home from this chapter, it is: *Go Get Lost and Stretch Your Edge!*

Earth Living

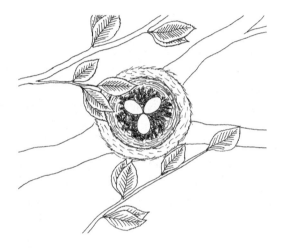

If you don't know who Cody Beebe is, odds are you never will. Cody has the raw, untamed heart of a wolverine matched with the gentleness of a humpback whale. He is prone to long bouts of disappearance from the human drama. If you try to call him on the phone or email him, you will most likely frustrate yourself. You would be better off driving out to his property, searching the secret nooks and making incessant crow calls. That's actually true. You would stand a much better chance of finding him. Wild things, it turns out, are curious. Make a racket and scare up a deer or a song sparrow, then become still and wait. Eyes will appear from behind the bush. So, too, with Cody.

I met Cody years ago and worked for him at his school for a time. He taught me much more than I can fit in this little introduction, and I will leave out those details. If your wild mind becomes curious about what isn't written, start practicing your crow call.

Tracking Cody's mind can be like trying to track the coyote. There are bursts of clear trail and ample sign. There are distinct patterns. And then there are large swaths of frustratingly indecipherable wilderness where the coyote seems to have teleported to another plane of existence. What is clear in tracking Cody is that he loves this bulgy Earth and he loves its children. He also, when the planets align correctly, loves taking adults deeper into their Earth living journey and will share some of the mossy, old teachings that had been shared with him.

On one such planetary alignment, Cody set up a three day wilderness camp for some of us who had been working with and for him. It was Easter weekend, and, that year, it was a cold time. We forded a couple waterways to find a secret spot along the bank of a fork of the Nooksack River. Our job for the weekend was simply to follow what some call "the sacred order" of survival: shelter, water, fire, and food. We scouted the area and made a plan, and then went in search of our individual shelter spots. Some of you reading this may have built or at least seen a debris hut before. If you haven't, it is worth exploring this squirrelly architecture. Tom Brown Jr. and others have written quite a bit about this form of shelter. It is wonderfully effective if crafted well: shedding water and providing ample insulation in the coldest of environments. I personally have seen countless kids excitedly dive into its creation and concoct many variations on the theme. I know of some schools who test the effectiveness of a person's earth shelter by dumping a five gallon bucket of water over it. If it is dry inside afterward, and it most certainly will be if made well, then it is a shelter to last at least one winter. Probably three.

So, my first major task was building my own debris hut. I intentionally did not bring a sleeping bag or blanket, so I had to build it well in order to not go hypothermic. The thing about the debris hut is that something like it can be made very quickly in an emergency and it will get you through the night. However, if you want to make one that will stay standing for a season, it takes some time. Most of what I know about these structures is from this experience and experiences that followed. This time by the Nooksack was to be my first time spending a whole night in my own debris hut. So, I fumbled around and scoured the land and assessed a few areas until I finally found a place that seemed right. The spot did not look like it would flood and there seemed to be enough materials close by. I prepped the bed by digging down and then laying layers of bark and debris that would provide bottom insulation.

This was something I did well. The Earth will suck the heat right out of you, and I am glad to this day that I spent the time with what was underneath.

I spent far too much time crafting the skeleton of the hut with sticks and it was afternoon before I had started with the gathering of debris. This most essential part of the process was more of a lesson than a success. The thing about being a novice is that your assessment without the benefit of previous experience usually ends up being something that you laugh at later down the line. I chuckle as I write this now. There was not even remotely enough debris nearby. A good debris hut needs *lots* of debris. Lots. Really. Three feet thick of debris on the outside is a good general rule. Then there's the stuff that's on the inside. If you don't have a sleeping bag and you want to stay warm, you have to stuff that thing like it's a giant stuff sack. The reason I know this is largely because of this Easter outing.

I settled for about a foot to a foot and a half of debris on the outside and a fluffy mass of leaves on the inside. This "settling" was largely because I spent so much time going so far out to gather debris that by dinner time I hadn't done anything else. I finished by making a door in the form of a leafy plug that I could pull in behind me and seal off the freezing night air that I knew was coming.

When I look back on that first night sleeping in my debris hut, the memory starts with my sense of feeling. The feel of the leaves pressing my body. A comfort that washed over my being: a secret intimacy that I refuse to try to describe—that only can be experienced. I remember the feeling of strange small-mammally wonder at digging myself into the leafy hole I had created. The nearly full moon night world out before me and my crisp steamy breath seeking the above. The sense of security and incubatory quiet as I pulled the door closed and was surrounded by darkness and the smell of leaf litter and loam. I can remember the feel of the cold air channel that was at my feet. I can remember the shivering and the huddling and the weak and frustrated attempts to pull my feet up out of the zone of cold. I remember thoughts as well: design tasks for the morning, which largely included gathering way more debris and fixing the cold drafty spots. I remember getting angry here and there at how cold it was. I remember waves of wonder at where I was. I remember feeling like I had crawled into the great person of the Earth herself.

I remember awakening and shivering during what must have been the witching hour, the coldest darkest depths of night. I wanted to get up and move but I was too cold. I thought for a moment that I had failed. Then the memory that I will never forget. It's as strong a pulse of experience as creating my first friction fire. Some part of me, some distant old and primal spark lit up from within. I breathed the loamy air and shivered the leaves around me into just enough warmth. Enough. A sentence came into my mind, "I am surviving." I realized that I had done enough. Just enough to survive a freezing night. Another sentence, "This is not wilderness living, but it *is* wilderness survival." A primal competency washed over me, and still shivering, I tucked deeper into the Earth and slept until morning.

I affectionately remember that shelter as my Easter egg. No poetics or prose can suggest toward the experience of cracking open that egg by pushing the door forward and feeling the new day's air. I may not have been skilled yet in those woods on the side of the river in the great Pacific Northwest. But I belonged.

Spending the Time with What Is Underneath

Faerie houses, forts, playing with a creek, hiding and seeking, sneaking, camouflage, throwing things, making leaf piles, finding good sticks, playing tag, climbing trees, scavenger hunts, imitating animals, beach combing, rock collecting, and making magic potions. This could be a decent short list for any outdoor educator looking for things to do with kids. Most likely, many of the things on this list, if not all, were some part of your childhood.

If you can send your mind backward and downward into your earthier memories, you might recall that intoxicating childlike spark of life coursing through your marrow when playing a chasing game; the inexplicable light in the eyes when witnessing another animal move like smoke through the woods; the ecstasy of being unseen; the thrill of when you are so entranced by hiding that you won't abide letting the wet or cold or aching body get in the way. What is this strange force within us?

When working for the outdoor youth mentoring program, we would hire new people here and there. When a new person was hired, the first season held very little expectations. The new mentor's job was to play and explore right along with the kids and to develop relationships with them. Personally, there was one thing that I would love secretly waiting and watching for. To me, this one little event was the primary indicator that the mentor had arrived. It revolved around a game called *Spider's Web*, which is debatably the most fun outdoor game in the solar system… at least the way that it evolved in our subculture. It is intoxicatingly fun. It involves hiding and sneaking and seeking and listening and creeping and stealing and planning. It has multiple options for roles that you can swing in and out of without interrupting the game. You can take breaks. You can spend time getting distracted by a berry bush you stumbled upon. You can run. You can creep. No kids of any age or gender, no high schoolers, no adults can resist the attractive gravity of this Jupiter of a game. And it was very important that, while we were playing, the new person would have *no responsibility* other than playing the game.

Mentor after mentor, sometime during their first season, there would be *the game* where that new person became unseen and ghostly silent. It would be the first game where I would not hear their voice talking to the kids. Where if a young person was having a problem and called out for a mentor, this person would *not* show up. In that game, it would be that new mentor who managed to creep at a salamander's pace through the thickest brush and an hour later, when everyone else was at their wits' end and no one had any idea where this person was, they would pop up unexpectedly from behind a sword fern holding a flag victoriously in their hand. And the spark in their eyes would be a brilliant starshine. A bold and unerring light of giving in to wild abandon. It was that light that told me that this person was courageous and untamed enough to invite their primal self into the world and to let it be seen by others. It was this spark that told me a mentor had arrived into our group.

Earth Living could be considered the personal practice of being an animal who can take care of her or his own basic needs directly with the natural world around them. It means being like just about any other being on the planet. Being native to the planet. As people, we have a wonderfully developed social system where we can play different roles and take care of one another. We have a fantastic simulation capacity in our little brains and we have these opposable digits that make for ample handsy creations. We can work together and make things so that we don't all have to be excellent foragers or hunters or shelter builders. That creates such a rich diversity of roles in cultures. It creates cities full of libraries and temples and laboratories and skyscrapers. It makes room for people like Bach and Shakespeare and Helen Keller and the Dalai Lama and Einstein. This cooperation is a great song of humanity. In industrial and neocolonial cultures, we depend on distant places and obscure processes for nearly all of our basic needs. In this situation, there is a pruning of the experience of directly tending to our own basic needs. We depend on the processes outside of our natural landscape and outside of our personal mental or handsy experience.

We can consider this book as a pause. A curiosity mixed with a keen natural discernment. Here, we can take moments to ask the question, *what are the consequences of this?* Nothing is absolutely good or absolutely bad, so what works well for us and what doesn't?

Let's start with the sacred order.

The sacred order is an *order*, meaning that it lists what you need most first. Shelter, water, fire, and food. Outdoor educators sometimes use the rule of threes to augment this teaching. You can die in three minutes without oxygen, three hours without shelter, three days without water, and three weeks without food.

The sacred order assumes that oxygen is present. That's fair. So then we start with shelter. Shelter means retention of body heat, which goes hand in hand with protection from the elements. Clothing is a form of shelter. If you have a good waterproof layer and a good insulating layer on your body, that could be all the shelter you need for many environments. Learning about shelter is simply learning what takes the heat out of my body and what helps keep the heat in. So water and wind and contact with the ground all become foci for study. They make you cold. Anything that makes you cold is a focus for shelter.

Anything that helps hold your body heat is a focus as well. With shelter, we learn the abundant plant, animal, and loamy offerings of insulation. We problem solve and we create our own little niche where the conditions are right for our own animal.

Water is trickier now than it was before industrialization. It is a deep and tender grief to spend the time to put our minds into the waters. To sit with the subject that is the creek or the lake or the ocean. To listen to the infinite songs they sing and to attune to our natural community that flocks to this life-giving essence. To put your lips to a spring and drink directly from the Earth is a kind of sacredness that happens so far below the intellect. It hits the bedrock of our being. To imagine nearly every creek and river being safe to drink, as they were not long ago, is to imagine such a greater sense of ease and belonging with the Earth.

In many traditions, a rite of passage ceremony includes spending four days alone on the land with no water or food. Those who go through this often say that their first sip of water became one of the most memorable moments of their whole life story. The appreciation for that water and realization of our dependency changes a person for life.

Now, drinking water directly from the living world means more work. And still, water is there for us. Water now means dredging through cultural karma, and that often means purification. Generally, the only flowing water that is safe to drink without purification is a spring with no vegetation around it. But such tribulations are not new to being a being with this billions years old planet. We have to adapt. Water means learning the ways to collect the rains; to find the sources; to know where to dig; to learn the plants that tell us of its presence; to listen for the kingfisher; to know how the mountains are carved and to read the watery story as it is currently being told. Water means knowing the seasons and reading the story of the sky. Water means knowing where the factories are and where the farm fields are sprayed. Water means tracking the animals, and learning where they drink. Water means crafting vessels with what is offered.

Hand in hand with water, now, is the sacred need of fire. With the poisoning of our waters comes the confounding of the sacred order. This is okay. We can't do anything useful by arguing with what is. We can't anger or cry our waters into being what they were. We have to work with them and us as we are. This confounding means that we're systemically confused and it takes a little more work to sort things out. Often times, fire is the purifier of water. It boils the biotics and that takes care of a good deal of the purification concerns. So, looking for water will have to come alongside having an eye for fire.

In this book, Fire and Food get their own chapter. It is just the way that this particular cookie crumbled. In this moment, let's just say that fire seems to have evolved into a distinct extension of humanity. It can also be said that humanity has evolved to be a distinct extension of fire. We are tropical apes with beautifully bare skin. We need ample offerings of the life community to stay alive. Shelter retains our heat, but in the colder climates we need some other source, at times, to build it. Our digestion long ago made a decision to partially leave the inner world of our private bodies and venture into environment. We cook, and in doing so, we open up a vaster world of food before us.

And food. There is no replacement for learning the food that is provided directly around us in uncultivated places. Knowing food and having the agency to gather it is a culmination of knowing oneself. It means knowing oneself as Place. The diversity and brilliance of the human diet is staggering. And every cuisine on the planet tracks back to an intimate ancestral relationship with Place. A full line of ancestry where, life by life, people paid attention and courted themselves into Place so that we could be intimately one body.

There is a fifth need that weaves its way through this fabric of survival. This sacred order of survival is passed down from intact cultures for children and the children's children to remember what is essential to living. Intact culture would not exist without the fifth need. It assumes the fifth need is there, just as it assumes air is there to breathe, and so it is not named. But we will get to that later.

Remembering

A question: why is the sacred order pertinent to us now, in a world where we can stare at our computer screen for days if we wish, order pizza, and adjust the thermostat?

We all answer this question in our own way. It is a real question. I would not ask it here if I did not clearly see, in my experience, that it is pertinent. I perceive a primal draw in every single human to understand these basic relationships. How could there not be? If we are alive and Earthborn, there must be some drive to learn to live with the Earth. How could life perpetuate otherwise? The drive may be diverted as soon as we are born and other cultural systems, like industry, take care of our basic needs. But the root never gets pulled out of the soil of our depth psyches. We have a primal essence that knows to its core that we need shelter, water, fire, and food. We become dependent on the systems of relationships that provide these basic needs. They are our life source. All systems, ultimately, depend on the living Earth. The living Earth is the root, the core of all basic needs. Every one. And we also know this. So, there is a drive for us to be able to draw directly from the source. That is primal empowerment. That is belonging.

We do these primal practices to remember. And remembering means becoming a member again. It is our birthright to belong with our Earth. It has been our birthright since we were single-celled organisms. When we lose that sense of belonging, a hole appears in the fabric of our being. A hole we consistently, on the deepest level, are trying to fill. There is never enough money or accomplishment to provide that deepest sense of security. If the industry goes away and the current fabric of society is rent, we have insufficient skill and resources to gain our basic needs. And, on varying levels, we all know this. This guides all of our subsequent actions. We reinforce industry because without it our basic needs of survival are not met. We are missing direct connection. We cannot think new thoughts, outside of industry and colonization without first tending to this depth of missing. We are missing conscious understanding and embodiment of our most primal relationships in the sacred order. We have a primal need to understand our Earth and ourselves in relationship to the basic needs of survival. It is our medicine.

The journey of understanding our personal, natural agency in attaining our basic needs without dependency on intervening manmade systems must include awareness and empathy. This starts by looking to other life forms to figure out how they have solved their puzzles of survival. Every being, if we look closely enough, is showing us some brilliant strategy of relationships. Every being shows the genius of innovating with the world in order to meet their basic needs.

Other beings are teachers. As I wrote earlier, if I need water, I listen for the kingfisher. It is difficult to imagine spending time with our undomesticated relatives and not developing an admiration for their adaptive brilliance. Tom Brown Jr. shares that his debris hut design was completely tutored by squirrels. When he and his friend asked his mentor about shelter building, his mentor simply told them to "go ask the squirrels." So they spent much time observing the squirrels and their homes and learning all of the nuances. Why not consult the being whose living completely depends on making a good structure with the immediate environment?

There is a warm seed that is planted with such an education. We are made in such a way, especially as mammals, as to be able to empathically get into the skin of another being. It is a powerful way to learn and connect with our surroundings. It is a brilliant flower of our evolution. When we watch the squirrel, some part of our being can actually feel in our bodies how it must be to gather a mouthful of maple leaves and skitter on our fingertips to a thick crotch near the trunk; to stuff and weave with our mouths and tiny hands; how it feels to curl up in that ball of protection, drift into slumber, and dream squirrelish dreams.

Those sentences and this book would make absolutely no sense if we did not have a mammalian brain with a limbic system. These parts of our anatomy help us to attune to other beings and overlap their experience with ours. Functionally and anatomically, we appear to have a triune brain. Three distinct "brains" overlap each other to make up our heady organ. In good evolutionary fashion, they are often labeled the reptilian brain, the paleomammalian brain, and the neomammalian brain. The oldest design, the reptilian, controls many of our most basic life functions, including the fight or flight response. The structure and function of our reptilian brain is pretty similar to the structure and function of the reptiles we are currently sharing the world with. The paleomammalian makes up the middle layer, and shows a slightly more complex design. Mammals seem to all share similar structure and function here. The paleomammalian seems to house a lot of the more primal emotions and to be very adept at attuning to other mammals. We can feel each others' moods and we, without cognition or volition, tend to synch up with the state of other mammals around us. This is sometimes called limbic resonance. It is a way we can tell if the cougar is hunting or relaxed, if the deer will run or feed or fight. It is a way that we very skillfully learn from and communicate with others of our own species. It is the reason one angry person in a room can change the whole dynamic. Vice versa, one person with calm abiding can help bring a whole crowd to their senses. We automatically sense if someone is angry or sad or happy, and that state bends each of our brains to share some of those emotional experiences. These mammalian traits are a great tool for efficiently learning how the squirrel builds his nest or how the deer makes it to the watering hole.

It is endearing to work with youth and adults and watch that soft glow of love and admiration emanate from their eyes as they watch another being performing her daily life tasks. It is sobering and impressive to watch the alertness in a person's eyes when they are stalking through the woods and attuning to the mink or the towhee. It is possible that, in empathy, we share not only sensation but also some primal life force. Empathically aware humans seem to have access to a stronger spark of vibrancy than others who have pruned too much of this power.

Empathy is work and overlaps with so many other processes of consciousness. When we go through our Earth skills journey, experience by experience, we build our capacities of empathy. We remember ourselves as part of a great web of life relationships. It takes time with the dirt to develop and hold this primal power. It takes a certain persistence and a willingness to be in new places. It takes getting lost and losing our way, then finding it again. A great tracking teacher here in the Pacific Northwest often says, "if you have been trailing a deer for two hours and you don't think you've lost the trail, then you haven't been paying attention." Remembering ourselves to the sacred order of survival and to our life community requires our sustained attention. If we are to enjoy the confidence and wholeness that comes with such remembrance, we must commit time and effort. As one of my kung fu teachers would say, "you are what you do the most." Without committing to some action, those ways get pruned and our perception narrowed. The primal need remains, but the trails leading to its resolution become overgrown and imperceptible. So, we practice in order to remember.

Some Earth Living Practices

I tend to think that the best practices and the most lively practitioners are guided by questions instead of structures. So, this paltry list is peppered with questions to ask yourself. The list is just to get your mind working in the direction. There are huge gaps. Let your curiosity fill them. What questions would you ask yourself to promote more Earth Living practice and knowledge?

Here are some ideas:

Sleep outside. Pick a good day and make it an adventure. Sleep in your back yard or any place that you feel inspired. Do it in a way that you feel safe and can relax into the open night. You don't have to do it alone. It makes for a great date. It's fun to propose to friends. It is an amazing family experience. It is naturally contemplative when done alone.

What trees shed water well in your area?

Try new types of outdoor sleeping systems. It really makes best sense to start with just stretching the edge of your experience. If you rarely sleep outside and it is an edge, try a tent for shelter. If you use a tent, try a tarp. I know from many consecutive weeks in the Tongass National Rain Forest that a tarp can be the only shelter you need in the fiercest of storms. Most people prefer it to a tent after some time. If you use tarps, then move on to making your own shelter out of natural materials. There are all kinds of options. You can ask around and do a little research and then just pick the one that seems the most interesting to you. Simple seems best. Choose something that is attainable and that you will actually go out and try. There is no harm in making it fun or having company. That said, doing it by yourself has a certain sense of empowerment that is irreplaceable. It is a potent life act to eventually build your own shelter. Something will change inside of you.

What is the traditional clothing in your area? What have people been using for thousands of years to give shelter to their immediate bodies?

Where do other species find shelter in your area? Ask naturalists and birders and just learn one or two things at a time. Then see where your curiosity takes you. It is a much deeper connection if you can do this while walking the land with someone knowledgeable. Reading about those shelters in a book or seeing them on a screen lights up the imagination. This is one step. The next deeply transforming step is to actually see these shelters in the natural landscape. Get close if you can and imagine yourself to be that animal. Study the shelter and ask why that animal chose particular designs.

Where does your water come from?

What are the waterways in your area? If you live in an urban or suburban environment, your city most likely has watershed maps available to the public. You may be surprised to see all the creeks around you.

Making an adventure out of walking a waterway can be a powerful, eye-opening experience. You learn that water so well, and you learn even more about the ways of water and land in relationship. This is, for reasons beyond my comprehension, dramatically different from visiting sections of a waterway. Actually walking it, through the tough spots, teaches so much. This can be done in any environment. Waterways typically start in mountains and often run through civilization all the way to the ocean. I have found that when I walk a waterway, some deep orientation part of my mind feels a certain relief and competence. It connects my understanding of where I am in a way that no other practice does. I am tracking the arteries of life that feed everything, including me, in my Place.

If you have never coal-blown a bowl or spoon or cup, I highly recommend trying it. It is magical. People become transfixed with this practice. There are nuances to it, but the practice is simple and intuitive. And then you have your own vessel that you made to drink and eat out of. It is curious how much pride and connection we get with a vessel we have made. It makes it real and loads it with story and that vessel lives in a wholly different part of the psyche than the ones that were bought.

Learn good fire safety and etiquette and start building them. You will learn what woods burn well and how. In my experience, people who haven't built fires before often can't identify wet or rotten wood from good wood. If you are inexperienced, it will set you up for success to build fires alongside more experienced people at first. Then just build them. Experiment and get curious and you will find that every fire is different and every fire has something to teach you about the environment, the materials, and yourself.

Start with good weather conditions when building fire and then try harder ones. You will be surprised at what the land offers even in torrential downpours. No joke that fires can be a frustrating challenge, but the potential is always there. It is surprising where the resources are for a good fire. The land holds some powerful secrets here, and you can learn them. Ask people around you. Just start with simple questions. For fire building, there is a typical order to your landscape. Usually, the fire lights best with one or two little "magic items" like paper birch bark or "fatwood" (if you are curious about fatwood, you should be. It is magic hidden in the rotten, wet depths of a decayed stump of a particular species of tree. It is nature's superpower for starting fires. In my Place, it is abundant. Other places surely hold their own secrets.) From there, there is often an order for the best twigs and then the best sticks. This knowledge is waiting to be discovered by you.

Try different ways to start fires, from flint and steel to a bow drill to a hand drill. Someone you know knows how to do this. They want to teach.

With wild edibles, I suggest starting with plants that are abundant and easy to identify. If nothing else, put some dandelion greens or chickweed from an unsprayed lawn or flower bed in your salad. Your body will thank you.

Learn one wild edible you didn't know before and use it in a meal. Then challenge yourself to learn more and increase your usage. You can make a game out of it or a personal practice depending on your disposition. You can do this solo or you can suggest a group meal where everyone does the same and teaches about the plant they used.

When you are confident with the easily identified plants that grow in your backyard, move on to more difficult identification or ones that require some adventuring or processing. Of course, this goes hand in hand with learning good harvesting ethics. Make sure you find good resource. Ask people.

Mushrooms can be deadly. Seriously. The first generation audio portion of the Kamana Naturalist Training program, which is offered by the Wilderness Awareness School, makes it abundantly clear not to mess with mushrooms unless you know what you are doing. Seasoned mycologists and lifelong mushroomers have died along with their families because of making mistakes. However, mushrooms can be eaten and they can be delicious. Just be very careful. Learn any poisonous look-alikes, and do it right.

Who do you respect who hunts and fishes? What can they teach you about the way those animals live and how people harvest?

What are the traditional ways of harvesting in your area?

You can get books and google all kinds of information on any of these subjects. Those resources already exist. Use them. They're great. More than anything, I highly recommend talking to people who are experienced. People love to talk about what they love. And there is a natural tendency for people to teach when courted by an open mind. Even the most curmudgeonly take on a certain endearing quality when they are coaxed into teaching. It also gets you connected with another human as opposed to a screen or even a printed page. It is a closer entry to the living world of your Earthy connection.

Primitive

Often people refer to Earth Skills as "primitive skills." I try not to. I am not an absolutist and, for those of you who know me, I might even call them primitive skills when in conversation with others. Good conversation is a jump into a bigger mind. Mind is a relationship. Mind is a community. Community means compromise and courtship. So, I need help from the big community mind in rethinking this term. I ask other minds to consider courting a shift.

Sometimes the term "primitive skills" hits my soma, my entire body-mind experience, the way a slander or a racial slur hits. There seems to be a deeply embedded problem with the story we perpetuate about our own ancestors. Even with some of the most egalitarian, community-minded naturalists, this sleeping demon asserts itself into the psyche.

Primitive denotes a relic of the past. This is very problematic for most people's innate confidence and for our right relationship with our planet. Stripping away all the trappings and all the luxury of ideas, Earth skills are simply the way of living as a being on and with our only home planet.

I propose that we commit real time and effort to considering this language and its way of thinking. As simply as we can.

When did being a creature that can personally exist with its own planet become primitive?

Culturally, we tend to harbor and perpetuate a subtle lie that our ancestors were unintelligent and graceless savages. I notice this in our language or at times when someone is telling a human evolution story from a Western scientific perspective. I don't believe that this way of thinking is accurate. Is the cougar graceless? Is she stupid? How did our mothers and fathers from so many millenia ago hunt the mammoth and survive alongside the saber tooth tiger? How could stupid and graceless brutes figure out how to make fire, to create burial grounds, to use plants as medicine, and to survive endless expanses of ice as a tropical ape? From this perspective, we humans *are* great apes, and I suggest never letting anyone, most of all yourself, discredit you and slander you into thinking this a mean and brutish lineage. We were born through the Earth and we hold this long life lineage, and we are made to own every chapter of our brilliant story.

Our ancestors were brilliant and full of grace. They were ferocious at times, yes, and we are as well. The idea of men communicating in grunts and dragging women by the hair has the same essence as the most deeply racist and demeaning ideas perpetuated by the frightened and angry of our current time. We often subconsciously or consciously attach this mindset to our brother and sister cultures who still hold the essential teachings of our human indigenous ways. This is a colonial mindset wrought by ravaged consciences who created a system of thinking that would collude with unjust and violent actions. The slander of "savage" and the delusion of empire-minded superiority are still very active in our world.

Stop reading and listen to a song sung by a human... one that brings tears to your eyes.

Did you do it? It is okay to pause.

Recognize that this is a great ape singing the fruits of a successful journey through time against all odds. Place by Place. Epoch by epoch. Culture by culture. Against all odds, a great river of ancient story. The hands of an ape. The tongue and eyes and heart and feeling of a breathtakingly beautiful ape.

This is us. Please do not ever forget it. Please do not ever degrade your ancestors and your identity again. You are something ineffably beautiful. Your heritage is indigenous.

Life has always been messy. The conditions may have been different. The depth and breadth of our consciousness has changed. We have grown in certain areas of complexity, and this is a wonder. To be loved and rejoiced. Sung in our songs, expressed in our art, and felt in our touch. However, with every shift in perspective comes a corresponding myopia. Pruning. Perceptual narrowing. We think the world *is* what we perceive. And we look back at our *own people* who lived and died for our sakes and we slander them because they did not share the same place in the spectrum of perception.

That slander is a seed of ethnocide and ecocide. It has been responsible for much pain and misery for many cultures who live closer to the land for thousands of years. It is also a lie. Just because our spectrum of complexity and perception changes, it does not indicate superiority in any way. Superiority is a dangerous delusion. If we continue to think that we are superior to other people, we eradicate major expressions of the human spirit. If we continue to think ourselves superior to the trees because we can easily kill them, we will continue to eradicate our own planetary lungs. We are all connected and we all depend on each other, and the delusion of superiority is slow suicide after so much hard work and love from our ancestors. The biosphere now needs an awakening from this delusion in order for us to pass on our seeds and care for this home as many species working as one.

The Wonder of Awakening

Watching a young person seem driven by strong invisible forces to build a fort, and witnessing the buoyant glean of pride and competence that beams from them when they successfully spend the night in their shelter creates a curiosity about the compelling forces themselves. Why are we so deeply transfixed by the creation of fire? When walking outdoors, why do people tend to admire knowledge of food and plants around them? Why are creeks and lakes such a powerful draw for human habitation and recreation?

Over the years, I have wondered more and more about this. There is a saying in biology: ontogeny recapitulates phylogeny. It is a succinct way of saying that when we are first born and in the womb, we seem to pass through the full stages of our evolutionary history: from single cell to notochord to having gills all the way to becoming a little primate. What if this trend continues after birth for the human being? We are strange creatures in that the limits of the size of the human pelvis have seemed to limit the maximum size of our brains. Some theorize that we then developed ways to keep growing when outside of the womb. As a species we have a uniquely extended development. Language, culture, and experience continue to shape us into maturity for a considerable portion of our total lifetimes. What if Earth living skills are an important ingredient in our development? What if these skills and relationships are as powerful as language for us and they grow essential aspects of connection to our biological community and our planet? What if, just as we grow in a particular evolutionary order in the womb, we also most skillfully grow outside of the womb if we have some experience of the recapitulation of our human ancestral story? What if we function best when we have a grown up with a relationship to the sacred order, our primal needs? If we skip steps, as many of us do in industrialized cultures, it may create havoc in our development and an unhealthy attachment. But, we are neuroplastic, meaning that humans never stop learning and growing, and we have the gift of the grace to reclaim what was missing in our development.

Stephen Jenkinson, author of *Die Wise*, says, "humans are not born; humans are made." This might be the succinct statement for the necessary human growth that happens after birth into the world.

There is a joy and an artistry in the making of humans. For those of us raised in industrial cultures without having those primal relationships as a part of our earlier development, the work often starts with permission. When working with adult counseling clients outdoors, there is often a moment when we come across something curious—like a jelly fungus or a bizarre and harmless insect—and the person will either assume that he can't pick it up or ask me for permission. When we talk about it, it suddenly seems strange that they should restrict themselves or ask permission to make personal contact with something new in their own natural world. Then they give themselves permission, and there is consistently a subtle deepening and lowering of the breath, a drop of the shoulders, and a release of tension around the eyes. They touch the witch's butter or the alder beetle and they seem to leave the world of our human-to-human contact for a few moments. Then, usually, the person looks up as if from a daze and begins talking again. But the content changes because their baseline has changed.

As we continue this journey and the person learns more about their own place, those changes in tension and breath become the new baseline. As a person develops connection, that person is literally, on the subjective level, walking through a completely different landscape. Where they were once surrounded by a host of unknown plants that may or may not be poisonous and a largely imaginary list of animals, that subjective reality is replaced by walking through a landscape that is ever-offering to their needs. They are walking on top of medicinal and edible plants, surrounded by shelter, water, fire, food, medicine, and tools. The world is an ally. Over time, as we walk together, they seem to naturally develop a multifaceted attention. We can delve deeply into psychological content because they are in a safe space and they have good foundations and resources *and* the two of us humans are only a part of a bigger attentional picture. The person seems to keep an awareness reserved for the workings of the bigger biological world happening all around us. This tends to create opportunities for more serendipitous moments where other beings are teachers. The person might spot a perching owl just as she is talking about her vision for herself. A conversation about the death of a relationship might be interrupted by the discovery of a raccoon skull. These other relationships are pertinent and they yield their own wisdom. This is possible because the Earth living relationships have been cultivated.

Speaking for myself and on behalf of the people I have worked with, we tend to become much better problem solvers as we develop our Earth living relationships. The more Earth living skills we do, the more we realize that everything in our Place has a usefulness. Even punky dead wood is useful for certain projects. Rocks are tools. We see all the creative ways that all the other beings work with their environment and we become more ingenious with our world. Everything in our Place has a use and our Place can provide for all of our basic needs. This can have powerful effects on our psyches. If we have this baseline awareness with the natural world around us, it affects the way that we feel about problems in general. We have an ingrained resiliency that can transfer to the psychological plane and the emotional plane. As this awareness increases, it eventually becomes reciprocal. We realize that we have a use for all other beings. We have value in and for the world. This changes the way we look at ourselves. It changes the way we look at and treat other people.

Let's pause again. Imagine, if you will, your Place that is immediately surrounding you. Try to picture the trees that are actually around you. Can you see them in your mind? Even if you don't know their names, maybe you can picture some character of them—the quality of their bark and leaf or needle. Picture the grasses around you and all of the little herbaceous plants interspersed amongst them. Where might you find the tiny tracks of shrews or voles or mice in a patch of mud or dust? Where does the cat or the coyote or the deer or the raccoon pass through? Even if you are in the heart of a city, the ecological world is shifting and moving and many little minds and countless planty fibers are moving and changing the world around you. Now enjoy a breath and realize that you are breathing together. Two halves in exchange. And then imagine all that this world is offering. Right around you, right now, the woody plants hold the secrets of fire and the hard yet carvable materials to make countless tools; leaves and flowers give food and medicine; fruits await the picking; the subtle green grass holds nutrients and vitamins that no cultivar can compete with; waters pool in secret, revealed only by certain plants and fungi and curious indentations; an old stump somewhere hides a hollow big enough for you burrow into; the seeds of flowering plants promise insulation from the cold. The world around you is teeming with what can heal you, feed you, and keep you comfortable. This is the world around you right now. You are surrounded by support.

Anxiety, depression, and loneliness are so pervasive in this culture at this time. These hungry ghosts gnaw at our vitality, if not seeming to affect us personally, then affecting those we are connected with. The economy of "not enough" claws at our psyches. So, one good step, it seems, is to widen our perception. We can change the way we think. And we can orient toward what is true and here and now. It will take time, but that is part of the change. Earth Living takes time—it operates on a geological pace. It slows us down. And that is a soothing balm. Patience is an antidote to panic.

Shelter, water, fire, and food are our primal needs. Nature has no room for dishonesty. You can't lie to a rain storm about whether or not you have a shelter. You can't rationalize yourself out of hypothermia. So, in the spirit of being ruggedly honest, let's address that there is a fifth need that we cannot live, or at least be fully human, without.

There are all kinds of examples that you can read about touch deprivation and its affects on infants. Frederick II, a 13th century Holy Roman emperor, sought to discern what the original language of humans was. So, in a frighteningly cruel experiment, he took babies from his populous and had them raised with their basic needs met but with no speaking or coddling or extra touching. He was hoping they would get to speaking age and then start speaking Hebrew or Greek or some other language. According to the monk who recorded this "experiment," those babies never spoke because they never made it to speaking age. The babies all died. Harry Harlow performed horrific experiments on Rhesus monkeys that involved touch deprivation and social isolation with all the basic needs met. These monkeys were either severely psychologically damaged or died. In the early 1900s, a leading American pediatrician advised parents to not touch their babies, as it would coddle them too much. In the years immediately following, there was a dramatic increase in infant mortality. There are cases of orphans who suffer similar situations and do survive. In these cases, the children do suffer from "failure to thrive." Attachment theory in western psychology, which we will explore more later, shows that human babies have a developmental need for skin to skin touch and loving gaze. Somatic psychology commits much of its attention to the human need for safe and loving connection. In the literature, and in praxis, it seems evident that humans need love and connection to be whole and healthy. Love is a fifth need.

In order to be human, we need love. We need safe connection to other humans. It is a basic inalienable right. We are not whole humans without it. We have a duty to each other and ourselves to make sure that this need is being provided. I suspect that this need also extends to our Place. When we feel love and connection with our Place, a part of our humanity is actualized. I suspect that such a connection with Place and with all the other beings with whom we co-create Place is a medicine for anxiety, depression, and loneliness. It is not a panacea, but it is strong medicine.

Love weaves its way through the sacred order in a mysterious fashion. So, too, in this book. Though it does not fit the "rule of threes" and doesn't necessarily fit into a dramatic survival situation, love is consistently required. Even as adults, we increasingly fail to thrive with its lack: our higher functions and our mental and physical health shutting down without this need.

Is it possible that the biosphere suffers from lack of human love and connection now? One could say it is our actions that cause the suffering:

cutting down rainforests, mountaintop removal, war, mining, petroleum extraction. But these actions are the results of a mindset and a "heartset." What if the Earth living skills build the connection to not only survive with our Earth but to extend our love and care into what creates us? What if, with enough attention, this creates a different identity where we are no longer thinking as if we are separate from the Earth?

Earth living is not just the living with the Earth. It is being the Earth living.

You Are Who You Eat

We humans are fields of living and dying. Moment by moment, within the bounds of each person, countless entities are ever arising and passing away. Through this personal field of collaborating ephemera, we each dream a reality of shape and characteristic: a tangible body. We dream ourselves into physicality. We seek to perpetuate the dream moment by moment. So we breathe. We pull the sky into the body and let it transform our field of being. The sky is swallowed by lungs and, with every swallowing, beings within the body endure, die, and are born. We drink. The waters of the world enter us and flood our field to birth life and wash out death. The specialized salt water of our blood permeates our being.

And we eat. We take in the Earth and our personal field grows dense and varies: bones, nails, organs, and hair... We eat the outside to grow the inside. We eat. We send the inside back to the outside. And we eat again. We eat beyond imagination. We eat the new, the never eaten. We, the human tribe, have invented ways to eat almost anything that we could fit inside ourselves. We eat the future generations, the seeds and eggs and mushrooms and fruits of almost anything that lives. And they enter our field. And they become our soil.

Our own deep seeds that we are made to carry, our sperm and eggs, stay alive and nourished from the eating. Inside the field of our bodies, we carry what contains the information for creating new human lives. The eating keeps our seeds alive. The eating propels humanity through generations.

Not long ago, our dominant culture had an idea that our daily behavior could not change the core unit of who we are: our genetic makeup. Now, through the field of epigenetics, we are witnessing that our daily experiences can turn on or off certain genetic traits. With a long life of eating from and nourishing our own fields, we change the core of who we manifestly are. Those changes can be imprinted on the code that we pass on in our seeds of future generations. As we procreate, generation by generation, little by little, we are authored in large part by what we eat.

In this chapter, let's wonder more about our relationship with food and consider how the wild Earth is a part of this process. It seems fitting to start where all of us start: with childhood. With the magic and the strangeness of the alchemy of eating. Perhaps you have a memory linked with a whole food. Perhaps somewhere in the child still inside of you is that feeling of when you first learned how cooking works. Maybe the first time you were asked to cut apples for a pie, or go out and pick some berries. Maybe you had or visited a garden and you can still, somewhere deepest inside of you sense your childy fingers grasping the green and plucking. Bring yourself back to your uncultured nature when you indelicately devoured beans or peas, when you shoved leaves into your mouth, or painted your lips with sticky strawberry red. Maybe you had access to wilder areas and your parents or some family friend handed you a rose hip and taught you to eat the outer layers with calculated deer mouse-like gnawings. Maybe it was bananas from the store, and you learned to peel the outer layer by yourself and mush the sweet innards between your happy teeth.

Somewhere in you is this memory of magic. Somewhere in you, the magic of eating still calls through the cosmos of your being, reminding you of the mystery of our interdependence. Everything we eat comes from the ground. It's not just a primal competency—it is a memory. We gather memory of who we are with hands in dirt, thumb and forefinger plucking leaf and fruit.

When you next have time in a kitchen, try this recipe:

Mix the ovaries of trees with the minerals of the ocean and ground up tree bark; mix the future generations of grasses with the fatty lactations of a grazing mammal and the energy-rich concentrate of grass bodies; place them in the protected center of the active hearth and let them perform the fiery alchemy.

This is apple crisp.

How different is it to look at a common dish with magic, wonder, and newness? Is it possible that language can get too efficient? Is there value in taking time to savor the story of our food? Is it possible that sometimes letting the mind quickly attach the labels of "apples, salt, oats, cinnamon, butter, and sugar" is not in best interest of our long-term efficiency? Is there room for wonder in a meal? What could be practical about it?

The Ethnobotanical Us

We will look at this wonder from multiple angles in this chapter. Ethnobotany seems like as good a beginning as any. This field looks at the relationship between human culture and plants. I interviewed ethnobotanist Abe Lloyd for this portion of the book. Abe grew up in the area where I now live and has been passionate about wild foods since well into his childhood. He teaches at Western Washington University and regularly leads trips and workshops around ethnobotany and connection to Place. I've selected some of the best parts of our interview in the below transcript. Let's take a wonder walk with Abe and see what he has to say about food and us:

Me: *Do you think it's important for people to eat wild foods?*

Lloyd: I think wild foods offer us something that we've really been lacking as a society that depends on industrial foods for the last fifty years and possibly, in some cultures and some communities, a lot more than that. Fifty years ago most people grew up on farms and had a real connection with the land that provided their food. Now most people don't grow up on farms; they grow up in cities and they have very little connection with the food that they eat. So, I think that wild foods, in some way, offer a similar opportunity to what farms offered.

But it goes a little deeper, in fact. What wild foods offer people is really a chance to interact with the natural environment: not just the land that produces food, the land as it evolved over millions of years, the land that actually supported human evolution in a number of ways. When we interact with that land for our vital nourishment, I think it sustains us in ways that we cannot absolutely understand.

Me: *What are some ways that you found that it sustains you?*

Lloyd: Well for me I find a lot of power in foraging from the awareness it brings to my environment. Every year I crave certain behaviors because the wildness of my humanity has evolved with those behaviors, and they are behaviors that I hadn't experienced prior to foraging.

Now, when it's fall, I just start thinking about acorns and salmon and blue elderberries. They're things that I crave and my mind goes there without even cognitively thinking, 'oh it's time to go and harvest acorns.' It's like my spirit is connected with the seasonal patterns in ways that aren't so cognitive and I think that that's really powerful for people who live in a very cognitive society.

Me: *One question that comes up might seem obvious but is there a health benefit to it? I mean sometimes when you say the word "craving", that's got a negative connotation, right? So, is it healthy and, if so, why?*

Lloyd: Yes absolutely. In general, I often tell people that wild foods are twice as nutritious as their domesticated analogs. Even things like blueberries that are noted for their high levels of antioxidants—you know, they're just packed with vitamins and minerals... blueberries are domesticated from a wild food—but their wild ancestors have twice the antioxidant levels. If we go out and we pick evergreen huckleberries, mountain blueberries, or cascade blueberries, they're much more nutritious than the cultivated ones.

But it's not just the nutrients in them, it's also the activity of harvesting them. When we go out and pick foods we're being active. The sedentary lifestyle is one of the big problems in American society. People are getting these diseases of affluence like diabetes and heart disease that not only relate to an improper balance of foods but also really relate to sedentism.

Another thing that foraging gives us is a diverse diet. When we're eating seasonally available foods and we're eating from the diversity of life around us we actually eat a much more diverse diet than we do if we just eat the same commodities year-round that are always available in the grocery store.

According to research by archaeologists at the Burke Museum, they found archaeological remains for 270 to 280 foods that were part of the Coast Salish diet. Those are only foods that preserve well within the archaeological record. But there are other foods that we're never cooked and don't preserve well and working with Elders they've been able to expand that list to close to 300 species.

And again I love comparing to our Western diet now, because in terms of diversity it's just not that rich even though we have the whole world to choose from. We can have a diverse diet but most of us are depending on a few species for the majority of our calories.

Me: *What do you think about the argument that some people pose where they say if you get too many people involved in foraging wild foods then it will have too great of an impact on the already taxed natural ecology? So, it's more of a preservation stance than a conservation stance. Thoughts on that?*

Lloyd: Yeah and I do get that question a lot, and it's kind of a juggernaut because the problem we're faced with in this crisis of biodiversity loss is really a problem of our industrial agricultural society where we have been able to grow our population beyond the carrying capacity of several different ecosystems by shipping food from one part of the world to another. People are rewarded for having big families in the farm economy. This is something I saw in Nepal when I lived there. In the lowlands of Nepal, malaria had been eradicated, so there was all this rich arable land available. So, people moved there and suddenly they went from a traditional family size of two to four to a family size of fifteen to twenty. In the farm economy, people needed the family help to clear the fields and to do the farm chores.

There's a lot of debate about this in anthropology: what came first, population growth or the agricultural revolution? Did people invent agriculture as a necessity to feed more people? I strongly believe that agriculture enabled large population growth because in non-agricultural societies there is a lot more incentive to live within the carrying capacity of the land around you. If you have too many children you have a hard time feeding them. In an agricultural society you are changing your lives so drastically that you can just create more food. So, the population is not as tied to the ecological wealth or the ecological heritage. It's more a product of simpler metrics such as soil and water and labor rather than the natural abundance of different species that might then depend on those things. People are eliminating some of that complexity.

So, we have this problem today: we're faced with environmental degradation and we see ourselves as the cause of that, and we don't know how to interact in a healthy way with the environment. We see all of our physical needs as taxing the environment in ways that are not healthy. We do not see ourselves as part of the ecosystem. And I think the solution to the problem is to help people feel like their needs can be produced sustainably from the ecosystem.

That's something that foraging can help us with. When we go out and forage, especially if we do it year to year, we are witnessing the impact of our behavior on the environment and we can moderate those impacts accordingly. I know that if I collect too many camas bulbs they're not going to grow back the next year. I know that if I don't steward the resources I'm eating then they're not going to be there. So, I think that we all can't necessarily go out and forage from the wild places that are closest to where we live because we've inherited all of these problems. We're living in these giant cities and if everyone just went to the nearest green patch to harvest their stinging nettles there would be no more stinging nettles. But the cities are a product of this industrial agricultural paradigm where it's easy to move resources from distant places into cities. Where people are disconnected from the places where those foods are being grown. The population is too high.

I'm not sure exactly how it's going to happen, but I think that foraging is absolutely part of the solution. It's a different paradigm. It's a way of getting our food without destroying the planet. I think we don't actually know if foraging can support our current human population because we know so little about these wild foods and how productive they are. We can compare a cornfield to a garry oak ecosystem. I don't know that anybody's done this, but it's something that I'm very interested in doing. We know that a corn field can produce so many tons of food per acre and we can calculate that, the calories per acre. But we don't really have a handle on how productive a garry oak ecosystem is in terms of acorn calories per acre. And that's just the beginning. We are so used to thinking about foods in monocultures and we're not used to comparing the productive value of one ecosystem to another, so really what we should be comparing it with is the farm ecosystem, which may be corn and beef. If we're growing a lot of that corn to feed beef, how many beef calories per acre are we yielding? And then compared to this garry oak ecosystem. Not only are there edible acorns to eat, but there's also deer. There might be camas growing [in the understory]; there might be squirrels; there might be wild greens like miner's lettuce and stinging nettle. So we can't just look at one food of that ecosystem. We really have to compare the whole thing.

And I don't know what the numbers are yet but we also have to think about the impacts on the environment of a corn field versus a garry oak ecosystem. A cornfield is losing soil and is requiring intense amounts of fossil fuels for fertilizers, running farm equipment, for petrochemicals, and for pesticides. But in this garry oak ecosystem, we're building soil and we're supporting biodiversity at the same time as ourselves.

And then one more comparison I want to make is thinking about the biosphere: biosphere being the whole geography of the ecosystem— so as deep as the roots go to as high as the branches of the tree go. In terms of food systems I'd like to think more in terms of the edible biosphere. Really the biosphere is bigger because of the insects and the birds that fly above, but we don't often eat those insects and birds.

So, a cornfield has a biosphere of about six feet. Corn has really shallow roots and grows to about five and a half to six feet tall, maybe eight feet. In that same garry oak ecosystem you might have a biosphere that could be a hundred feet tall. So even though one acorn is much smaller than one head of corn, the productive area of that corn field is very tight. It is very dense, that productivity is amazingly concentrated, but I think we need to start thinking about diffusing our demands on the ecosystem or on the land around us.

One thing that my friend Elise Krohn says, who does a lot of thinking about indigenous food systems, is that everything from whitecap to whitecap is producing indigenous foods. So, the whitecap of the mountains to the whitecap of the sea. And so, foods from as high as a mountain goat can climb to as deep as a halibut can dive. There's this huge range of edible landscapes out there.

The edible biosphere of native food producing ecosystems both taller and more expansive so it doesn't have to be as concentrated on the land around our communities. If we think about it from a watershed perspective, if there are all these food-producing ecosystems from whitecap to whitecap, each one doesn't have to be so productive.

And while we're foraging from these landscapes we're eating

healthier foods; we're living a more active lifestyle; we're connecting more deliberately and in a number of different ways to the natural world around us; we're building a culture of stewardship instead of this colonial paradigm. We're building a sense of place. I think colonial cultures do not want to have a sense of place because they need to be able to move from one place to another to exploit those resources. And that translates into individual views in all of us where we don't know the land around us intimately; we don't depend on our knowledge of the land around us for our wealth. We depend on knowing general things that can have relevance in a society anywhere. In our society, in fact, we often have more opportunity if we leave. We go away to college. When we finish college, we go away to wherever there's a job, and so we learn these skills that are not place-based at all.

We're encouraged to go where the money is and I think that's absolutely a colonial mentality. And we don't do colonialism as a government, but we still do neocolonialism as a capitalist society, and that gets a lot of environmental critique. I think that the personal colonialism is not getting enough attention, and that is people that just abandon their homes and their families and their knowledge of place for opportunity.

Simple Wisdom

A simple, everyday wisdom around our food that is spoken by doctors, dieticians, naturopaths, and healers of all kinds is this: *go back to the land.* If we use the lens of the Western scientific and historical perspective, human beings have been farming for about 12,000 years max. The oldest of our ancestors of the human genus, *Homo habilis,* seems to have evolved around 2.8 million years ago. Our ancestors before that were a long line of about 12 million or more years of hominids. With those numbers, that makes our agricultural heritage one thousandth of our hominid evolutionary story. Every one of these grandmothers and grandfathers for the other 99.9% of the time foraged directly from the land. Organs shaped with the plants, fungus, and animals that were creating them. They grew together and the shaping of hominids to humans to *Homo sapiens* was wrought with what grew wild and unmanipulated on the Earth. Millions of years of shaping caused a community of organs that worked optimally with the natural diet. No different than the deer or the cougar.

Anthropologists have a lineage of works dedicated to understanding the ramifications of agriculture on human beings. It is a fascinating line of curiosity that a book on Place and Wonder can only barely touch. It may be worth asking questions and doing research around physical diseases that seemed to co-arise with agriculture. This could beg questions of the medicinal value of simply eating a wilder diet. As Abe suggested in the above interview, with agriculture came an increasingly narrow diversity of human diet. Over time, we stopped regularly eating countless species from a diversity of plant families—each with micronutrients we most certainly have not yet identified.

If you have one, open up a book on edible plants and note how many plant families, let alone species are in that book. Then, if you're curious, research how many plant families are in the average diet of the dominant culture. You may conclude that we, as a species have gone through a kind of nutritional narrowing. If, as it seems, psychology and biology are bound together, does that mean a correlate psychological narrowing? There is a lot of research, more every day, on the effect of nutrition on physical health. We see this in the increased marketing of superfoods from traditional diets. In this book, I propose that we also get curious about the living, subjective relationship between humans and wild food. I propose we think past just physical health and wonder about the behavioral, social, psychological, and spiritual aspects of these relationships.

Eating wild foods is not often easy. There is a good reason we chose to cultivate particular foods in contained, easily accessible places. Wild food can fight for its life. It can be hard to find. Thankfully, the more we know, the more we see the abundance and the more we enjoy the entire journey of eating from the wild landscape.

If you have ever been stung by stinging nettle, you know that plant well. I have semi-traumatic memories from my childhood of going to a boy scout camp where, during our "free time" the oldest boys formed a club and vowed to torture all the younger people. They put on gloves and roamed the trails armed with stinging nettles. If they caught you, you were sure to be covered in welts. I distinctly remember long lines of crying little kids with welts on their arms, myself included, waiting in line at the water fountain to douse our arms in cool water for some momentary relief.

That trauma aside, it turns out that stinging nettle is now, quite possibly, my favorite edible plant. Nothing in this world compares to the delicious vigor of a bowl full of steamed nettles. Nettle lasagna puts all other lasagna to shame. Inevitably, when plucking those young plants, no matter how careful you are, you end up getting stung, and that ends up being a part of the harvest as well. Those plants are potent, and they make sure we know it. And for all that orneriness on the outside, they fill our insides with a vibrant life-affirming tide of "yes!" It might be worth researching and asking around about the medicinal quality of these wonderplants as well. Ingesting them is good for helping with allergies. The stings themselves are said to be very good for arthritis. If you are very brave and sufficiently foolish, you can roll in nettles in the spring to have a full flush of your circulatory system. If you decide to do this, avoid your face and tenderest bits, wear soft clothing afterward, and be prepared to be very energized and a little uncomfortable for three days. Let me know if you try it.

I am personally very thankful toward those camp hellions for their unwitting introduction, no matter how terrifying it was.

Aside from nettles, there is a host of fairly easily accessible wild foods in your ecosystem. If you live in a city, you may have to venture a bit further to get foods that are relatively toxin-free. I wonder how we would treat pollution and toxins if we had a depth cultural understanding that *every* spot of Earth can yield precious food and medicine. Many of the "weeds" that inhabit lawns and disturbed areas are edible and/or medicinal. I've heard some offer the perspective that this is the Earth offering healing to a suffering section of the bios. I know our dominant culture does not like to grace the Earth or many other "things" with consciousness. Regardless of how we choose to define "consciousness" it seems evident that the organisms working together to create the biosphere harmonize into a dynamic and creative response to conditions. Much like our own bodies. Made of cells and organs that don't seem to directly hold or contribute to our subjective conscious experience, yet so many bodily processes are quite brilliant and intentional. If you have ever been seriously injured, you know this intimately. It is awe-inspiring to witness how the body problem-solves and act in order to heal: inventively fighting infections and mending tissues. Often, in these cases, the personal consciousness simply registers being tired and in pain. Can greater biological systems work with the same responsiveness and intentionality?

I wonder if our perceptual narrowing has made us dull to certain nuances of our experience when relating to our biological family.

Years ago, in a different place from where I live now, I decided to try catching salmon in an older fashion. I made a spear out of oceanspray and spent a good amount of time preparing myself ethically and relationally so that I could do this with good conscience. I made plans. I researched the fish. I spent time with my own spirit and I fasted the night before. I took this very seriously. My partner at the time was (and is) a very talented and brilliant human being. She was a bodyworker by profession. She was very supportive of this endeavor and she volunteered to go with me. She wanted to stand with the fish and appreciate the landscape. So, we headed out, found a good spot, and split up. I hunted for a long time. I spent time hiding and sneaking, waiting, working to empty my mind, and finally striking when the time was right. I learned, through a lot of attempts, that the design of my spear needed to be altered and I finally recognized that I would catch no fish. I said some thanks and headed back downstream.

There I saw my partner standing on a rock and gutting a salmon with a small pocketknife.

Frankly, there is a frantic little monkey that lives in my mind and likes to mess things up. It saw this and started clambering about how unfair it was that she was successful and I wasn't—how I had gone through so much preparation and she just came along and caught one without doing anything. Thankfully, at that time I had learned enough to not listen to the monkey for too long. I sighed and I remember overtly thinking, "she's my teacher. Go learn from her."

So, I did. And she told me her story.

She was standing among the fish with a camera and taking pictures. She stopped taking pictures and just stood there in the stream admiring these beautiful and powerful beings. As she stood there and stayed with these fish, they slowly moved closer and closer to her until they were swimming right alongside her. She noticed one large fish right next to her feet and she told me that in her mind she said to the salmon, "you would let me pick you up, wouldn't you?" She slowly bent down and let her hand enter the water. She swam her hand alongside the salmon. With a bodyworker's attunement and grace, she gently stroked her hand along the salmon's body until she came to the caudal fin. Once there, she gently, with one stroke, lifted the salmon from the water. The salmon never struggled once, just remained in placid freeze as she carried the fish across the water to the rock where she was standing as she told the story. In another fluid motion, she swung the salmon in a great arch and broke through the skull, ending that life in one stroke.

I cast my spear aside and devoted the rest of our time to learning this way. I learned, on that day, that attunement to the salmon means a quietness of body. I learned that I had to drop the project of my identity and let myself feel salmonish: let my hand drop in to the secret pools and swim as a fish doing her last great dance. The salmon taught me very directly and very consistently that if there is one moment when I try to use aggressive force or my mind seeks to quickly grasp, the salmon will swim away. There is simply no way that my hands can overpower those brilliant beings. The only way is to stay clear and attuned all the way through. And if it is done right, the salmon would not even flip once when pulled out of the water. There is no way to do this kind of thing and not feel a deep respect and gratitude for those salmon. There is no way to do this and not feel a debt for taking the life of such a being. It awakened a protector in me, for the salmon and the stream. It also taught me the difference between taking through technology and concentrated force as opposed to attuning.

Taking a life is ethically challenging. Fishing has many rules and regulations for very good reason, and in most places this kind of fishing is illegal. So, if you read this, please don't just run out and try it. Do your work first and make good decisions. Know that the river or creek is being fertilized with the next generations of these vital biospheric life-givers and that you could crush the eggs—the last work of entire life journeys. Ethics, debt, and responsibility are part of eating. If we accept them and feel them, ethics, debt, and responsibility become a part of identity. If we depend on the salmon and the wild plants, they become a very real part of us.

What happens when we wrap our food in petroleum products and raise our children's finger to know the sacred connection of food is through oil? That to harvest our basic needs, we must first harvest a federal reserve note—an abstract community debt? What happens when we live under the delusion—and it is a delusion—that we are not dependent upon wild foods and wild systems for our lives? What happens when we outsource the soul-wrenching ethical challenges of having to take other lives to sustain ours—when we can have others far, far away do the killing of invertebrates, rodents, and more necessary for industrial farming? When we can buy meat and never meet the eyes of the being while life vanishes?

We may be in a geological blip of time where, as a species, we get to defer these primal processes that have been a part of us for our entire heritage. I suspect that some deep part of ourselves still knows this. There is a Zen saying: *there is nowhere in the world to spit*. Some cultures in the global economy can avoid the immediate witnessing of the impact of our actions, but the deep mind knows and there is an uncomfortable dissonance. There is only one planet. And we, as a species, must eventually eat everything that we create. This is a kind of biospheric karma that we can never get around. We are eating both the good works and the suffering of our ancestors, and we are leaving good works and suffering for our children and for the children of all species. How much oil will they need to eat? What can we teach them of the beauty and grace of their immediate home? How can we support the passing on of the knowledge that food and medicine are the product of the entire face of the Earth? What happens when we look at our lawns and forests and begin to see a sea of food and medicine with no inherent interference? Can we find a way to not let property and money obstruct this empowered identity? Can we be adaptive and creative with this problem?

Cultivating Culture

I wonder how much the debt and the responsibility of eating has crafted human cultures over time. I suspect that many people share the sentiment that it is hard to remain feeling, to not deaden oneself or avoid certain sensations that come with harvesting. Eating is the act of becoming. And in becoming, we are causing another being to cease becoming. If we consciously access any compassion or empathy at all, this becomes a deeply moral consideration. It can hurt to harvest empathetically. I wonder how many songs and rituals, art, prayers, stories, and cosmologies are a way to help us hold this. Food keeps us alive physically. The act of consciously eating might just be a lynchpin of staying alive psychologically and spiritually.

Can you think of a culture that does not take pride in a certain food? Where food is not a part of identity?

When we take in food, it creates our bodies and our whole baseline of physical sensations. It crafts our moods. A Place-based cuisine is akin to the color palette from which we paint ourselves. It makes sense that we would weave an identity with the food that creates us. Food and identity have a primal link.

Ben Greené, maker of the film, *Survival Prayer*, spent time in Haida Gwaii paying attention to the land and people, listening, looking, and asking questions about food, language, culture, and identity. I interviewed him for this section of the book. During our interview time, we watched clips from his movie. In one clip, Margaret Edgars tells an old Haida story about the eulachon. Eulachon is a very fatty staple food fish that was abundant in the Haida Gwaii area for thousands of years, but then left. Since that time, the Haida people have traded with others to keep this fish in their diet. I suggest buying the film to witness Margaret, the land, and other people share their story. You won't be disappointed. Here are the words that Margaret spoke, "we did have a story told by one of our elders. We used to have eulachon on the island and they said it got made fun of by someone. So, the eulachon just disappeared and never came back to the island. As God put this food on our island for our survival.

During our interview, Ben shared something told to him by a Haida elder: "You don't make fun of anything. Be thankful that your food is there in the forest and in the sea. We have to have respect for everything, they used to tell us."

The Haida people have been living on, with, and through that island for upwards of 17,000 years, depending on estimates. I suggest pausing and taking a breath here. Pause from reading and take a look around. Listen to the sounds and feel the air across your face.

Then consider just what that number means. Try to put your mind into how long 17,000 years is in one Place. Think about your own very short life and how you've grown to know the places you've lived the longest. Imagine so much time without industrialization. Living and eating directly with the landscape. Wouldn't you just grow into each other, like the cougar and the deer? Wouldn't your people's voice be, in some ways, a voice of the land? Not the only voice, but a voice. Like speaking for your family, of which you are a part.

Dig enough into your ancestry or the ancestry of any human being on this planet and every line leads to a similar relationship with similar teachings and stories. The voice of land and people growing through one another.

That voice says, through different tongues, not to make fun of anything. That message was passed down by the Haida as a vital teaching for countless generations. Why?

Greené: We can talk about all kind of things: what is being harvested, what it is used for, etc. There are a lot of different kinds of data that interest anthropologists. But there's also the experience of doing it. [...] Harvesting takes time. It's out in the elements. It's cold. It's windy. Sometimes it's uncomfortable. It has a rhythm to it. [...] It involves our hands. So, there's this literal contact between culture and Place through harvesting. Providing sustenance but also a cultural experience that is about identity. Because people talk about, if we couldn't do this, then who would we be? We would be just like everybody else. Harvesting is about who we are.

I asked Ben more about this physical act, about the tactile relationship.

Greené: I was very interested in not just the atmosphere and the rhythms of harvesting but the tactile experience. So, getting close on the people's hands so that people in the audience could have almost like a tactile experience. To almost feel like their hands are pulling these supple berries or snapping the thimbleberry shoots or cutting the slippery seaweed or pulling the salmon out of the net; cutting the salmon. The tactile relationship is the literal interface between culture and landscape.

Greené: We have a huge amount of our brain that is devoted to our hands and if we're only interfacing with abstract data with our hands through computers and so on and we're not using them in a subtler way that actually involves feeling and subtle manipulations, it feels to me like a life that's less human.

Greené: There's a cultural/spiritual sustenance that comes with these kinds of experiences of harvesting. A physical connection, a set of sensory memories associated with activities that become a part of a person, that they deeply care about. And if that went away, something is lost, right?

In the film, Barbara Wilson, says, "if we didn't have wild foods or the foods that our ancestors eat and we didn't have the words that go with them, which is our traditional knowledge, we would be just like everybody else. We would go to the store, we would never know where our food came from, we'd have lots of diseases—we do anyway because we've taken food from other places into our system—I think we'd be very poor. I think we'd be very poor socially, mentally, physically definitely. Because I really believe that our bodies crave the sockeye by the time spring gets here. I know what a treat it is to eat the seaweed—black seaweed—it's like popcorn. It's the best, you know? And if you think about eating clams and cockles and all those seafoods and all the joy we get from eating them, life would be so sad. Life would be sad without wild foods."

According to Ben's research, one in five people on Haida Gwaii had diabetes at the time of the filming, which is much higher than the national average in Canada. Ben points to what some people on Haida Gwaii call the "poisonous foods"—industrially produced junk foods like chips and hot dogs. They say they are literally poisonous because they give the people diabetes. He points to a study done in the nineties where they got people to engage in learning how to embrace their traditional diet again and start eating traditional foods. Their glucose levels stabilized and they got positive outcomes. So, there's a health movement now to turn back to the traditional foods.

Ben also reflected on the role of reverence.

Greené: Reverence being respect for something that is larger than ourselves, a feeling that we're a part of something bigger than ourselves. I think that is really important for letting us learn how to exercise restraint in how we interact with the land."

In the film Margaret Edwards speaks, "my grandmother was always talking about how blessed we are to have all this food around us. That's one of the reasons why I get up so early in the morning to see the beautifulness of the sun where the daylight is beginning. If you're out somewhere where you're out in the open and you can hear all the birds and all the life around you. You wouldn't know how much life there is until you get out there."

Me: *"So what I'm hearing through your work, the voices of the people you talked with, and this conversation is that the plants and the animals are food, but the actual act of harvesting is a food or a nutrient in and of itself."*

Greené: "I think so. Inherently valuable. I think harvesting, to these Haida people who I've filmed, is inherently valuable. It goes way beyond the utility of the end product.

(Ben pauses)

The food is also a gift. It's a gift from the land and it's a gift to the elders.

(Pauses again)

How do you want to live? I think it comes down to how do you want to live?

I think harvesting makes you love Place. Love is attention. Love is touch.

Right now, people are working to keep our foods and our relationship with the land healthy and vibrant.

In the southern end of the same continent, a grass is digging its vibrant wanting roots through vast swaths of the giving ground. The ground and the roots have known each other for as long as ape songs have been gracing the winds with their sweet and strange calls. This grass has been cradled by granddaughters and grandfathers, by mothers and uncles who give it word and whisper tales of its grace into the ears of the generations. Word by word, child hand by child hand, the grass and the people have learned each other and grown through one another, changing shape, twisting their organs, swimming their body-minds into ever-new oceans of chemistry, bending their seeds toward each other. It is a marriage of depth faith through the terrors and tides that all relationships must storm. It is a commitment so long and true that the each of the two would no longer be who they are without the other.

The humans told tales in many languages and many shapes over many eras of how the grass was born and how it bore humanity. This grass grew long heads filling with succulent seeds that shared a full palette of worldcolor. The grass gave up itself to the human hand, and the human hand held it more precious than any deep metal. Just as the algae and the fungus grew together to make the lichen, the two species took the long faith and committed to being two as one navigating the ever-creation of the wildernessed, changing body of the Earth. It is a vessel of humanity. A greatest accomplishment of human learning and blending, of being the world and loving the being. It is corn.

What did the ancient ancestor of corn feel like in our ancient ancestors' hands?

What is the root of our cultivars? What happened? What is the story?

It has taken serious genetic tracking and problem solving for western scientific culture to track corn to its ancestor, teosinte grass. By this method of tracking, it is estimated that it was about 9000 years ago when corn split off from the teosinte grass to start its journey of formation into the current cultivated species. People estimate that around 4000BC, selective breeding by Mesoamerican people enlarged the seed pods of corn to about 1 inch long. This process continued for another 6000 years until an "ear" of corn grew to the size it is today. Now, after all that growing with human hands, corn cannot reproduce without human assistance. We are that linked.

For over 3000 years, Indigenous American people have been soaking corn in alkali water, water mixed with ash, to liberate the B vitamin, Niacin. Corn without this treatment is a poor source of niacin, and if it is not treated this way and there is not another major niacin source in the diet, a health condition called pellagra can occur. Pellagra is a serious deficiency of niacin and can cause severe diarrhea, dermatitis, dementia, and eventually death. People learned, through deep relationship, how to use other earth materials to pull this vitamin from corn and create a source where there was once a deficiency.

How did people figure this out without the same means of knowing that dominant western culture uses? No machines, industry, or scientific method.

In a deep valley in Mexico right now seed-protectors have established "corn reserves." Farms in secluded areas are guarding the diversity of traditional strains of corn from the area of the world currently known as Mexico. Year by year, they keep these heirlooms alive and do their best to guard their precious DNA from genetically modified pollen that inevitably catches the wind and works its way into their being. Scientific evidence and good rational thought reveal that the best defense against climate change and other challenges is biodiversity, despite claims from the dominant corporation for genetically modified agriculture, Monsanto.

This little piece of this chapter has some tough content. I suggest you take a break and breathe the air. Find something you appreciate about your immediate landscape. Something you love about the Earth that is your home. Then, as you read this, I suggest noticing what your body is doing. Do you have emotions? Do you want to run or fight—avoiding the words, fighting them, imagining fleeing from the problems, or fighting the institutions and systems that made them? Do you feel helpless? Do you feel grounded? What can you do to stay grounded?

Monsanto is a company that has strongly affected the lives of people worldwide and changed the genetic heritage of our planet. The corporation has been around since 1901 where it made a good amount of its money selling saccharine. It has since introduced aspirin, PCBs, essential work on the creation of nuclear weapons, Agent Orange, Zyklon-B gas (a chemical weapon used in WWII), aspartame, synthetic bovine growth hormone (rBGH), Roundup, a host of herbicides and pesticides, and now genetically modified seeds that are pesticide and herbicide resistant and are genetically designed to not reproduce. It would be worth researching the history of each of these products and the host of law suits and bans that have followed their introductions into our lifestream.

The seeds that Monsanto currently bioengineer can only be bought from Monsanto. Monsanto genetically modifies the seeds so that they cannot reproduce, and, therefore the farmers must buy new ones every year. Monsanto proposes that engineering seeds that resist dying from the toxic chemicals that Monsanto sells to cover our food is the way to create a steady, healthy food stream for the planet. Ample research shows that perennial applications of these chemicals onto soil eventually kills off the biota, the essential micro-organisms that make a soil fertile. Areas of India, Africa, and South America that have had fertile fields for millennia are becoming deserts due to this strategy and people are committing suicide because of it. They cannot save their seeds to replant the next year, they must buy the chemicals, they go into debt, and the land dies.

If you can, ground yourself and take a moment to recognize how much vibrant and beautiful life is currently around you: the unfathomable force of uncountable beings that are right now creating this whole planet. Think about your immediate community and how the people, even when making mistakes, are generally striving to hold some sort of ethics and goodness. People don't want to suffer. When people are healthy, they don't want to create suffering for others. That's a wonderful gift of a baseline for humanity. Think about all that is supporting us. Breathe the world and come to your senses.

The ways of thinking and the current systems that reward Monsanto's actions are a problem for our biosphere and our humanity. Just one problem. And a problem contains a path of solutions when the mind is willing to see it clearly and to think new thoughts because of it.

It is up to each of us to discern the problem clearly. I suggest, without losing your ground and getting too activated, seeing clearly what Monsanto's history is. You can research every lawsuit and ban and see the history of competing propaganda that Monsanto has put out until it was no longer economical to do so. Clearly speaking, Monsanto is a company that has mostly produced toxins and has currently shifted its focus to chemical warfare with arthropods, micro-organisms, and plants. The battlefield where Monsanto dumps these deadly chemicals is our food. We are eating these products. Our digestive systems contain a host of microorganisms that are similar to what is in the soil. We are eating this suffering and it is killing parts of the micro-organismic community that makes up our bodies. We are becoming different in our bodies and minds because of this. This is a problem. Let's figure out a new way.

Many in Mexico are actively fighting Monsanto, Dupont, and others to protect the genetic integrity of corn. Some evidence suggests that all strains of corn have been infiltrated in some way by genetically modified DNA, but still the strains are mostly intact. However, legislators are allying with the corporations and passing laws that forbid farmers from trading or selling seed. As in the U.S., Mexican laws are being passed to make the infiltrating genetically modified genes private property. This strategy results in the violent takeover of small farms that have been infected by the pollen from genetically modified products.

How is this affecting our physical health, how we think, and our ecological body?

What happens if we cannot save seed? For the first time, more people in the world are in cities rather than in rural areas, so we don't grow up deeply understanding the vital connection of saving our own seeds. What if we took the time to remember this? What if we pause and recognize that no seed means no people?

Svalbard is a Norwegian island close to the north pole. It is the location of the Svalbard Global Seed Vault. The seed vault can hold up to 4.5 million seeds. This vault holds seeds from all over the globe and has a mission to provide a safety net against the accidental loss of our vital genetic diversity. It is in one of the most remote and stable places on the planet and it is holding our greatest treasures. It is not filled with gold. It is not filled with oil.

You Are Who You Eat

I heard the following story secondhand before I met the guy who actually authored it. It turned out he lived a block away from me, and he confirmed that it really happened. So, let's just say that this person is and was very excited about wild foods and was in the stage of exploration where he realized that there are actually very few toxic plants and a great abundance of food growing wild out of the Earth. He was ecstatically chomping every new species that came his way, and found to his delight that he felt happier and healthier as a result. He went down that seductive road of the utopian wild and began doubting more and more of what the dominant culture warned against. Finding the idea that most plants are poisonous to be a fiction, he became cavalier in his experimentation.

He ate of the land and he shared his abundance of wildharvesting with others.

Like most in his culture, he also had a garden, a house, and regularly shopped for groceries. Wild foods were a passionate perk. So, one day said gentleman went out to his garden which he had somewhat neglected. Other passions and demands of life turned his head from the wanting bed and he found himself very late for planting. He also found a curious thing. Volunteers! Plants in his garden that had planted themselves. Being a fan of the wild processes and the unmanipulated bounty that the world offers, he took a good look at these volunteers instead of pulling them out as weeds and trying to make room for his store-bought cultivars. He noticed that these plants had thick carrot leaves, and, as he let them grow, they proved to be very interesting and potent forms of carrots. He admired the journey the seeds must have taken to find their way to his bed, and tended to the carrots just as carefully as he did his bib lettuce and his lacinato kale. They grew tremendously large and he was excited to see what kind of root they would have. Their stalk had beautiful purple blotches and he imagined that some fancy strain of colored carrot with rarer genetics had wandered into his life.

The time came, eventually, for the harvesting. He worked his bare fingers down the fluffy soil alongside the carrot's root, grabbed the stout stalk, wiggled and pulled until the deep root was birthed into the airy upworld. It was a proud and unique carrot indeed. Whitish, like a long thin parsnip, but with enough girth to promise a delicious meal. He broke off the foliage and cleaned the roots, then took them inside to prepare them.

He had it all planned. These wonderous journeyman who happened into his life would become a culinary tribute to the delicious between of the wild and the cultivated. He had bought the other ingredients and set out to transform these roots into a great batch of kim chee. He held back from eating them raw, wanting to use every bit for the batch. He mixed the ingredients into a large glass jar, covered it with a cloth, and set it in a warmish corner where it would perform its month-long transformational ferment. Slowly bubbles could be seen and the microbe-rich broth promised a delicious, spicy tang.

After one month, the time had come. Fortune had it that he was invited to a pot luck party thirty miles to the south, and the community of people there were exactly the type who would appreciate this kim chee's lineage. He took an empty quart jar and began filling it with his treasured creation. He paused halfway, thinking that, though there was a certain poetry to trying it together with others for the first time, he did want to make sure it turned out all right. So, he took a small bowl and filled it up for himself.

It was kim chee through and through and the wild carrots had a strange but somewhat inviting bitterness to them that was balanced rather well, to his palette, by the spices and ferment. He finished filling the quart jar, got in his car, and took the drive south on the highway.

According to him, it was about halfway into the drive when he started to feel a little funny. He had a swampy dizziness and there was a strange surge of energy concentrating on his core. It was night, and, as he kept driving, he noticed that the lights of the passing cars were beginning to do strange things in his visual field. The lights became streaming beams and he noticed that when he turned his head, his visual field took some time to catch up. He, of course, became very concerned. Not a good thing to experience while propelling a one ton hunk of metal at seventy miles per hour. He thought about pulling over. Then he noticed that the edges of his vision were starting to go dark. He pulled over and called 911.

I honestly can't remember what happened after that, though I will admit that I have shared this story with plenty of other people and embellished an ending with getting his stomach pumped. That might have actually happened, but I won't commit to it in a writing. What is true is this: he was poisoned and it was bad. In fact, this fine fellow had unwittingly attempted a Socratic ending to his life. Just like Socrates, he ingested one of the most deadly plants in North America: poison hemlock. A wonder of the carrot family.

Plants are potent. They involve risk and they demand that we pay attention. We can't narrow our perception or tune out our attention when harvesting. A good amount of wild mushrooms and a few plants, like poison hemlock, will kill you.

That kind of reality with our food wakes us up. Potential death or suffering is one sure-fire way to encourage perceptual widening. We are made to pay good attention to things that can hurt or kill us. Just like the cougar to the deer, having a predator grows us. We become very attuned and we learn how to live skillfully with that being. If we live with the land, we know the plants, and if we know the plants we know what we can eat and what we can't. We even know what to do if our little ones eat something they shouldn't. Children learn to identify plants with astounding proficiency.

So, let's go back to the woods to find what our bodies are made to eat. Go to the beaches or the meadows. Go to the creek's edge. Learn and remember.

It is not just nourishment. It is also medicine.

Who Eats Who

My friend, Kelley, recently taught me my new favorite word: xenohormesis. She sent me an article that explains this fascinating movement of nature inside and outside of the body. Lacking the same degree of movement that animals have, plants have become far more brilliant chemists. Since they can't get out of the way of something or move themselves to a new location, they change the chemistry of who they are. When plants are stressed via a pernicious influence or an environmental condition, they release particular compounds that might fight off the bug or handle the freezing temperature. Xenohormesis is a term for what happens when a plant's biochemical health response is ingested by animals so that the animals can enjoy the same benefit. Attuned to the plants and to themselves, animals have been observed intentionally eating stressed out plants. It turns out that there is evidence that these stressed out plants can maximize the yield of health-promoting plant compounds. These compounds affect the animal's overall longevity and fitness and help with the animal's own immune responses.

We use a similar principle in our Earth-based, non-industrial medical heritage. In the pacific northwest, the douglas firs tend to produce a decent amount of sap when their bark layer is penetrated by woodpeckers or environmental damage. The sap flows into the wound and covers it. That sap has antifungal and antimicrobial properties that help protect the tree's living layer from infection. It is the tree's immune response. Human animals have paid enough attention to the trees to long ago notice what is happening. So, our clever little minds and hands have learned to collect the sap and use it for our own antifungal and antimicrobial purposes. If we get a fungal infection on our skin, a salve or tincture or just the sap will do wonders. That is one very simple example of countless. Medicinal teas and tinctures are the basis for so much of modern medicine. It seems that recently our culture has been recognizing that industrially isolating compounds that plants provide does not often work as well for our beings as eating the plant itself.

Our systems consume and provide for one another. That is what it means to be alive as part of a biological community. When we pay attention, it is amazing to see the variety of life that other beings actually eat. The gentle deer is often thought of as a pure herbivore. The deer ingest a vast web of plants for sure. However, I have seen some serious mushroom consumption in the Pacific Northwest. It is also worth noting how many bugs and other fungi the deer must consume along with all that foliage. Those bugs and fungi may make up a small percentage of the diet but they almost surely provide some essential nutrients that the deer cannot get from plants alone. I have even heard from trusted sources that deer have been seen eating newborn rabbits if they stumble upon a nest. Though we may not want to envision a deer eating babies, it happens and it is actually a testament to the messy jambalaya of livingness that we all stew in.

There is a frustratingly clever community of deer mice who persistently find ways to share my office space. Treasured articles of clothing, handmade fabric, gifts, feathers, and sea charts have all been victims to the merciless maw of the mouse. One spring, a mother mouse found out that a drawer I rarely open was a perfect place to raise her newborns. Until I opened it. Honestly, part of my problem with mice is that I tend to be a softy when looking at the mouse eye to eye. I have no doubt that the damned mouse senses this and feels a somatic invitation to do whatever the hell she wants in my office space. As angry as I have gotten at them, they are so clever and cute that I can't bring myself to do anything but mouth threatening words, relocate their nests, and try in vein to mouseproof my space.

So, I couldn't even bring myself to relocate this mouse's nest when I saw the little eraser-sized pinky babies all cuddled up in a warm home of insulation and gnawed pieces of my favorite scarf. I told the mother that I would wait until the babies were just big enough, then I'd remove the nest and mouseproof again. As I waited, I became fond of occasionally peaking in to see the little brood of future troublemakers squiggle and peep. They were damned cute. Then I noticed something very interesting. The brazen mother mouse who had my number completely and was not afraid of being seen, began sallying forth to feed herself while I was working. Hearing the stress-inducing sounds of nibbling rodent jaws, I looked around to see if I could find the cause. I saw this mother of mice, her mammaries fat, gnawing the toes off of a great blue heron claw that I had displayed amongst other nature curios. Over the next week, she chewed up and entirely ate three toes worth of desiccated claw. I imagine that all that milk takes a lot of stuff out of her, calcium being just one major ingredient. And I imagine the claw created a mother capable of making milk that would make more mice.

The great bear is a wonderful exemplar of varied diet and varied being. The bear would not be without a particular seasonal dietary progression. When bears come out of hibernation, their bodies are wholly different from what they were when they went in. The bear has not eaten and has not defecated for that whole time, and the system needs particular help to get things going again. The bear hungers for particular plants. The ones with roughage that will give him energy and work like a toilet brush through those plugged up intestines. The bear's diet changes with the season, and the bear's body morphs. Building on a lot of plant-based nutrients, among other things, in the summer, then more proteins and fats to prepare for the next cycle of hibernation. This means a shifting diet of everything from grasses to berries to mushrooms to insects to little critters to bigger game. With a very easy shift in perspective, the bear could be seen as an expression of these foods and of the land's season. The bear is one way that they continue their wander and wonder until and they become soil again, waiting for the seed.

Tracking who eats who is tracking the entire web of life. It could be the most skillful question toward understand the living relationships in our biosphere. A deep practice of following this question over time must yield a transformation in our view of death, subjectivity, and individuality. Lots of creatures would gladly eat us, given the chance. Just as we eat lots of creatures. Micro-organisms and fungi are making meals of us all the time. When we die, our conglomerate of experience, unique in the whole universe, unravels and disperses in mysterious vectors. That strange binding force that we call "life" seems to disappear: the unity of our cells, the community of organs, and that saturating dream of "I" unexists. Yet our stuff makes food for the extension of more "I." What is to say that we don't share "I?" What would change in our actions if we changed our perspective about living? What if being healthy was a way of offering the world a good meal when we die? The sentence, "I am a very good meal," can be a wonderful point of pride and a brilliant strut before our biological family. Why not be a good meal if you're going to be a meal no matter what?

This chapter is almost over, so I suggest pausing again. Wherever you are, take a moment to soften your vision and open your hearing. Listen with your eyes and look with your ears. Turn away from these words and be the world for a few breaths. The world as it is.

What is alive in you?

What if we pause for a moment as a people? It would have to happen person by person. It would emerge like spring, one bud at a time, and only well into the movement would some label of Spring emerge in our minds. What if, as a people, we pause momentarily from our technological advances and our ways of relating to other beings we share Life with? What if we just pause and take in the bigger picture? What if we listen? Take breaths to consider our actions and notice the results before moving forward.

There are a lot of thoughts about food in this chapter and a lot of proposals for shifting relationships. It's good to take a moment and honor the truth—that changing relationships takes time and effort. Sometimes the patterns are quite entrenched and the problems seem unsolvable, but I have yet to be in a relationship where it's not worth it to at least make some aspects a little bit better. Even at the end of a relationship, when it is clearly going to be over, a step toward kindness and compassion on both sides seems to always be worth it. I suspect that we actually cannot feel hopelessness in the exact moments when we are experiencing something changing for the better. The shift in relationship is like light in the darkness. It doesn't promise to go on forever or vanquish all darkness in the world, but in that little spot of the cosmos where our gentle eyes are shimmering, we experience the calm of appreciating the here and the now. We are blessed with seeing this little bit of our lives a little bit more clearly. Hopelessness comes after the fact, when the simulator of the mind creates ideas of the bigness of a problem and projects all these potentials for a future. But here and now in the moment of change, Life can be good. Life happens here and now.

I once heard Eliot Cowan quote African elders in saying that they are concerned about the intake of foreign foods into their cultures. I wish I could be more specific than locating the source as somewhere on the vast and varied continent of Africa. So, please forgive me elders, and let us simply hold the thought with curiosity in our minds. These elders are concerned because they say the people won't know whose ancestors they are eating. When we eat something from southeast Asia, whose ancestors are we eating? And vice versa.

This is a curious one to hold, indeed. Ancestors are relationships through time, and they are the foundation of identity. How can we understand who we are if we are eating and becoming who we don't know? Globally, most of us are now facing these conditions. There must be a new way of thinking and relating to help us work with this. And, I think it is worth considering.

Perhaps a part of the different way of thinking lies more in a completion of an incomplete identity.

In the United States, we are most often addressed as consumers. Since World War II, this has been, in some ways, an intentional and trackable shift in policy for our governing entity. Consuming is exactly one-half of the story. As we experience more "stuff" in our lives and diseases like hoarding become more prevalent, I wonder if we are actually craving the other half of our identity. I wonder if the abolition of the provider identity has created a kind of collective hungry ghost of our society. We keep eating, hoping to fill the gap of meaning, but the more we consume, the more we need the balancing consciousness of ourselves as providers. Debt begets duty. Simply eating seeds is eating the future generations of so many beings. This is a great sacrifice. It is a debt. It is a true debt for the ecology—the deep and true economy. When we take lives, we accept the debt—the duty to tend lives and raise the children that survive. When we consume, we grow debt and we hunger for the balance of duty. Perhaps it is time to consciously act under through truth that we are the ancestors and we are making the soil for the children of our world.

I wonder if this kind of consumer hunger is responsible for our grasping at superfoods from other cultures. The superfoods are often marketed as a central food for a culture that maintained a deeper sense of identity and Place-based connection. This morphs into the examination of micronutrients so that we can prove, in a culturally relevant way, that such relationships with land and food are nutritious. We then grasp. Superfoods become a brand of spiritual materialism, shopping for meaning and connection in body, mind, and spirit.

Instead of shopping for the embodied experience of another culture's ecospiritual identity, why not just fall in love with the superfood native to your area? If you are in the Pacific Northwest, fall in love with the salal berry. Fall in love with the taste and texture and get creative with it. Get to know this plant, then realize that it is growing wild all around you. You can plant it in your yard if you have one. If you don't have a yard, there are plenty of people interested in restoring natural habitat who would graciously accept your helping hands. And, over time, you and your children can eat the fruits of your labor. So can other beings. If you have a yard, there are programs in some areas where you will be given the plants or the money to buy them. You will be very pleased to soon realize that native plants grew up with this environment. They need almost no work from you to grow. They've been growing here in many cases for longer than human memory.

The consumer vacuum makes us frantic, and, perhaps more than anything, we forget to listen and feel. Remember, every one of our fully human ancestors listened deeply and felt enough to figure out food preparations and combinations like soaking corn in alkali water. This is a power of humanity and we absolutely can do this.

How do we listen to plants? The answer may very well dwell in the perceptual wilderness, the realm of perception that is beyond the narrowing.

The wisdom of the farmer is that you are not farming plants, you are farming the soil. You are tending the biota and nutrients in the soil. The more you pay attention year after year, generation after generation, the more you realize that the subtler processes beyond the vision are where the greatest life force does its work. In Western Culture, we have done miraculous work in extending our five senses (more so the vision and hearing) through tools and using our cognitive abilities to understand the world. This is a wonderful power. And, it seems that it is not enough. Our actions show that, even with these great powers, we are making some poor decisions that are hurting ourselves and our world. I suggest that, when such a condition arises, it implies a systems problem. It implies, to me, that we need to look for other ways of knowing and relating in order to balance the wonderful powers we already have. No sense in condemning a power and trying to make it smaller in order to find balance. We can't uneat the apple. No one can uneat an apple.

But we can grow new abilities that will yield balance.

One sense that has been largely armored off in consumer culture is the felt sense. Felt sense simply means physical sensations within the body. We all feel them. They are absolutely integral to our humanity. In fact, strong science, Buddhism, many indigenous traditions, and many other wisdom traditions recognize that what you actually feel in your body is a great source of information and the seat of wisdom.

The tightness in your stomach, the fluttering in your heart, the sinking in your gut, the heat in your head, the electric tingling in your fingertips are all a deep and present contact with experience. When they are conscious and felt, they are a direct form of knowledge. Neuroscientist, Antonio Damasio suggests that the body is a ground reference for understanding the entire world around us. He states, "our most refined thoughts and best actions, our greatest joys and deepest sorrows use the body as a yardstick." Felt sense is that yard stick. It offers data on the current state of the organism's being as that being contacts the reality of the present moment. Damasio calls this the "proto-self." It is the wordless knowledge that underlies our conscious sense of self.

It is entirely possible that every emotion and cognition has a correlate *preceding* sensation on the body that we have often pruned out of our awareness. Buddhism, a two thousand and five hundred-year-old sustained subjective inquiry into the mind, has come to this conclusion. If our thoughts and feelings are preceded by sensations, then wouldn't it be a worthy extension of our consciousness to be aware of those sensations?

Perceptual narrowing simply means we have narrowed what we are aware of. It does not mean that what is outside no longer exists and is no longer affecting us. We may not have any conscious awareness of radiation from a reactor leak, but it will kill us anyway. If we develop an awareness, we can choose to change our behavior and maybe save our lives. Being aware of the sensations in the body is the same thing. Most of what happens within us are blind reactions. When we can actually feel what is happening, we develop the ability to choose whether or not to do anything about it. We potentiate new options. We move from reaction to authentic action.

With food, when we are really attending and embracing our full humanity, we work with the felt sense. The felt sense teaches us the "song" of the food. The sensations teach us the true and deeply personal effects on our being. When we feel, we feel the food song through us. We feel the difference it creates in our beings. This is the root of our whole ancestral lineage of food and medicine. We are on a thinnest moment of human history where the objective approach is dominant and de-sensitization is rampant. The objective is a wonderful teacher, but as Barbara Wilson states in *Survival Prayer*, "we have set aside our ancestors' ways a little too severely." The result is not in the future or past—it is here now. The result is not feeling. It is cutting off our primal sense organ for our deepest relationships.

Food is feeling more than anything else.

It is our reactions to the feelings of our food that craft so much of our behavior, and consequently our clever more superficial consciousness comes up with explanations for all of this. If the consciousness can no longer feel—has numbed felt sense—then the explanations will be confused. We are asking ourselves to understand something with insufficient information. Like trying to explain city traffic patterns without being able to perceive the traffic lights and signs: searching for some elaborate mathematical explanation for why cars seem to all stop and move in patterns when all we have to do is extend our perception to see the obvious explanation. This may be why we are mystified by our indigenous brothers and sisters and our ancestors who figured out such elaborate relationships with natural food and medicine.

We have the ability, every single human. It is as innate as breathing. The sensation has been culturally pruned. When we bring the felt sense to consciousness with food, then we cultivate a greater capacity for discernment and also a certain degree of equanimity—which begets a depth of authority over our own actions. We don't blindly react, but we have the capacity to see longer term connections and we can *choose* actions with greater skill and capacity.

We begin to feel the root of our addictions and we feel how they correlate to other sensations and this opens the door to conscious understanding of the roots of our behavior. We learn to navigate food addictions. We learn to appreciate and choose what is truly healthy. We do this from the bottom of our consciousness, our soil, upward.

We develop a deeper, slower appreciation for the healthful song of wild whole foods. The mind discerns poison from medicine with greater accuracy.

This can change eating habits. Which can change cultural decisions. There is a true challenge for many of us in choosing to eat cheaply or eat healthfully. In some cases, we don't even have that choice. Sometimes we are gleaning from the food bank or feeding our children with whatever we can. Wild food can be just a tiny part. It can help in all the ways detailed in this chapter and in the book as a whole. Even gleaning dandelions in urban centers may not be an option due to toxins in the soil. This is a hard situation, and it will take real change to help heal these areas. These Places, beings, and people are us. The answers will come if we have the courage to shift our ways of perceiving and relating. We can make better choices now. Each of us, to the best of our ability. And it will take many minds from many Places and many positions to work through the systemic problems of feeding ourselves well and being good soil.

If you have the means, fast from other acquisitions and invest in your own soil, your body/mind, and the soil of the planet that we are leaving the planet's children. Eat food that feeds the planet. When those with means shift this value—it helps to enhance the value itself and to see the need for those without means. Social obligation grows from good, nutritious soil.

With growth, this can evoke the realization that we support food that supports land. Because land and water support life.

Feeling might be the only way that we can establish our living relationship with our world. Through listening with our full beings, not just our intellect and eyesight, not just through machines that extend our cognitive and perceptual powers. Through listening and feeling we can understand our plant relatives and we can work with the strangest shifts in our biological plane. The bioengineered strangeness and morphing microorganisms are a part of the wilderness of our cosmos, as we are, and we bend to the same rules. And we sing songs, new ones yet uncomprehended.

We can listen and calm our frantic hands. We can cease the harsh shoves we give to our living world, and we can receive the teachings. We can grow with our world and all of our relatives.

The Fire Within

BOW   SPINDLE   HAND HOLD   HEARTH   NEST

The western redcedar has been known as the *tree of life* in many tongues, and for many thousands of years our human tribe has been making ropes, clothing, tools, boats, ceremonies, fire, and more from this ever-nourishing organ of humanity. She splits naturally into planks with the grace and ease of a monk bowing. Some have said that when you are ill in any way, simply sitting with your back against the trunk of a redcedar can help heal you.

In redcedar country, you can wander the woodlands for a relatively short time, and you will inevitably find an old cedar stump with a spire of slender planks of seasoned wood. The planks are usually the perfect size for a fire by friction hearth. As if a gift. You can harvest this gift, and from one plank, you can make a hearth and spindle. From the crotch of a cedar tree you can make a handhold, and with a little sap or nose grease, you can make it slick enough to work well. From the inner bark of cedar you can craft a beautiful and strong rope. From the sweetly drooping branches, you can find a perfectly bent bow. From her outer bark, you can harvest and craft a fine duffy nest.

You can then take a moment and breath. You can give thanks to something and hold it in your mind. In this way, you can remember who you are.

You can smile.

You become Now. You can bring forth fire.

Fit the spindle in your bow. Situate your body so she is efficiently and skillfully balancing her weight, providing support, and poised to put sufficient pressure downward. Grab your handhold and position it comfortably in your palm. Set it on the spindle and lean your weight into it. Breathe. Focus. Power all comes through the Earth and is directed through your core. Not your shoulders. Your shoulders are easy passages for the force to move through. Begin with a few light strokes to get the feel for the spindle and hearth. Focus on keeping the spindle vertical, then begin long, fast strokes with some pressure. Keep going and when you see smoke, keep the same speed. When the smoke becomes dark, you can speed up. Wait until the smoke is quite dark and consistent, and consider going for a little more if you want a big, reliable coal.

You are tired and your arms are shaking.

Stay focused.

With precision and care, take the spindle out of the notch and set the bow, spindle, and handhold in a place where they won't get in your way. Kneel low before the smoking pile of cedar dust. Bow to that fire inside that is a magical gift. Though you are shaking, find your breath and stay controlled. Add a gentle and precise stream of your human breath and pay attention. The smoke will tell you how much. Just pay attention, and keep gifting your breath. This is a relationship.

When the pile gets smoky and you can see the dim reddish light of a healthy newborn ember, stop. You feel an electric excited pulse through your being, and you want to rush in and grab the ember or fall into fear that it might die if you don't act in seconds. The baby is healthy and it can take care of its own endurance for some time. Stop and breathe. Look around and up toward the canopy. Breathe again. Look for your nest and get it close to the ember. Gently work the ember out of its womb on the fireboard and use a thin shaving of cedar to take the newborn home to its nest. It is young and small yet and it needs a home where it can be nurtured. Hold the nest gently between your hands and tuck the ember into its barky home. Smile. Breathe your gentle and directed stream of breath onto the smoking newborn. It needs your breath to grow. Keep blowing and watch the baby grow. The nest fills with smoke. Keep blowing. Cradle the nest close enough to hold the growing fire-child tightly. And then, a bright flame flares and a moment of joyous wonder uprushes from some deepest source within your body. You are lit from within by the birth of such light and heat. The ember has become a fire. Set it on the ground and feed the fire small twigs. The nesty home burns to an ash that will fertilize the soil for the redcedar trees surrounding it: its ancestors and its future generations. Now, feel the deep awe and thanks for the fire before you.

There would be no humanity without our relationship to fire. I suggest taking a moment to pause and think about all the fires we have going right now around the world. Place your mind into the subtlest ones happening in metal chambers or in the basements of buildings. Imagine, if you can, what the world would be, and who humanity would be without these fires. It is a strange vertiginous contemplation if you let your mind truly approach it.

Though it is tempting to fill this chapter with nothing but stories of how I have experienced and witnessed the wonder and empowerment birthed from creating fire directly from the land, I choose to start with a different story. A story of failure. It was hard to choose which failure story to tell. There are plenty others that have played a very strong role in creating me. The truth is, learning fire means a long path of failed attempts, of frustration, of quitting and coming back to it, of being severely humbled.

One night in eastern Washington, a dear colleague and I were in the midst of running programming for a camp. It was a full moon night with a gentle breeze and I was seated by a lake's edge listening to the wind in the pines. Soon, a group of about seventy people would come around the corner. These people were almost all from the inner city, and a night walk through the woods was, in many cases, completely novel. Fire by friction, for many, was a myth of cave men rubbing sticks together. The reason for such a large crowd was that the word had spread that the night before I had demonstrated fire by friction in the middle of the night. Everyone who was available wanted to see it this time around.

In my stomach was a deep unsettling. My chest was tight and rattly. The reason for this was what had happened hours earlier. My colleague and I had created a large, all-camp game that was meant to bring fun, excitement, and connection to everyone participating. What we hadn't anticipated was how our game held the power to invite some of the worst aspects of competition. We hadn't anticipated a thinly-veiled war in which rules were bent or broken; where tears and anger flooded the field. It was, for me, a saddening and frustrating thing to attempt to mitigate. When the game was over, it felt like the charge of war was still in the air. We learned later that this was a typical result of this all camp game. We learned in the consecutive season how to mitigate this ahead of time and design a game that would not have the same possibilities. However, in the moment, I felt a deep disturbance throughout my body and I could not shake it.

I did not want to sit there and create fire for the people. I did not want to be there at all.

And then they came. I did not feel the warmth in my heart that often comes before I start a fire for people. I could not find the full shape of my breath in my body. I was too distracted to give myself the moment to look around and admire the landscape. I took a short breath and waited for people to all seat themselves. Then I spoke. It was amazing to me how much attention I pulled, and I could almost feel the group expectation. They had heard that I was going to perform a magic trick and that the world would burst into a brilliance as I ignited the nest before them.

I did what many fires have taught me to do. I tried to find my own center. I worked to slow my speech and take pauses between the sentences. I gave thanks in a way that made sense to the audience, then brought our minds to the moon and how it was carrying the reflection of the sun's fire. I worked, through words to court the sense of presence and awe that seems to invite the fire to come into existence. And through all of that, I just didn't feel right in my body.

So, I started, and almost immediately the spindle popped awkwardly out of the hearth. I felt a tightening in my stomach and could feel the expectation of the crowd. In my mind, I asked the fire to come, and I still just didn't feel centered. And then it cascaded. The spindle popped out again and again. The hearth resisted. I worked hard and placed it back over and over again. I worked until my arm gave out, and nothing but the smell of light smoke graced our night expectations. Finally, my colleague, with all the care in the world, asked me to stop. I could feel the disappointment in my being and in the air.

Fire does not come automatically. Disorder in the people makes for disorder in the person. Disorder in the person makes for disorder in the actions. Disorder in the actions is the death of skill. The fire does not come to such disorder.

What else but the fire teaches these lessons? Who are we, as a people, when we stop learning them?

The Fire in the People and the People in the Fire

Over the years, I have been graced with witnessing many people work at fire by friction for long enough that they do get their first fire. Any words I type here are but an utterly flimsy wreck of stick figures desperately trying to point toward that epiphanic experience of first fire. Something cosmically aligns with a first fire. And it happens *inside* the person. What I mean is that, when a person gets her or his first fire, almost without fail, as soon as the person becomes conscious that they have actually succeeded, the exhaustion and the singular focus drain instantly out of them. A geyser of elation erupts through their being. And then, something very interesting happens. I swear I see this every time, and I would love others to look for it as well. I'm certain I am not imagining it. I distinctly remember feeling this myself with my first fire. Some deep underlying anxious tension in the body simply releases. It is difficult to say what exactly changes in the body, where the tension was, or even what it felt like. It was a tension that was always there, and because of this, it just seemed to be a part of being a being. But, in the moment of first fire, that essential tensioning force, unexpectedly and inexplicably vanishes. The person feels a relaxation that she or he has never felt. And the strange thing is, it is not temporary. That particular vein of tension is gone for good. A deep underlying anxiety is lifted.

What if this is the birth of a primal competency? What if it is below the intellect? What if it is the whole, deep animal of the soma and the time-depthed human spirit knowing that it can create its own fire? The being then knows that it does not have to depend on other humans' knowledge or resources to attain this most basic need of human existence. The human fire lineage is many hundreds of thousands of years old. The human soma knows the need for fire, and it knows to be anxious when it is depending on other people and other systems to attain this basic need. When a human can get fire directly from the land, the primal system has no need to hold on to such anxiety.

Look into almost any tradition, and you will find the myth of how the people found fire. Often, it is a theft and often it is a relay. When we make fire directly from the natural community, this makes perfect sense. Making a fire by rubbing wood against wood is a truly mystical experience requiring a community of species and some mythical explanation. A question I once heard asked at the moment of the birth of a fire, and one I have since asked countless people since is "where did the fire that's in the wood come from?" It is a fascinating question to ask groups of kids or adults alike. Oftentimes, the response in the U.S. is some version of a scientific explanation of how friction created heat. But if we stick with the question, and really get people to look, we notice that friction is not a sufficient answer for where the fire came from. Friction released energy that was already there. It takes just a bit of bending of cultural training before we see the simplicity and truth in the question. The fire, call it heat or energy if you would like, got into the wood somehow or was part of its creation. It came from somewhere. We have a beautiful diversity of human story that shares answers to this question. Maybe it was a god or coyote or a crow that stole the first fire from another fire. Maybe they passed it to another creature who passed it to another. The western scientific story can be seen as yet another theft and relay. If we ask people enough how the fire got into the wood, they tend to say that the wood grew with the tree. Where did the tree get the fire? Many will eventually say it was from the sun. Where did the sun get the fire? Many will eventually see that the sun is an ember from the first fire, the Big Bang. So, the fire we pulled from the wood is the fire of the Big Bang. And the relay is that fire passing through cosmos, through planet, through species. The thief is our little human minds and hands in cahoots with the other species we work with to craft our firemaking tools.

In the western scientific story, we have been making fire since before we were the species we now are. Species ago and mythically far back in our memory, we learned fire thieving. Earliest claims, though disputed, say we learned 1.7 million years ago. There is clear evidence that our ancient relative, *Homo erectus*, had controlled use of fires 400,000 years ago. And 125,000 years ago there was widespread control and use of fire around the globe.

I invite you here to pause and take a breath. If you can, look outside, and even if you can't, then simply extend your senses and your imagination outward. Remember that you are here with the planet. Think about the length of a year. Imagine all that happens in one planetary

trip around the sun, then all that happens in a human lifetime. Imagine
what your land looked like 300 years ago. Pause. Breathe. These numbers are so easy to consume without actually digesting. If you give them
time, as you would a meal, you will find deeper nutrients. Imagine 3000
years ago. There may have been between fifty and one hundred million
humans on the entire globe then. 30,000 years ago, woolly mammoths
and saber-toothed tigers and a relatively small population of humans
roamed together. Now take look at the numbers in the previous paragraph and try, just a little more than you usually would, to imagine how
long ago they were and how they fit directly this same planet where you
are alive and holding the story. The fire in your electrical outlets has
been passed on, taught and warmed human hearts and hands for all this
time to make its way to where you are now. The relay is still going. We
are living the myth.

Fire is a part of our being. Richard Wrangham, a Harvard archae-
ologist, puts forth that homonids developed small jaws and big brains
because of the mastery of fire. In one dimension, we can look at fire as
an extension of our digestive system. As our ancestors used fire more
and more to cook food, we were able to eat a greater variety of foods,
a greater abundance of nutrients, and with less work for our internal
digestive organs. The fire became, in a way, our first stomach. It started
the digestion before the food entered the mouth. Some posit that this
allowed our evolution to make choices to send its energy elsewhere in
the body. The gut requires a lot of energy. If we could use our minds
and hands to outsource that energy, then the nature of evolution could
choose to put more energy into developing our brains.

Of course, there are ways to eat raw and many people do it beautifully. That said, if we are in temperate zones or beyond and we eat
directly from our land all year long, we have to use fire. This extended
stomach also has made it possible for humans to live outside of the
tropics. And, while it helps with digestion, it also provides heat for the
body which is essential to life in colder climates. Fire is a part of the
body that is outside of the perimeter of our skin.

As we have grown into fire and fire into us, it is a curious pursuit to ask questions about human development in relationship to fire.
Having worked with so many young people around this element, it is
hard not to see the innate, primal fascination. The element pulls developing human attention with powerful internal force.

Daniel Fessler, an evolutionary anthropologist, has some interesting perspectives here. He questions whether adult fascination with fire is a direct result of not having mastered it as a child. It is interesting to start fires in front of modern adults. We fixate on the fire, and, if you pay close attention, you will see other arms literally twitching when someone else is feeding the fire. People watch how others do it and many feel deeply compelled to experience the act of feeding the fire. Each individual human being has a bunch of mirror neurons that are watching and subtly replicating the experience. As if drawn by an irresistible force. Fessler suspects that humans have evolved psychological mechanisms directly dedicated to controlling fire. They are part of our development. When that development doesn't happen, when we don't grow up making and tending to fires, there is a lack, and that lack creates a fascination. Hence a lot of western people standing around a fire and staring fixatedly at it. To pursue this line of inquiry, Fessler looked into cultures where people currently do develop with a direct mastery of fire. Interestingly, he noticed that in those societies, mastery of fire seems to happen around age seven. After that, the behavior of fire play seems to die down. Fessler says that "the modern fascination with fire may reflect the unnatural prolongation into adulthood of a motivational system that normally serves to spur children to master an important skill during maturation." He compares this to how human children all go through a phase of fascination with predatory animals. Human evolution seems to require for their health and safety that they learn about certain things.

Anthropologist Christopher Lynn has found an average of a five percent decrease in blood pressure when people are watching a fire. He suggests that this could help reduce anxiety. He also found that people who had higher scores of prosocial behaviors, like empathy and altruism, had a greater relaxing effect from fires. If we think primally here, this makes perfect sense. The presence of a fire means the presence of an essential element of our humanity. We don't have to worry about its lack. We don't have to use as much intrinsic energy to create heat, to digest, etc. and beings directly know that in the moment. Lynn points out that humans learned how to use fires thousands of years before they learned how to start them. Keeping a fire going, especially when you can't start it again, is a very important task. Over time, such a task would have to have evolutionary weight. Multiple people can tend to a fire much better than a single person. So, it makes sense that the people who were social also tended to be the people who had more fires in their lives. The people who had more fires in their lives received the benefits of fire more consistently, and this makes for stronger, healthier people. They had to work together more. In social life around the fire, our people grew up smoking food, tanning hides, making tools, making medicines, having ceremonies, and even using the fire to clear land so that certain plant communities can grow. So, in this sense, fire seems to have co-arisen with prosocial behavior. Fire cultivates human community. Invite people to come stand around a fire, and you know this is true at the experiential level.

I distinctly remember an experience a group of us had while I was teaching a college class. As a class, we had been inquiring into the role of environments on our bodies and our social relationships. In one particular section, we had been contemplating Marshall McCluhan's statement, "the medium is the message." For McCluhan, a university is a medium, as is a classroom. The medium shapes us into how we take in information. We become the medium in many ways. We decided to have an outdoor class and to pay close attention to how this different medium affected us. Midway through the class, we started a bow drill fire and gathered around to have a discussion. Our bodies lowered, our voices deepened. There were more pauses between speech. Many simply stared at the fire, and, when they spoke, it was as if their words were offered directly to our one collective hearth. We noticed that the balance of speaking time had shifted. People seemed to be leaner and more heartfelt with their words. Those who rarely spoke, shared more vocal time, and those who often talked seemed to ease their habits. Was that medium shifting us? Are people around a fire the same people or the same community as people under fluorescent lights seated in desks? Does fire call forth our more egalitarian nature, thus changing *who* we are individually and collectively?

I also wonder now how human capacity to focus and the mastery of fire co-arose. Mastery of fire means the growth of what we call skill and discipline.

I distinctly remember an adult friend trying a hand drill for the first time, and becoming consumed by the task. He worked and worked, failed and came back. Stretched. Breathed. And finally, his face brilliant red, his skin slick with sweat, his arms shaking uncontrollably, he produced an ember. This is an impressive first attempt. He looked stunned, then looked around him, clearly disoriented. After some time of processing the event, a giant smile bloomed on his face and he said, "I have had ADD all my life and it's almost impossible for me to focus on one thing." His breath dropped. Then a clear expression of wonder. "I've never focused that hard on anything in my entire life."

If you have ever tried making your own fire in the direct way, you know how much time and effort it requires. It is a journey. Even for my friend, who enjoyed success on his first attempt, there were many steps of that journey left to walk. When working with fire by friction, we have to dedicate ourselves to moving beyond perceived failures. We work and work. We first work to simply get the technique and to teach our bodies how they can actually transmit their force with accuracy and efficiency. We work until we get smoke. We discover all the ways our technique has been off, creating problems where the dust does not collect correctly or the spindle gets caught and slows down. We learn to feel gladness for the smoke and then to shift our focus toward getting dark smoke. We learn to keep working again and again until the smoke becomes black. Then we learn that if we stop at that moment, even though there is ignition, our ember will die. We need to keep going past the point of "success" and feed more fire. We learn all the ways the fire can die. Learning how fire dies again and again at our own clumsy hands is the only way we can finally become midwives. And birth by birth, and nurturing by nurturing, we learn how to carry fire all the way through its process until it becomes fully formed. Again and again we practiced this way for thousands and thousands of years. And those that had the discipline and who could develop the skill were the ones who grew up with fire. They are our ancestors. Fire ignites human discipline.

The Community of Fire

When you make a friction fire in front a group of people, they almost always get excited afterward. Inevitably, since you were the one performing that ancient and sacred task, people have a tendency to compliment you. The compliments are sweet, and, if you keep making fires and you pay attention to the truth of the matter, they are often a bit misplaced. Personally, I feel some wariness when I hear someone speak highly of how "I" made a fire. It just doesn't seem accurate. In an interview with Krista Tippett, the Irish poet, Michael Longley, quoted his spouse's great wisdom. She says, "accept compliments but don't inhale." True of compliments about "making" a fire for sure. If we make enough fires and we are honest, we find that we are utterly dependent on so much in order for that fire to blossom into shimmery existence. The compliment is a beautiful twig of human thanks handed to you, and your job as the fire midwife is to put the twig in its right place so it can illuminate the world. My honest response to such a compliment often seeks to accept the thanks and then pass it forward. I try to point to the whole community it takes to make a fire: everyone who ever passed this down, all the species who contribute, and the environmental conditions that allowed for it. This is not false modesty. This response has been birthed from experience. In fire making, the individual is humbled by repeated failures enough to recognize that it depends on a whole lot of things greater than you to decide whether the fire will come.

If we orient toward the truth, we can see just how strange it is to consider anything an individual accomplishment. If we used a knife to make our kit, who made the knife? What kind of skills and lineage come along with that? Even if we use a sharp rock, what kind of rock did we use? How did we learn? Who taught us fire? How did we learn about the different woods? What lessons have these woods taught us? The question "who made the fire?" is utterly mysterious. Kneel and light a fire enough, and a small ember will grow within your soul. Experience by experience, kneeling again and again, this little ember will grow and shed light on your world as only you see it. You will actually see, as you look around, that you are surrounded by an interdependence of uncountable beings. Each one the leading edge of every ancestor that has ever graced this planet. You will see that you are in a great council that is in session now. And you are kneeling. One small and beautiful part of a vastest. Every time one of us lights a bow drill fire we are keeping a single fire burning. It is the fire of memory. It is the fire of ancestry. It is the witnessing of the Big Bang itself. It is the fire of Who We Are.

Fire ignites the consciousness of to an identity that transcends and includes our personal selves. If we pay attention to our relationship with this primal force, we experience a revelation of the most essential work-ings of ourselves and our cosmos. When making a friction fire, it begins with such an archetypally masculine expression. Your whole body and your whole mind must be singular, focused, directed. You are a tremen-dous amount of force driving through resistance. You drive through the resistance of the fire board and the handhold. You keep your technique as consistent and focused as possible as you experience a rush of resis-tance in your own muscles, which call to you to cease. You drive through and from that direction and focus, and through the resistance, the fire is born. And exactly at that moment, when the masculine expression feels the joy of success. Exactly at the peak, the whole of your being must embrace the archetypally feminine. With equal commitment, you become the nurturer, the listener. You take in all the forces acting on that little ember, and with unfathomable skill, you offer a soft nurturing breath; you pause and tend to the way the dust sets on the pile. You pay attention and perceive exactly what the ember is asking for and then you use the slightest and most precise movements to gently allow the existing forces around you to care for the growth of this little being. You are aware as you separate this being from its home in the notch and place the being in its nest. You add exactly as much breath as the being needs. No more, no less.

The fire demands that we do this. That we not only embrace, but cultivate and express these aspects of ourselves. And this is the only way, for millenia, that we could have fire for the community.

There are many traditional views of what fire making means on the depth spiritual levels of being. I suspect it is very much worth it to consult other people and learn how they have come to understand the deeper aspects of this act. Through paying attention, fire making has become a ceremony. If we pay attention to any life-affirming act enough and we invite awareness of the depth of our being and the breadth of the cosmos, it becomes a ceremony. Naturally, insight will evolve and the actions will bend themselves accordingly. The mind and the spirit will gather with greater concentration. With each ceremony, consciousness will increase. Love and truth will infuse us more and more.

The way this happens is different for each culture. Different leaky boats to that same distant shore. For some Apache, I have heard there is the following meaning: The bow and the cord are the expression of the four directions and the circle of life. The handhold is the great and loving hands of creation. The spindle is the expression of the masculine. The hearth is the expression of the feminine. The notch, where the two come together, is the womb. The dust, which is the product of the union, is the physical body. The ember is new life and future generations. And the nest is nurturing Mother Earth. Each time the ceremony is consciously created, each person who participates is re-minded on the depth level of these essential aspects of our existence. Each time this happens, the consciousness transcends and includes the personal ego. We re-member ourselves with the unfathomably vast currents of being, and we are an expression of this one big story. The point of this paragraph is not to appropriate the beautiful ways of the Apache or anyone else. The point is that a ceremony that is authentically meaningful and relevant to the person and the culture, that is wrought from paying attention and serving love and truth, will beget transcendent human consciousness. It will do this in a way that is also personally experienced. This is a vital nutrient for what some would call the higher functions of humanity.

The fire ceremony repatterns our consciousness in ways that are transferrable to other experiences. We know, at the depth level, that we have great powers of both feminine and masculine principles. We know that we are part of a great cosmos. We know that we are a tapestry of relationships with our life community, that we are Earth and sky and more. Such experiences lead the mind to Mystery, and we develop a personal relationship with Mystery, in whatever form makes the most sense to us. When challenges come in life, or deep confusions, we know how to make fire to light that darkness. When we have spent time physically working through the masculine force in ourselves, we can call on this. I know there have been times in my life, when I have literally been exhausted, in a canoe, in a storm, on a dangerous ocean, and that same directed force that won the fire coursed through me, and only with that force could I keep putting my paddle in the water. There have been times when I have been very directed and focused with a loved one, and I suddenly realized that I must change myself. In exactly the same way I have been *taught* to shift when I have an ember and need to be my feminine, I have shifted. I have opened up my vision. I have listened and paid attention. I have realized that the moment was calling for me to receive. And the dynamic changed instantly. There was a softening and a release. It was because of me having learned how *I* can change to meet what was needed. It was because of learning my own depth and breadth. The fire teaches the uniquely human art of living. Life becomes a dance of lighting and tending to fires.

When you or I use a lighter from the grocery story, what happens in our consciousnesses then?

What if we paused and breathed the air at this moment. If you can, look at the sky. So big. A container holding us, the fragile and brilliant us, as cupped hands to protect our little being from the coldest life-crushing space surrounding. We are, all told, a small and finite place.

Only one in all the universe.

How many lighters and matches do you imagine are in the world right now?

Do we gain primal confidence from their use? Do we experience the ceremony that reminds us of who we are? Could we?

These are real questions.

One factor that may be causing serious systemic problems is the issue of primal dependency. When a lighter or any other industrially manufactured good is the source of fire, then we become dependent upon industry for a basic need of human survival. Though we could engage with this relationship on a predominantly intellectual level, I suggest that we consider what is happening below the intellect. We are not just dependent. We are primally dependent. This means that the dependence happens at the core of our human systems—the deepest evolutionary identity of our organism. The core of us that survives in relationship with the planet knows that it cannot procure a basic survival need without an intervening system. Industry becomes the source, the only dealer, of our primal need.

This creates a condition where, if we do not perceive that we have the power to change the system and we do not have the direct ability to create fire ourselves, the primal part of us will fear anything that threatens the integrity of the industrial system and the global economics that it uses to distribute these needs.

On a primal level, we recognize that each basic need *is* our survival and our primal processes are organized toward securing those needs. The challenge becomes more complex when we recognize the depth of the relationship between our humanity and our basic needs. As we can see, fire and humanity are not one, not two. Please consider, then, that these basic needs of shelter, water, fire, and food are essential to the survival of Earth-based humanity itself. They are integral to fully human consciousness. If we lose our Earth-based humanity, our resulting behavior may make us lose the life-supporting conditions of our biosphere. Each individual knows the need and knows herself when she has a direct relationship with that need, a relationship void of systems that intervene with her connection to natural planetary processes. If an individual has a direct, agentic relationship with a basic need, then parts of her consciousness come alive. This is why the British banned the Indian people from gathering their own salt; it is why Gandhi and others organized a mass protest focused on the people gathering their own salt directly from the ocean.

A fire within ignites. It is the fire of human agentic wildness. We become uncaged. We have authority over our own basic survival.

If you find yourself intellectually skeptical of these thoughts, then that is wonderful. We must all think this through and come to our own conclusions. We must each choose the actions that best serve our inner integrity, our loved ones, our greater communities, and our whole ecological identity. I do request that you actually work through the experience before you intellectually otherwise conclude. I am quite certain that the experience of a direct primal relationship with fire will change you; it will change your entire baseline of thought; this will change your conscious explanation for reality. Please try it and discover for yourself as yourself.

You can start with the wonder of witnessing so many people respond to fire. Have a fire and ask other to join you. As you sit around a fire, ask yourself what it is that draws me and so many others to this source? Why do we stare? How do I feel in my body? How has this shifted the group dynamics? Is there less anxiety in the group and in me personally? Why?

I can see in my mind's eye so many times when I have introduced fire, particularly a friction fire, to a group of people. In my wilderness therapy trips in Alaska, each time it would dramatically shift the group's intentions: the participants would act as if they were gravitationally pulled toward the fire and toward the knowledge. I can see my most recent mentee, who spends most of his free time playing computer games, witnessing his first fire. I can see the actual trembling of his hands as he excitedly gathered sticks and stared at the fire's center. I clearly recall him saying, without any prompting by me, "this is all the excitement of a video game, but it's in the real world!" Why did he say that? Why? This is what we ask ourselves and the fire. This is how we come to know ourselves as individuals and as a world.

I can feel in myself, and see in my memories the stories of so many people gaining skill and knowledge with the fire. They gather their own wisdom and power twig by twig, stroke by stroke, breath by breath. They gather the world of trees and rocks and fibers and human muscles in such an alchemy that they create momentary starburst of energy. And some of that starfire stays in them each time. It grows, and you can actually see it in their eyes. I think, I hope that each one reading this knows what I mean by that. Do you know that spark that I speak of? When you look into a vibrant person's eyes and they seem to shimmer inexhaustibly. They are awake and alive. And I have seen and felt that knowing the fire is one way to cultivate that fire within. It is a primal confidence and belonging.

Of course, there are beautifully awake, vibrant, whole, honest, and loving people who have never learned the fire in this way. I am so thankful for these people, and I hope you are too. I am not suggesting that there is only one boat that will get us to the island of awakening. As the priest said, we are all choosing the boat that leaks the least for us. I am saying that relationship with the primal need of fire can be a very skillful means for all of us, given our shared heritage, to understanding some of our deepest aspects of self and world. I am asking what many others have been asking as the industrial growth society overtakes culture by culture, language by language, landscape by landscape, waterway by waterway. Why are we so hungry? Why do we seem so scared to slow down? What would happen if each of us spent time cultivating the fire within? Have we set aside our ancestral ways a little too severely?

For the Birds

Right now, somewhere in every yard, there is a feather lying close to the ground. If you got up right this moment and searched the closest yard very hard, you could find it. It is aging. The barbs are starting to fail and invisible mites are probably hard at work taking the whole thing apart. If you come at the right time, you may even see an ant taking a piece of this feather back to his nest. The feather belonged to a bird—maybe an oregon junco or an english sparrow, a house finch, an american crow, or even a northern flicker. If you stare at this feather for long enough, you would begin to think about the bird who left it. You would wonder where the bird is now. Maybe it is flying at this moment, maybe perched on a twig, maybe sleeping in some dense foliage, maybe he was eaten by a cat or a cooper's hawk. You could look at the feather to find some clues. If you look in the right way, you would notice whether or not the feather was shed or if it was plucked out by a predator. You might look around to see where the bird might live or the path the local cat likes to take. This is happening right now in your back yard. That feather, that is out there, is the beginning of a whole path of adventure. If you kept asking questions about it, you would find yourself walking the path of knowledge of your whole Place—every mammal and bird and plant. You would find yourself developing powers of awareness that could take an instant picture with your mind and recall significant details with high precision. You would know how to move like a cat or bound like a deer. You would learn how to make your mind still as the rocks. It is all there… connected to that one feather… all you have to do is look and keep looking. The more you look, the more you see.

Right now, feathered wonders swim oceans of air above us, looking down at our innate tininess. A bird near you is flying through forest at sixty miles per hour, and somewhere in the world, a peregrine falcon is reaching the speed of two hundred miles per hour as she slices the atmosphere. Twenty-nine thousand feet above ground, flocks of migrating birds are connecting the continents of the planet. The king penguin is diving seven hundred and eighty feet below sea level to find food. Birds are dancing now. They move the world with the head pumping dance of mortality, sending alarms and threats across the globe. The dance of love is being played by the crane, hopping, bowing, and twirling before the grace of future generations. Birds around us now are ever-hunting and ever-harvesting the living globe—from the death grab of the talon to the hooked beak that pries its way to seed. Owls are bending the night air into silence with specialized wings that eliminate the vortex of noise; listening with an ear so sharp they can capture a mouse in complete and utter darkness. A hummingbird's eye is greeting a world of four primary colors—impossible for a human to envision.

Right now, a sharp shinned hawk's eye works with such skill he hunts full speed through thick forest, catching birds from their perch. Flocks of birds are creating a communal sphere of awareness, sharing eye and ear so that each of the whole can enjoy full and vibrant lives. Flocks are banding together to create a defensive force far greater than any individual; driving hawk and owl toward some distant, unseen limb. Acorn woodpeckers are working together to store food for the winter in a common granary. In one snag, they shove as many as fifty thousand acorns into the cracks, holes, and crevices. Other birds are voraciously stashing caches of seeds into the earth, the occasional farmhands to plant anew the forest. Birds are gathering stone, mud, branch, twig, feather, hair, spider silk, moss, and more to bend the world into a curl of a home in which children will be born.

Now, raptors are tending nests built near an ant colony and enjoying health as ants make a meal of bird parasites. One the same platform as the red tailed hawk, a house sparrow is building a nest. In some strange agreement, the two are living together, the usual predator with the usual prey: the house sparrow enjoying the protection of the hawk and the hawk enjoying the nest-guarding alarms that the sparrow chimes out at the site of any egg robbing predators.

Rails are moving through marshlands with an other-worldly silence and incomparable speed, compressing their bodies to slivers that do not disrupt a stem of grass, then sliding into water without a ripple. European starlings are advancing across landscapes in a tide of ominous brilliance. These backward birds are sporting bills that are stronger in the opening than in the closing; they are sporting vision that can shift to binocular at will; they are now infusing their colonial nests with medicinal plants that fumigate mites. Finches are using wood splinters and cactus spines as tools to dig for grubs. Green-backed herons are fishing now—throwing insects and berries and twigs and human food into water and waiting for the fish to come.

The globe is being ever-bathed in a ring of spring chorus. The song is the song of us—co-evolving now. The avians, in a great co-author-ship, are storying our entire world into being.

Birds and Us

In considering all the ways birds and humans are not one, not two, it's skillful to consider this from multiple perspectives. When I think of this topic, I think again of my friend, Josh Lane. I wrote enough about him in this book to make me think I should just call him and let him speak for himself for a bit.

So I did.

And what follows is some of what Josh had to say about (and for) the birds and us:

Me: *I was wondering if you would be willing to share a short description of your journey with deep nature connection and how birds have played a role in that for you.*

Lane: I grew up in the suburbs in Connecticut on the East Coast and pretty much grew up playing video games—and that was kind of my world. I didn't have a lot of nature access as a kid, but my grandparents and my parents were gardeners and my dad would take me camping, so I got a little bit of nature access that way.

But I would look out the window or be outside and just look at the trees and get the sense that there was something more going on kind of right in front of my eyes that I couldn't quite put words on or even describe really. It was that desire to know. "What is that tree in my yard right there? What is that plant growing on the lawn?" It was this sense that there was a greater story happening that I wanted to plug into.

Eventually I ended up connecting with some people who had trained with Tom Brown, Jr. He is well known for being called The Tracker, and was trained by an Apache mentor in a native lineage of nature connection. Through that experience, over time, I started to learn some different ways to actually connect to that story of nature.

Jon Young, who is one of Tom's prodigies, ended up helping me really learn about that world of the birds through their voices, their behaviors, what he calls "bird language." This was something that took many years to cultivate for myself, to be able to plug into that story of what are the birds doing? What are they telling us through their postures and their vocalizations? What are they telling us through the subtle feelings that our body detects on a primal level that might pass us by if we're lost in our thoughts, we're lost in our head and we're not paying attention to the moment with all of our senses?

This set me on a path that I explored for the past 18 years of connecting with the birds that are right outside my door, sometimes deep in the wilderness, sometimes right in the suburbs, right in the forest, wherever I happen to be, but finding these universal patterns of behavior around the world.

Me: *Somebody listening to this conversation might think, "Well that's great for birders, or people who go to the Audubon Society, or just people who really like nature but why would I need to know that?" How was that journey applicable to your everyday life?*

Lane: Looking back on it all, one of the things that really got me sparked was sort of that mystique that you might say comes with the ninja, or that idea that it's possible to sense things at a distance beyond what you apparently think you can perceive. A simpler way to say that is that birds become an extension of ourselves in a sense, and what we can see and hear. Because a bird that's posted up on a branch a hundred yards away can detect things that we can't necessarily detect from our vantage point.

In a way, they become like a tool, or an extension of our own awareness. So when they alarm at something, that becomes an indication to us that we can detect something moving that's beyond our normal periphery. There is a theory put out there called the Extended Mind Theory, maybe ten years ago or so. It looks at that idea. You think of a primate that's using a twig as a tool to find ants or to find food and you know that if you're using a tool like a rake or a hammer, that you can actually sense, peripherally, through that instrument. It's like it becomes an extension of your own senses. You can, in a subtle way, feel what's at the end of that instrument that you're in contact with.

In this way, the birds become that for us. They plug us into this larger tapestry of sound and motion and intent. So, what I find happens with bird language is that we go beyond just the identification. We go beyond those questions of, "is that a robin? Is that a Junco? How many are in that flock?" That is a key part of it, to be able to identify that, but a lot of people just stick to that level. Sometimes when they get into birding, it's like, "Let's go from this bird to the next bird," which is great for census reasons, just for connecting and getting out, and seeing who's moving in your neighborhood. But when we stick with that one robin that's on the lawn, now we go beyond just identification.

Okay, we know that's a robin, but what is the robin's behavior? What is it doing day-to-day and what is that telling us about the larger environment? When that robin is singing, that's telling us one thing: that

that robin is not under pressure in terms of predators at that moment; it's safe to do what it wants to do in terms of defending its territory or attracting a mate. But when that robin stops singing and freezes, looks up in the distance and then all of a sudden utters an alarm call and disappears, that's telling us something entirely different. That's activating our extended mind network. So, it's like we become part of the landscape in a much deeper way through sensing the robin's behavior.

And it plugs us in, it really plugs us into the moment. It builds curiosity, it builds passion for what is happening and it gets us really excited to actually feel like we're part of that story because now we're reading part of that story through the bird's lens as much as we can as a human being anyway. For me, those are some things that, I think, really merit our attention, that can really benefit us from tuning into the birds.

Me: *Why bother being more aware? What does it do for us? What does it do for you?*

Lane: Why bother being more aware? Yeah. One thing I think we can all relate to these days, is that it's so easy to get lost in our plans. We have endless things we have to plan, or do, or get ready for. Or it could be even things, like doubt or worries, that are coming up. There's a lot of internal chatter that can direct our attention, and we might focus on all these plans we have to do. Suddenly, a whole day goes by or maybe it's a week, or maybe it's a month. Suddenly, we look back and say, "Where was I during all that? Was I even present? What happened?" Because we get so lost in the world of the mind, sometimes. These days, especially, with so much on our plates. It's easy to have that happen.

I find, for me, value in practices, like bird language, that invite us into our senses. They give us little challenges and little reminders that help us to step back for a moment from all that busyness, and take a deep breath, and let it go—let that busyness go. Let that stress go that accumulates with that. Actually get into our body and go, "Woah! My shoulder is tight." Then you take another deep breath and let that go. Then you listen a little bit. You go, "Wow! I can't believe it, I didn't realize there's been this robin singing outside my window this whole day I've been working at my computer. Wow, I could tune into that if I want to." Then, eventually, after doing that a lot, you realize, "Wow! I could be tuning into that all the time. Even when I'm working."

So it brings us right here, right now. It's a doorway to the moment.

Me: *When I listen to that, I think of mindfulness. It's a buzzword nowadays in our culture. There's a certain cultural paradox there. I hear "awareness" and I think of effort. I hear words like "mindfulness," or "pay attention to your surroundings," "receiving," or "feeling how your shoulders are," and I think of relaxation. In some ways, culturally, there's that paradox of effort and relaxation. Is there any way you can unpack that difference? If I'm working at the computer, in one way I could think, "Oh jeez. Now I've got another task. Now I've got to also listen to the robin outside my door and have to pay attention to where the cat's going. How the weather is and all this other stuff. I'm already busy." How does that work to actually relax you?*

Lane: A great question. To me, what I've seen work really well with that is to think of it as a natural progression. You could have this really high bar, sort of that ninja level bar, this ultimate awareness, that we reach for everything that's going on in us, around us. But the reality is we start where we are and we can hold that high bar for ourselves, but we don't have to stress. We can add little things every day that add to our awareness, that add to our sense of peace, that add to our life. One by one, just bring those pieces in and integrate them, and when we're ready, add another.

In qigong and energetics, this is thought of as regulation. You learn how to work with a certain type of breath or certain movement until your subconscious from your body-mind integrates it. Then it's just like driving, you don't have to think about it anymore. But it just happens because it's trained.

We can do this with our awareness of the birds, of the natural patterns. So, a sit spot is a great way to do that, where we literally can just sit on our front porch or out in the garden, and just sit there for five or ten minutes a day. Just give ourselves the space to tune into the birds, tune into the wind, tune into the sensations on our skin, and the smells drifting across the lawn.

In that five minutes, we're training that faculty of releasing the tension, of opening to what's there, and building a bridge, literally, with what's coming in and contacting the senses.

All the time, there's tons and tons of data but only a few bits of that are reaching our conscious mind. So, we're just building a little bridge, one day at a time, one piece at a time. So that eventually, when we do that enough, we're going to be working on our computer or whatever, having a conversation, but because we've built that bridge, our awareness is tuned into that bird that's outside the window. Even if the window's closed. We'll start to notice all these things that have always been there but now we don't have to try so hard because we've already built that bridge. Does that make sense?

Me: *Would say that when you do that, it just does take a load off of that task? Because what I'm hearing is that that's an extension of my mind. If my mind's really micro-focused and it's really narrow then this computer task is the one thing that I'm doing and all my time and effort is going into it. But if I extend my mind, then it kind of takes a pressure off of it. The task is part of something larger. How does that sound for you? Does that make sense?*

Lane: Yeah. Well there's different ways to approach it. It could be something like when you rest your eyes periodically when you're working on the computer. Every ten minutes or so you want to ease them from the distance. When you do that, you can use that time to just really consciously tune into the sounds as well. What's happening with your breath? What's happening in the room around you? What sounds do you hear outside the window, in the next room even?

So that's a time when you could really consciously engage that. But what I found after a long period of practicing bird language and seeing people who are training in this, is that, after not too long of a period of time, the mind will just pick up those sounds. Even if it's not consciously engaged in it. Because you've built that bridge. It's like when you're in a room in a big party. There's a hundred people in the room all talking. You can't really hear any of the individual conversations but if somebody says your name, all the way from across the room, you're going to tune into that right away. You're going to, even if you're in the middle of the conversation. I think it's the same thing that happens with the birds when we build that bridge to an individual bird, or to patterns of sound. That we just don't have to think about it. It actually self-regulates so we start to just absorb it and realize it's happening.

Me: *That makes good sense. Another question that comes up is identity. I'm wondering, for you and for others, if connecting with the birds in this way and taking part in the larger connection journey has shifted your sense of identity?*

Lane: Absolutely. Yeah. There's an expansion there that happens. It's gone through many permutations as the practice has developed, as I have grown in my life in different areas. But, at times, it's empathy. Really feeling for the life of that bird; what they go through just to survive. The awareness of what they have to hold because there's a cooper's hawk or a sharp shinned hawk in their neighborhood. It's there every day. The strategies they develop to actually survive in the face of that. How tuned in they have to be to the other birds to get that early warning that that hawk is on the wing, heading towards them. So, there's that feeling of empathy, at times, that really arises, tuning in that way, which can translate into just how to connect with other people. Helping me to see a bit more through their eyes in different situations and getting out of my own box as much as I can. So, bird language transfers that way. That's a big one, I would say, that really has just stuck with me.

Also, is the sense of Place that develops with bird language. Understanding the larger patterns that are playing out, day in and day out, and then how they shift through the seasons. It's really an amazing feeling to be able to go somewhere and, even if I have never been there before, whether it's a neighborhood in a different side of the country, or even going to a whole other Place, like in Botswana, where I've never been—I don't know the names of any single bird there—but because I've become tuned into certain patterns in the vocalizations, being able to just know right away, "Oh, there's some kind of bird, like a cooper's hawk over there. I don't know what it's called around here but I know that there's one over there because the birds are getting really quiet in a certain way." Or, "Oh wow, all those birds that were feeding in the canopy, they all just got quiet and ducked down. I think that there's a red-tailed-hawk-kind-of-bird coming." Then it zooms over and the birds return to their eating again.

So, even though I don't know the names necessarily of birds in certain places that I'm visiting, these patterns are still holding true. I still feel connected to this larger story, even though I don't know the particulars, necessarily. So that's a really cool thing, too.

Me: *That's great. Then I wonder about the bigger picture. We tend to be so personally focused, as a culture. We have a mostly individual psychology. It's just where we're at. I wonder about that sense of Place and a connection with the birds. How about on a macro level? If more people practiced this in our contemporary society, how would that affect the greater world? Our ecology?*

Lane: Yeah. I think there would be a number of transfers that would happen from that skill set. One thing we know is that the conservation movement in America, in particular, has been fueled in the past by hunters. Which is a really interesting thing. Now the number of hunters is decreasing, so it's an interesting question as urbanization increases, as well. How do we continue to connect people to the natural world? One of the things about hunting is that it gets people out there. It gets them experiencing that Place.

So, what is it that gets people outside? Really sitting still and connecting with their senses? Waiting each moment, observing, being there? Bird language is a really natural way to get people out there, consistently, in the same place. When you learn you want to, especially in the beginning, go to the same place over and over. Same park, same backyard, wherever it is, and sink into a particular place that you sit each time. Get into your senses and get to the know the local characters that live there. Who is the robin that lives there? Where is the bluejay? Where does that bluejay rest at night? What happens in springtime when that jay is around, looking for eggs? How does the robin's behavior shift? You get all these little nuances, kind of like a soap opera.

What we've found is that people just tune in empathetically. That they tune into that story, just like people get so excited about a soap opera they watch each day. They want to know what's going to happen to their robin. They keep getting out there. Now there are kids in a preschool at the Presidio in San Francisco, who go out there and do bird sits every week. After a few years of this, even these little kids that are 3-5 years old get so tuned into the local characters and the goings-on, just from their bird sits.

I mean, I think it's got a lot of potential. It's giving people empathy. It tunes them into that larger story of the ecology of a Place. They fall in love with that Place and want to care for it, as well.

Me: *That's wonderful. That's wonderful. Well, any further thoughts?*

Lane: If folks want to go further into bird language, I have a free e-course on birdlanguage.com, so that's one resource for people. Then just my own website, creativeemergent.com, for folks who are interested in going deeper on those kinds of journeys through personal mentoring. But there are just a lot of great resources out there. Jon Young's book, 'What the Robin Knows: How Birds Reveal the Secret of the Natural World,' is an amazing book. For this skill set in particular, 'The Stokes Field Guide to Bird Behavior' is several volumes that get into the little subtle things, like how birds flick their wings and what it means, and all kinds of common behaviors you can see right in the back yard. So that's a really handy one.

So, I'm just thinking of resources and really the best resource is the bird that's right in your back yard, that you see every day. When you're out in your garden, or going to your mailbox, or whatever. Taking those little moments while you're out there just to tune in with them and check in on what's happening for them each day. Over time, you'll get to know their stories. You'll get to really see what's going on in their lives and probably have a lot of questions, more than anything else. That's important because those questions are going to build some curiosity. Then it becomes effortless because when you have a need to know. You have a curiosity. That's going to naturally open your awareness. It becomes effortless. So, mindfulness becomes this really natural thing.

I suggest pausing for a moment before you continue into the next section. Can you extend your awareness beyond the immediate focus of your attention. What are you not noticing? How big is your world actually? What is happening all around you right now? How is your breath? How are your shoulders? Where are the birds right now?

Birds as Teachers of Relationships

This book has an orientation toward an honest and a holistic perspective. That means it includes the difficult and the dark. Let's now step into some darkness together.

In rites of passage, we often say that it is in the darkness where we find our gifts.

Here is the true tale of the passenger pigeon:

To begin this tale, we should first give context for the era in North America from more of a bird's perspective. In this case, we'll focus on the plume trade. In 1886, the plume trade in Manhattan was at its peak, and, according to one observer, in one place, on one day, about five hundred and twenty-five hats were flaunting plumage of over forty native species of birds. The growing middle class had appetite for nonessentials, and feathered hats were a prime target. Feather traders marketed the remains of around sixty-four species from fifteen genera of birds. We were mad to don the sexually-charged breeding plumage of other beings. In 1902 the accounts of the London Commercial Sales Rooms recorded enough heron plumage to equate with the killing of 192,960 herons. That was just what was recorded in London. Plumes were literally worth nearly double their weight in gold. In 1900, the millinery trade employed one in every thousand Americans. The American Ornithologist's Union and the Audubon Society were hard at work trying to educate people and help shift their behavior.

At this time, the passenger pigeon was a great song of the land. The passenger pigeon was, in all probability, the most abundant bird on the planet. Many observers remarked that, when a full flock passed over, it darkened the sky. One great ornithologist estimated that one flock consisted of two billion birds. John James Audubon watched a flock pass overhead for three days and estimated that, at times, over three hundred million pigeons flew by each hour. Native Americans and early settlers harvested these birds with the ease of wandering into a colony and picking up birds who fell from the nest.

Soon, the abundance was noticed by the ever-hungry economy, and it drove men to slaughter the pigeons and sell them. They fed them alcohol-soaked grains; they lit fires of grass or sulphur under their nests to suffocate them; they captured pigeons and sewed their eyes shut— then set them on a stool in the forest to cry out their pain—then killed all the birds that came to the cries; they knocked them from their nests at night with long poles; trees were chopped down or set on fire in order to catch more birds.

Eventually they killed so many that existing pigeons would abandon their colonies and not breed for the season. With the rest of the spoils of the railroad came more pigeons from farther west. One single hunter in Michigan in 1878 was recorded as shipping about 3 million birds.

By 1889, eleven years later, the passenger pigeon was extinct in Michigan.

No efforts succeeded to maintain flocks. In 1914, the last known passenger pigeon died in the Cincinnati Zoo.

What can we learn from this? Where is the gift?

I am reminded now of a young person, Caleb, who I worked with for a while. Caleb was suffering from serious social anxiety and a sense of isolation. His body was held tight. He expressed uncertainty about how people reacted to him and what impact he actually had in other people's lives.

Caleb also seemed charmed. Nearly every time we went out together, we would have a close wildlife encounter, often with a type of bird. As this happened, we took advantage of the moment and used the birds to practice understanding how to read the impact of our actions and noticing what cues we had within our bodies. The brilliant thing about approaching a bird in this way is that there are all kinds of cues happening all the time. The overt behavior of the bird, such as a feather ruffle or a bobbed head would tell Caleb that the bird was getting a bit nervous. Caleb then felt inside his body and noticed where he felt tension and nervousness. He started to be able to recognize that some of the sensations seemed to be his own, others seemed to be more empathically based. He could feel when the bird was getting nervous. He learned that, as he approached, he could change his behavior, his mindset, and the way he reacted to sensations in his body in order to help calm the bird. Over time, Caleb recognized that the same general pattern held for people.

Step by step and bird by bird, Caleb practiced his own internal senses, his social awareness, and his sense of empathy. Caleb saw directly that he does have power and effect in the world. His actions clearly mattered and he could see how they alter the world around him. His teacher was primarily the birds themselves. Since birds are everywhere, Caleb learned at the experiential level that a counseling session is not the only place where he can experience this, and another human is not the only species that can serve as a teacher for him. Is this not empowering?

John Muir famously wrote, "when we try to pick out anything by itself, we find it hitched to everything else in the Universe." Each bird we meet is the center of a universe, and if we deepen our relationship, we can learn endlessly about ourselves, others, and the world entire. Most birds have a good knack for being elusive, and I suspect this is of great benefit to human beings. In order to get to know a bird, we have to work for it. In working for it, we learn so much about ourselves and the rest of nature in the process. A favorite quarry I will often give mentees is to figure out what bird is making all the racket in the bushes. I make sure that the bird is a spotted towhee. The spotted towhee makes so much noise you would think he is four times his size. He also is just elusive enough for beginners that he teaches the need for patience, restrained approach, and a quieting mind. At the same time, he does not demand a high degree of any of these qualities. Just enough. If the person is too direct and too fast, the towhee will disappear and, at best, make an annoyed screech. But as the person slows down mind and body and learns to open up her senses, the towhee becomes more frequently visible. I then give the person the challenge of seeing the color of the eye. This makes a close encounter essential. For that close encounter to happen, the person will almost definitely need to exhibit a small bout of stillness and patience. Interestingly, more than the pursuit, it is often the stillness that draws out the bird. If you are more still than the bird in mind and body, the bird will often come to you to check you out.

As we relate to birds as a center of the Universe, we find so many life lessons. The anatomy teaches physics and the relationship of form and function. The songs mentor us in the wide world of music and language. The flocks, if we attend to them teach us how to expand our minds and see the great web of long range communication happening all around us.

We witness birds as teachers of movement and embodiment. We learn the sidestep, the side-straddle, the hop, the stride, and the double scratch. We see that each movement contains the story of the behavior of ancestors, from birds who spent long time feeding on the ground, to those who took more to the trees. We learn the unmatched grace of a penguin with his short feathers and dense bones, swimming ocean depths. We understand the kingsfisher dive as she punctures air and sea to snatch her prey. We enjoy the american dipper's lessons on walking slippery creek surfaces and invading the frothing rapids.

The birds engage with the world in ways that inspire us to change our own behavior or thinking. Birds are a wealth of interesting ideas for the art of being, and we have evolutionarily grown up being bent into behaviors by birds or bending our own shapes to match them. Trackers, martial artists, musicians, artists, spiritual traditions, and cultural ceremonies show how the birds have shaped humanity again and again.

The birds: the great symphony of Earth; the masterpiece of color and motion; the ecological expression of genius. We wander the colors of being through the regal epaulets of a red winged blackbird. We learn camouflage and countershading. We impress members of the same species with our shape and palette.

Birds teach deep strategies of survival. They perform the great distraction displays to lure a predator from a nest: they feign a broken-wing and flail on the ground or they perform a "rodent run" by dragging their wings, erecting their feathers, and squealing.

Birds respond to environmental conditions within their deepest body. They conserve energy in winter by entering a regulated hypothermia. The red-tailed hawk drops his core temperature by five to seven degrees. The mighty hummingbird body enters torpor, in which she can endure a cold night by dropping her temperature fifty degrees for several hours.

Bird wings cut air in such a way they can create lift. The secondary feathers make an airfoil. They flap arms with a great force to create thrust. Wings vary for sustained high speed or soaring or high maneuverability or quick takeoff or powerful swimming. Bird wings can be so strong that the strike of a swan or goose wing can do considerable damage to a human being. There have been incidences of swans hurting and even killing boaters to protect their nests.

Birds move the whole world. During migration, birds can lose one quarter to one half of their body weight. Most fly at night, and some travel nonstop over open ocean. In the U.S., there are four major "flyways" of migrating birds: the Pacific, Central, Mississippi, and Atlantic. About one hundred and fifty species of birds come north from tropics to breed. These are arteries moving Earth. In each bird body and each bird mind, the earth of tropics moves north and mingles with temperate zone earth. A great tilling of the one field.

Beaks sport endless designs of specialized tools: cutting, serrating, grasping, carrying, scratching, fighting, and digging. Beaks filter water, preen, nest-build, egg turn, defend, attack, display, hatch, and climb. From the hummingbird probe to the falcon's beak to the pelican's great pouch to the woodpecker's pickaxe and chisel. Feet are long or short, webbed or unwebbed, feathered or bare, made for clutching tree trunks, digging holes, or breaking backs. The birds eat the world through a gizzard: a special muscular section of the stomach lined with horny plates and ridges. Grains, nuts, and hard shells are crushed, aided by sand, grit, and pebbles that the bird swallows. Birds, finally, define themselves to the world by the existence of feathers. The unique feather. Between one thousand and twenty-five thousand feathers per bird. The magical feathers work to trap air, resist water and sun, insulate, focus light and sound, display, protect, rudder, lift, and camouflage.

Birds are teachers of the diversity of relationships.

Birds are artists of courtship. Some courtship feed, in which one adult feeds a delicious catch to another during mating season. Usually the males gift the females, but in some species it is the females who court. The courtship feeding can begin before copulation and continue through egg laying.

Some birds are termed "promiscuous." They do not form pair bonds and only court and copulate briefly. In these case, the males usually have limited to no apparent investment in their offspring.

Some birds are polyandrous. In this birdy way, the female mates with multiple males, but male only mates with one female. Here, the female courts the male and the male does most of parental duties. In some cases, birds have invented "cooperative simultaneous polyandry" in which multiple males mate with one female and a single clutch of mixed parentage is raised cooperatively by the female and the males. With polyandrous jacanas, the female will practice infanticide and kill the offspring of previous females, their new male lover attempting to defend his young from a previous relationship.

An estimated ninety percent of birds are termed "monogamous." This means that the male and female pair bond. They do this for a single nesting, a whole breeding season, or for life. In these relationships, various degrees of nest building, feeding, defense, and young rearing are shared between the two. Sometimes the monogamous behavior has been observed shifting to polygyny or promiscuity when environmental conditions change. This indicates that monogamy could be considered a bird strategy of social partnering that is dependent on conditions. Monogamy does not necessarily indicate fidelity or clear parentage. With some regularity in many species, females will lay eggs in other birds' nests so that others will raise their young. In many monogamous species, infidelity is not infrequent. This suggests that many monogamous pairs end up raising children with different genetics than their own.

Polygyny is where the male mates with multiple females and female mates with only one male. One way to perceive this is that females have a limited number of eggs in their lifetime and the eggs are relatively large cells. They are a big investment for the female. They must be laid and tended to and they take a half or all of a season to become birds. Males have abundant sperm. A male who mates with a female whose children don't survive has spent little investment. A female who mates with a male whose genetics are unfit for the situation loses a tremendous amount of investment. From this evolutionary perspective females should be choosier. Oftentimes, polygyny happens in situations where a male holds a territory that is abundant and luscious while other nearby males have poorer territory. The female then chooses to share being a mate with the male with rich territory.

However, birds like african weaver finches craft even different mating ways. They live in areas with superabundant resources; There is no territoriality. They have colonial nests and minimal defense or child-rearing needs from individuals. Here the female chooses any male, regardless of his other mates.

Grouse and other game birds have created an annual mating ritual in the form of leks. Males congregate at traditional sites and undergo their ritualistic dancing display. They "pop" "gobble", "boom", and strut. The females line up on the outside to choose their mate.

Birds are representatives of the breadth of possibility in community. Some birds choose colonies as a way. In this way, they reduce the chances of predation for each individual. Birds can roost together at night, and in this process, they seem to incorporate a certain mentorship by older birds to younger birds on how to find food. All night roosting community birds enjoy increased security and warmth during the sunless hours. When food resources are best shared, colonial nesting happens. Birds agree to live together and share information of resources and protection for the good of each and all. Cooperative breeding happens in about three hundred bird species. Mature nonbreeding birds or birds with some mixture of shared parentage will help rear and protect the young. With some jay species in some places, the incubating female is fed by her mate and by auxiliaries. Nestlings receive more than half of their food from auxiliaries: the aunties and uncles.

Some birds, such as the European Cuckoo or the brown-headed cowbird entirely rely on other species to raise their young. The mother will toss out an egg from a nest, then lay her own, then disappear from the scene. The foster parents will dutifully raise their far-oversized young cuckoo or cowbird until the bird is mature enough to go out on its own and eventually repeat the same reproductive strategy.

Stand on a beach for any length of time and you will witness piracy among birds as well. Crows and gulls constantly work to rob each other. This "kleptoparasitism" happens across the board. Turkey vultures will bully herons into vomiting their food. In one case, a sparrowhawk was witnessed losing its food to the merlin, who lost it to a honey buzzard, who lost it to a peregrine falcon.

The incubation of eggs can be done by both parents taking regular turns or going in longer shifts, by solely the female or solely the male. About twenty percent of bird species vary the pattern of who incubates depending on the circumstances. Birds seem to communicate and adapt with a keen situational awareness.

Commensal feeding happens when birds feed with other species of birds or other animals. Often a "beater", like a deer or a bear, will stir up prey by walking through waters or through the landscape. "Attendant" birds will follow and eat up the little fish or insects. In North America, hummingbirds, warblers, and kinglets will follow a sapsucker around and drink sap from the oozing wells it leaves in the tree.

Birds express the world as musicians and artists. Crows and ravens riddle bird behaviorists with their trickster ways.

Birds make us look up. They live the trees. They dance the air. They lift human spirit. You know this if you have ever been in a group of people who witness, up close, an eagle hitting the water and coming out of the spray with a writhing salmon in its claws. Before any thought can intervene, the people will cheer. Some even clap. What great spirit arises in that moment?

Birds gift a weave on the tapestry of existence.

If you are ever lost for meaning, find the place where the heron have their rookery. Become a small, not-knowing thing. Enter the woodsy edge as if you are entering a church. Pause and discover your own senses which you had been forgetting. Shapeshift. Walk as the silent bear along the giving ground. Receive the living world as she reveals herself to you.

Watch a mother heron sliding through the sky, landing on her lone pyre of a nest, gifting her hungry young fishy kisses. Feel the presence of the great ones above and feel small and vulnerable, like a mouse scurrying among the hawks. Caress the treasures you will find in the snowberries below: a frilly breast feather and half of a heaven's blue egg. Hold them in your palm with the knowledge that you can deliver them to a child's hands; where they will be felt and the human child's eyes will drink them into their being. You will meaning them with the gift of a Story of what you witnessed.

When you do this, you realize what it means to be a witness. You witness this wonder. You then come back to the human world to report that the sacred is out there. Hiding in the tops of the alders on a late May day in a place where the ocean, the sky, and the land all embrace. You bear witness as this coughing strip of reducing ground, encroached by Progress in the form of buildings and bulging lawns, holds a last magic. But it holds it. Like a seed. The magic is there. And you tell the children of what the world actually holds. Storycrafting them an umbilicus to this world, to their world, to our world. Remembering our children to the heron, the sky, the broken egg, and the great blue beyonds.

Sticks and Stones
and Breaking Bones

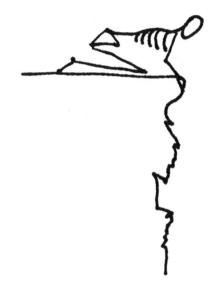

Sometimes, I think that being human is simply being a story carrier. Every day brings stories, and we are sharing them in every conversation. But, in life, you get a few Big Stories. You only get a few. Some people get more than others, depending on how much Living you've done with your life. But those Big Stories are yours to transport and to share with the right people at the right times. They are the food beyond the body, beyond the individual. They are the nutrition of Peoples, what gets sent on long after your death and what finds its way into the hearts, hands, and minds of the coming generations. Big Stories are, perhaps, what we get to curl around and remember one last time on our death beds.

So, I received one big story from Tom, my first kung fu teacher. I have shared this story with many people at what seemed to be the right times, and I share it with you now. The time is right. And you are the right person.

In my early twenties, I found kung fu as a Way. I was in Rochester, New York, and my teacher, Tom, had a school in the industrial section of the city. Tom grew up in the middle of the city, and, through unusual circumstances, had found kung fu when he was very young. He had made it his life's focus. He was probably around sixty years old when I met him. Tom was very short, bent over, and balding. No joke that his hair was a lot like Yoda's. He was, to me, an Italian-American city kid version of Yoda. A grittier version. Tom smoked cigarettes with tenacity. I have an ingrained association with the smell of tobacco and my teacher's tiger claw grip against my face. It's a sweet memory for me. I love that man.

I had joined in with a lot of other gritty, heavily tattooed city kids and, through a curious set of circumstances, we had all become deeply invested. There was a kind of sisterhood and brotherhood in our practice space. We pushed each other to grow. And we all did. Quite a bit.

Tom's teaching style remains mysterious to me. It is one of the reasons I have dedicated so much of my life to the art of mentoring. Tom didn't seem to do all that much. Of course, he showed us techniques and gave us very useful and successful advice. He crafted every class. But, there was this sense that he wasn't really doing anything, and that it was up to the students to make sure anything actually happened during practice. If your ego was seeking attention from Tom, it was exceedingly likely you would witness his back as he walked out the door to stand alone in the hallway. He would often show one technique and then sit in the corner. Occasionally, he would appear by your ear and make a joke about how terrible your form was. Then a quick correction. Then back in the corner.

One day, Tom was quietly observing the class struggle through a technique.

He began to pace and look irritable. This was not normal.

He called us to attention abruptly. "No. No. You're all missing it. You're not extending your bodies from your center, so you have no power or control. Extend the body. Know your center." He shook his head. "Everyone line up at the back of the room."

We all shuffled to the back wall.

"Not you, Matthew." I glanced at Tom, nodded and stood by him.

He put his hand on my shoulder. I smelled tobacco. He spoke softly in my ear. "Matthew, I want you to do exactly as I say. Go to the opposite wall and sit down with your face to the wall. No matter what you do, do not move a hair once you are there. I'll tell you when to get up."

The funny part about this story is, from this point forward, as a witness, I can only tell you what I experienced while facing the wall. I did not see Tom pacing back and forth in the kwoon as he spoke. "Know your center. Be your center. Then you can extend as far as you want with skill and power." Everyone else was silent. Then I heard the sound of metal clanging from one of the weapons racks. Then some shuffling.

I trusted Tom, but this became a practice of trust that was greater than Tom. I made the decision to stay still no matter what. My heart was beating stronger.

Then I heard a whooshing sound. The air in the room was being cut by a large object. Tom's voice, "a weapon is an extension of the body. An extension of the center." The whooshing got louder and closer to me. I did everything I could to let the concerned thoughts pass away as they arose in my mind. I focused on the wall and took deep breaths.

Then I felt the whoosh coming right for my head. I felt something slice the air just above my head, striking my hair. It passed. It came again.

Three times the hair on the top of my head was struck. My skin never touched.

I heard the whooshing subside. Then Tom's voice, "Matthew, you can get up and turn around now."

Tom was standing in the center of the room with six-foot-long poleaxe gripped in his right hand. He had a blindfold over his eyes.

In kung fu, they say that a weapon is an extension of the body.

Ani Difranco says, "every tool is a weapon when you hold it right."

The opposite is true as well. Every weapon is a tool when you hold it right.

It is always how you hold it.

It is always *who* you are.

Anxiety, Unpredictability, and Uncontrollability

We swing sticks. We throw rocks. We fall and trip and scratch and break. We climb and move our bodies toward cliff edges. We run fast down hills and over obstacles. We scrape ourselves on the ground and cut ourselves on thorns. We duck, we dive, we roll, we swim, we cry.

We are magnets to the edge of our fears. We are grooms to navigating the unpredictable. We are brides to knowing ourselves in situations we cannot control. In this way we learn wildness. In this way we awaken our ability to be the wild.

Let it be known that there is one clearly identifiable part of my job where I feel the most helpless and the most inspired to pray to the entirety of Being that the person I am with stays safe. It is tree climbing. Tree climbing with another person in my care is an exercise in faith for me. My faith is always challenged. Mostly because I know that faith and foolishness are twins who I cannot always tell apart. However, I do climb trees with people. I do it because I perceive that it is what is most needed in the moment for that person. Though it is frightening, I am serving the moment and that person, so I do not get in the way. We climb trees.

I have a strong memory of being with a group of adolescents for an exploration by the Nooksack River. There were eight boys and three mentors, and we were exploring as well as helping to clean up the area. Along the banks of the Nooksack, black cottonwood covers the earth and some of the larger trees bend themselves to hang over the river bed and catch the extra light. It's a risky move for the tree, as it must clutch the sandy, waterworn earth with increasing tenacity as the tree stretches progressively outward. Eventually, with erosion or wind, the cottonwood's hold on the earth gives way and the whole tree tumbles into the river.

One such tree was still clutching fairly strongly. This tree had leaned out so far that it was a full arch, connecting the bank to a sand bar in the middle of the river. As the other boys explored pockets of vegetation, tracks of mink and racoon, or eddies filled with small fish, Chris found that tree. Chris was typically a bit quieter than the rest and he was fairly physically adept. He was exactly at a time of his life where he found deep meaning in testing himself physically. All the mentors had discussed at different times how to provide a good growth edge for him.

That day, we saw him find his own edge. He climbed up that tree, and I remember distinctly watching him and thinking, "he's going to keep climbing." I watched as Chris shuffled himself further and further along the trunk, and the risk got greater and greater. The apex of the arc was about twenty feet in the air. So many times I felt a wave of impulse in my body that wanted me to shout and call him back, but some deep part of me knew that this was very important for him. When he hit the apex, I looked around and saw the two other mentors also looking at him. All three of us, from different angles, watching this boy take a very real risk. All three of us remained silent. Chris scooted further and further and began the descent of the arc of the diminishing trunk. By the time he got close to the bank, he switched to hanging from the tree and side-straddling his way toward the tip. He made it and dropped. The smile on his face was calm and deep with a touch of mystery. It was the smile of someone who had just discovered himself.

All the mentors discussed this quite a bit afterward. All three of us shared the same internal experience. We all wanted to call him back but we all resisted because we all knew that it was important for him.

This call would not have been defensible in court. If he had been injured, I can't expect any parent to support it. But I know in my bones that it was the right call. I am sure Chris knows that too.

Why did Chris do this? Why did three different people, each sharing responsibility for Chris's well-being, stand by and witness? Would it have been different if one of us verbally intervened and started coaching him? If he had been safety harnessed? If he had a helmet and had padding laid at the base of the drop?

Ample research suggests that in order for a person to undergo a truly transformative process in such contexts, they have to overcome high perceived risk. The standard for providing such experiences is creating situations of high perceived risk but low actual risk. In this brilliance of human design, we create situations such as ropes courses where people feel as if they are facing a potentially mortal danger of falling at great heights. Safety mechanisms and structural features, such as harnesses and nets, create situations where the actual risk of injury is very low. This method works wonders for individuals. They experience the physiological process of a high degree of threat. They have to face their mortality and they have to rely on their own actions to preserve their lives. A person experiences the courage to override debilitating fear. A person undergoes an experience, at the depth level, where they have taken care of themselves in a potentially deadly situation. This creates a deep level of organismic confidence.

That said, I wonder about the answers to the questions in the earlier paragraph. If Chris was harnessed, helmeted, netted, or coached, he still would have overcome his physiological sensations of danger. He would have known that it was only his being that could keep him moving and keep him gripped to the safety of the tree. He would have learned about himself and found a new confidence. And, it would have been a bit watered down and redirected. Chris's being absolutely knew that there were no safety features. There were also no intervening human systems. It was Chris, the tree, and the hard rocks below. No coaching. No coddling. If Chris was coached, his being would have to recognize that part of the successful event was having an older human directly guide him. This is different than doing it completely by oneself. If he had safety mechanisms, then his being would know that human intervention and risk reduction was a part of his experience. He would not know if he had the confidence to do it without these mechanisms. Entangled in the success would be the dependence upon other humans or upon human fabrications. When it is just Chris and the world, his deep primate knows that he is a successful organism as he is and he belongs in this world. When he knows he does not need these human interventions, then he does not feel anxiety at their lack. He does not have to hold the question of whether he can take care of his own being without them. He can, with a clear mind, both value his relationship with the natural world and choose the extent of his interdependence with human processes.

Relationships always change for the better when we stop clinging out of fear.

The wilderness is risky by nature. The environment is not modified by humans to reduce risk and increase comfort. The environment is unpredictable and uncontrollable. This is a recipe for anxiety *if* we do not have the capability to respond successfully to the changing conditions. We are primally programmed to seek risky situations so that we may experience success and, consequently, the sufficient confidence in our abilities to take care of ourselves as an organism in our natural habitat.

I am not advising that we all take such risks as we did in our mentoring of Chris. I am not suggesting that such risks will ever feel comfortable or be defensible. I am suggesting that such risks are a primal recipe for the emergence of empowered and connected humanity. We must decide individually and as a whole how they fit into our lives at this time.

Risk reduction and safety promotion has done wonders for decreasing accidental deaths and injuries in our culture. Over the past fifty years, we have seen a dramatic increase in the use of safety systems in home, school, and work. I am wondering how we balance this with providing enough risk for empowerment in each individual.

If have spent time around plants raised from seed in a protected greenhouse environment, you know what it means to "harden a plant off." Plants in the greenhouse will look beautiful and strong. Bright greens, healthy thick stems, broadly reaching leaves. The plants in the greenhouse are models of health to the eye.

If you want to sell a plant that will actually grow in a farmer's or gardener's field, you cannot sell these plants as they are. You have to take every one of these gorgeous beings and move them outside for a few days, preferably in moderately bad weather. What happens next is fascinating. As soon as the wind starts to pick up, the sun goes down and the air gets colder, those beauties become frighteningly weak. Every plant folds. If a plant could wheeze and cough, they would be doing just that. They look like they are about to die. A good farmer casts a cold eye on this, and lets those plants work it out for themselves.

And they do. Day by day, they begin to develop the strength of stem and the fortitude of chemistry to deal with the wind, rain, and cold. They meet the challenges, and they become strong at an inspiring pace.

They are made for such strength. All they needed was the actual challenge.

The hardened off plant never forgets. It has changed and it will ever meet the weather with embodied knowledge.

The Kung Fu of Wildness

Kung Fu translates to time and effort. A baker, an artist, a mathematician, or a janitor can have good kung fu. Through working with one aspect of the world in a disciplined fashion, people with good kung fu have committed to a life's education of learning how their actions affect the conditions of their internal and external worlds.

Broom stroke by broom stroke, day by day, ache by ache, healing by healing, insight by insight, we learn the way of being. Kung fu is the way of committing to one thing long enough to see that it is the center of the universe; that it contains all of the lessons available to a human experience. This process reveals personal power and how that power is connected to the rest of being.

As a martial art, Kung Fu is a way of studying conflict. What happens when forces clash? How do they respond to one another in the ensuing moments? How do they resolve? What are the exact aspects in each force that is creating the conflict? What is my role in this?

Some of the best teachers of navigating conflict are the nearly unchangeable forces. The ground. The rock. The limb. The thicket. The scree slope. The river. These forces act with a constancy. When we are struggling to stay standing in the river, we cannot change the river. When we are colliding with the earth, we cannot change the earth. We learn to change ourselves in that moment when our bodies meet a force far stronger than them. We learn how these forces work and how we work with them. We begin to see that if we fall directly into the force of the earth, we hurt ourselves. We bruise a tailbone or whack a head. However, we begin to understand that if we change the angle at the moment of contact, we can use our muscles and skeletons to convert a vertical impact into a horizontal motion. We learn to roll out of it, and we don't get hurt. We distill a greater principle: where force meets force directly, the greater force always wins. We begin to see this principle in our everyday lives. We learn to roll out of conflict. This is good kung fu.

In a park in Bellingham, among the many folds of the chuckanut formation, there is a drainage with a massive sandstone boulder. This boulder is situated perfectly in the center of a clear vista of the sword fern-carpeted woodlands. It is an odd shape, as boulders tend to be, and it teases the eye with a host of possible routes to its peak. But the eye is deceptive to hand and foot. The boulder proves a puzzling challenge, where grip and foothold seem to be ever fractionally too shallow or too far away. With this boulder, I have witnessed many human beings work through a path to understanding the nuances of this immovable force and of the force of their own bodies. It is the Training Rock. And even after an ascent is managed, this rock offers as many other challenges as the imagination and the body can craft in harmony.

Just over the ridge, there is a great ocean of nettles who tower over six feet tall by mid-June. These nettles stand as an indomitable guard to the secrets that lie in the pockets of cedars and salmonberries beyond them. In the spring, they offer delicious food. In the Fall, they offer their bodies as cordage. But in the Summer, for human kung fu, they offer their sting. Cody Beebe, who I mentioned earlier, has a wonderful response when a child comes to him crying about a nettle sting. He kneels down in front of the child and looks at the sting. His eyes sparkle with kindness as he nods his head and listens to their pain. He waits for the pause and then offers. "Do you know what I've found to be the best cure for nettle stings?" The child looks at him. His kind eyes glimmer with care. "Time." The nettles teach this lesson and more. They teach how to manage discomforts and to recognize that they will pass. They teach how to have grace and move gently and skillfully through their maze. They teach how to have courage. Spend too much time being ginger while trying to harvest a nettle, and you will only get so far as the stinger. You will get stung again and again. If you decide to pick a nettle bare handed, you have to commit beyond the sting. You have to grasp the nettle with surety.

Two ridges further, and there is a secret trail that leads along a short sandstone cliff that seems to disappear. Follow the trail and you will discover another hidden section of the cliff. It tapers up to a remote part of the ridge, and the passage is full of scramble, grip, and thicket. Slip by slip and problem by problem, this cliff reveals herself with veins of red and grey and sculptures of air-carved sandstone. She offers horizontal vine maples as holds and bulges of sword fern as grip. She offers places where she will seem impassable. She offers a beyond that drives the human body through the impassable.

Above her, on the remote ridge, the forest offers a thicket of tree, shrub, thorn, and frond. The shrubs so thick that a human must wedge himself between thin gaps. A human must learn the arts of ducking and crawling and gliding in her passage. And if a human makes it through the thickest part, they receive the other side. As if a gentle gift, an opening filled with unimpeded sunlight, nodding flower, and clandestine nest. A place of secret peace.

We need resistance to grow. We need to feel the branch against our arms, the ground slamming onto our skeleton, the rock against our heels. Every last person of every gender learns the world through pleasure and through pain, and our living, unedited world offers the harmony of both.

Over time, working with youth in our species' natural outdoor environment, a wonder settles into a person. You notice that very early in human development, a person picks up a stick and swings it. You watch and see that every person, as if compelled by an internal and unseen force, begins to test how the stick extends. How it works through human manipulation. The person's internal development is expressed through this behavior. This person is becoming a person through the stick. This person is remembering the story of humanity. Just as ontogeny recapitulates phylogeny in the development of the human embryo, we experience such a movement in our development outside of the womb. A human moves through the experiences of standing on two legs and learning tool. We learn the stick and rock, the throw, the bow, and the sharp edge and we remember the long lineage of who we are. Ontogeny recapitulates Anthropogeny. To truncate the lived experiences of human evolution is to arrest development.

Watch groups of youth, and you will see the stick turn from tool to weapon. The difference is not the stick. It is the wielder. The wielder learns that the stick is an extension of personal power, and that personal power can be used to serve any impulse.

This turns to battles and fights. When humanity is held by the generations, and the container of culture is created, the battles and fights are often expressed through games. If not through games, then through arguments and mediation. If you look into the etymology of *competition*, you will find that centuries ago, the meaning of the term was "to strive together." Look back further toward the root and you will find that a petition was a prayer for something better that was written to divinity. The deep root of *competition* is "to pray together for something better."

When we engage in such conflicts, we learn to manage our aggression toward one another. Any parent knows these impulses begin by being expressed very bodily and very clearly. Fight is clearly fight and flee is flee for young children. When two children with sticks play at attacking and fleeing, they are learning about themselves and one another. They inevitably learn lessons about power and they are forced to make decisions. They have direct experience of the power of empathy and direct experience of the power of domination and submission. When they have direct experience of these powers, then we, as adults, can help guide them to make truly agentic decisions about how they will act in life. This is a primal pattern of the birth of morality and ethics.

Oftentimes, the young boys I've worked with, and some of the young girls develop some degree of fascination with war and playing at war. This, of course, begs serious questions about gender and about cultural conditioning. That aside for now, I am curious about working with the phenomenon as it is. I suspect, if guided by family and community, it is one of the ways young people can begin to work out complex moral issues that lie at the heart of humanity. In some ways, each person is moving toward working through the same core question that is riddled through many foundational texts and teachings of wisdom traditions around the world. How do we live ethically and morally in a condition where much of our ancestry has engaged in warfare? Where we are still at war? Beneath that, I suspect there are the questions of Earthy existence: humans eat to live, and to eat we must kill—be it plant or animal. A child's fascination with these topics is the sign of a morally developing human being. It is an opportunity to help the child develop her own personal morality.

The next time you are around a herd of young people playing tag, watch for the negotiations they are enacting. Watch the whole herd and see how they are deciding, again and again, where they stand in the whole and how each person uses her own personal power. Watch just one person in the herd, and you will see a personal living system learning how to navigate sympathetic arousal with greater resiliency. Sympathetic arousal can be short-handed as fight or flight, and it always precedes experiences of the freeze state. A person learns how his body works when he runs from the predator. How he ducks and dodges and successfully evades. A person learns how she hunts, attacks, and successfully takes her prey. A person learns about freeze. How it feels in the body when the predator is upon you and you have no option to fight or flee. How it feels to be tagged and to release yourself to a small psychological death. We learn over time how to behaviorally minimize freeze in a situation where it is not opportunistic. We learn to more successfully navigate fight or flight and how to come out of freeze when the being needs to. We learn to choose and commit consciously. We learn ourselves in primal action. We provide, through experience, essential nutrients for the development of our nervous systems.

We learn who we are and the extent of our personal power through primal engagements with the world and with each other. We are primally formed to learn these lessons through breaking branches, bumps, running, dodging, cuts, and even larger accidents—regardless of gender or culture. Everyone has potentially traumatic experiences repeatedly throughout a lifetime, especially in childhood. If we don't experience enough successful navigation of fight or flight impulses, then we don't learn how to tone our systems and become less prone to trauma. If a child has a big fall that overwhelms him, it usually means the deep and primal systems of the body decided, in moments before impact, that fight or flight were not options. So, the body went into freeze. When the child survives the fall, that freeze feels like helplessness and powerlessness. So, in a way, the child needs to reclaim his sense of power and agency on a deep level. The body need to shake, which is true for every mammal, and the breath needs to do its unimpeded work. Oftentimes children will cry or scream while feeling all the feelings coursing through their being. This is a child, in part, resolving all the energy that got stored up in that moment of freeze. This is a child negotiating himself out of trauma.

In trauma, these fight or flight impulses have been impeded and the body never got a chance to process them. The neurology, the larger body, and the subjective experience (which are all intertwined) get stuck in their own way. The impulse gets stored in our bodies and minds; it is unintegrated energy. This creates a host of problems long term. While it is a brilliance of the human being that we can store such impulses for a later resolution in a safer spot, it is a costly endeavor. We can continue the rest of our lives, but we are always spending energy holding that traumatic content in check. We are always amped up in a way, and this can manifest as problematic behaviors and even lifestyles. Over time, unresolved trauma has serious health effects.

Interestingly, a consequent successful resolution of a fight or flight situation or a skillful navigation out of a freeze can help us to metabolize old traumatic content. This is a borderline jargony way of saying something that we all have experienced in some way. If you got an injury from jumping over a rock one time, and it was a bad injury that you didn't fully process, you may notice that the next time you try to jump over a rock you hesitate to a degree that is dangerous. Your muscles shake with competing impulses. You might even feel compelled to avoid jumping over any rocks. If you work through it and teach yourself to jump over rocks again, you become skillful at it. With consecutive successful attempts, you find that the inhibition is gone. You have metabolized a trauma and gained more agency at the same time. Since life is full of sticks and stones and breaking bones, not to mention breaking hearts and terrible losses, it is so important for us to learn how to move through such experiences.

If a person insufficiently learns to successfully resolve a fight, flee, and freeze responses and protect their own being, they build a persona in which they cannot protect themselves. This is a primal anxiety. When people hold trauma or anxiety, it changes their behavior in maladaptive ways. Cycles of domination and suppression can become externalized into the community and the world. A personal system that cannot successfully regulate itself tends to then look outward. It seeks to reorganize external conditions in order to not trigger the trauma or anxiety. It wants to assure itself that it has control. Unfortunately, it seeks to do this by attempting to control the uncontrollable, ever-changing world around it. Other people, or the land itself, can be damaged by the actions of a disorganized person seeking some way to resolve their trauma or anxiety. If a person cannot control something that he feels he needs to control, then the next maladaptive option is usually to destroy it. I wonder if, on some level, war and mountaintop removal are expressions of disorganized systems that cannot resolve themselves.

Other Animals

On the east side of Lake Whatcom sits Stewart Mountain. It is a humble mountain compared to its larger siblings further east, and it is often overlooked by any aside from nearby residents, loggers, and hunters. Stewart is a maze of trail and lumber roads. It sings through a bubbling choir of creeksongs. Near the top, it undergoes a strange shift to nearly subalpine environment and spreads itself thick with blueberry and salal. If you are up there in the open blueberry expanse as the sun is setting at certain times of the year, you can witness the strange hunt and chase of the nighthawks. They do not make secret of their presence as they shriek and bolt through the sky. The juncoes, jays, and thrushes below dash from shrub to shrub. The insect-eating nighthawks peel the sky apart with their terrible dives, and they often make a loud roar with their wing feathers as they pull out. They chase each other with cries, sharp turns, and talons outstretching. The air is thick with the hunt. They eat well on those nights.

Look and see the bear scat strewn about the land. The scat speaking of feasts of vegetable matter and of the occasional animal. The bark of conifers on the land reveals scars from the bold tooth of the bear. This giant moves with such grace and careful paw that it is, along with the mountain lion, among the hardest of the large animals to track. So quiet when he wants to be. So much a phantom. And the lion, when she deigns, moves like mist through the foliage. Ramble along Stewart's drainages, and you will find a splay of deer hair marking the end of a blacktail deer's life and the continuance of the lion. The bobcat, the mink, the racoon, the snowshoe hare, the mountain beaver, and the countless other residents reveal the dance of living and dying with the wilderness.

On Stewart, humans hunt. Hunting is a matter of continuing ethical debate, and perhaps it always will be. Can we be human and hunt without feeling a challenge to our morality? Is hunting, by nature, a moral struggle that requires each person to decide where she or he stands? Harvesting animals can feel closer to home for humans than harvesting plants, and this can create more consideration of the value of this behavior. If we hunt other mammals, we know that they feel and emote similarly to us. If we take a racoon's partner and we watch the other racoon staring at the dead body, we can feel the pain in our being. It is not an easy thing to do. If we are present and the heart is engaged, if we are fully human, then taking a life is never an easy thing to do. This is the character of an awakened and dynamic morality. No one reading this has exactly the same experience or opinions on hunting, and that is the fabric of an awakened and dynamic ethics. We are all here because of hunting. We survived ice ages, and we live outside of the tropics. We endure winters, and that has required meat. If nothing else, at least the meat of small animals.

We are in a strange place here where we all are faced with a need to consider and deeply communicate our ethics around hunting and meat eating. If we live outside of the tropics or in population density or in any kind of civilized lifestyle, we depend on agriculture. I remember a friend telling me a story. She was a small-scale organic farmer and she was exceedingly skilled at her job. She produced more vegetables than conventional agricultural methods could have and she increased the vitality of the soil at the same time. She did till and that meant that, even in this lower impact relationship, she killed. She told me one time, with a heavy heart, about running the tractor through the fields in springtime. As she ran the tractor, she saw the voles running from her in abject terror. The tilling time is the same time that those little voles make kind burrows to birth their sweet young. As the blades progressed, they sent those little mammals back to the soil. She told me that her heart couldn't take it when she saw one vole so terrified that it went into freeze right before the tractor. It would not move. She stopped the tractor and picked up the vole. Placed her in a sanctuary spot. She checked the spot the next day to see the vole dead where she had placed her. The terror had killed her.

I suggest pausing if you can and feeling in your body. Imagine that vole. Imagine my friend with a kind heart trying to feed people in a better, gentler way. It is a hard thing to hold, is it not? Imagine those underground taking blade or suffocation. The roots of our vegetables digging into them a month later. If you do feel something here, it is the feeling of morality working. Morality is not easy and mechanical. There is no unchangeable standard. Morality is alive. Morality is created every moment. Morality needs to be exercised.

Now, we can live a vegetarian lifestyle. And, the hard morality is that, outside of the tropics, this requires petroleum and all of the systems of transportation that go with it. Eating vegetarian is also a moral struggle. Such deliberations are best considered by many minds in congress.

Even if we do not hunt, we are who we are because of hunters. Not just human hunters. Have you ever seen a rabbit actually crawl to sneak away from a potential predator? It is not even crawling. It is more like slithering. It's almost unbelievable to watch what they can do with their bodies. Have you seen a deer slide through a minute opening without making a sound, or jump a six foot obstacle? Watch the racoon climb. See how the lion dances the land in soundless grace.

For so many generations, humans have watched their non-human relatives to understand the movement and spirit that these beings embody. Trackers will practice walking like the animal. They will embody the movements they see on the ground. Whole sets of martial arts have been crafted by studying the ways of other life forms. The tiger. The crane. The mantis. How many cultures have dances inspired by our animal relatives? We learn through our animal siblings how to be.

This is a story about a battle. It was witnessed by a great naturalist and the guts are true, though, as with everything in this book, I tell it in the way it naturally comes through me.

It takes place on a mountain field far away from any human civilization. On a sunny day with the buzz of insects and the shifting voices of leaves. On that day, a human was in swoon with his Earthy animal and was wandering and wondering with the landscape. In the distance, he noticed something and paused. A great plume of smoke was rising from the field. He watched it carefully and took a breath, as natural animals do. He noticed how localized it was, and wondered if some strange wild phenomenon had just created fire. His wonder pulled him, and he made his way through the field with as much grace as his being allowed him. When he got close, he managed a view.

And there, to his surprise, he saw that the smoke was not smoke. It was earth: great plumes of dust roiling through the air. And the dust came from an anthill three feet wide. The ant hill was under attack by a tenaciously digging badger.

The human stilled and watched for some time, witnessing Badger and learning.

Then, some strange tug in his body caused him to look further down the field. And he felt a jolt of energy in his body. He saw across the field, directly approaching the plume of dust, a great grizzly bear. The bear walked with the confidence of an undefeated warrior.

The human checked the wind, ducked his body, and became one with the blades of grass.

He witnessed.

Bear approached the dust and saw Badger. Bear's head dropped and his shoulders bulged for a moment. He walked in a focused path toward Badger. He came right to Badger's rear and sniffed. Badger did not even turn around. Badger was focused on the ants and nothing more.

Much as a king who is slighted by his subordinates, Bear gave a snort and bulged again. Badger did not turn around. Bear took his massive head and, in one graceful strike, shoved Badger away from the hill. Badger's body flew in the air, landed on the ground, and tumbled. Badger turned to Bear, fury in his eyes.

Badger charged Bear.

Bear, startled and confused, wiggled for a moment, then turned and ran away. Badger ran after him until he was away enough from the hill. Then, without another glance backward, Badger went right back to the hill and dug and ate of the delicious and nutritious ants.

Bear stopped and turned. As if remembering himself, he shook and looked at Badger. Bear's head swayed low and back and forth, and his muscles seemed to pulse with power. He walked at a fast clip right back to Badger. Without pause, he again placed his head next to Badger and struck. Badger flew in the air, but this time was ready. Badger hit the ground, tumbled, turned, ran toward Bear, launched himself in the air, and bit down hard on the bear's snout.

Bear roared.

The human's heart pummeled his chest.

Badger did not let go. He hung from Bear's snout as Bear roared and shook his head. The blood of Bear painted the nearby land.

Bear took his great claw and raked Badger's body. The blood of Badger painted the land.

Badger did not let go.

The human forgot to breathe as he witnessed.

Bear slashed and roared. Bear's and Badger's blood poured. Badger was deeply wounded and bit down harder. Bear struck again and again until shreds of Badger's skin were hanging from his body.

Badger's body became limp. Bear shook his head.

Badger did not let go.

Bear slashed at the dead body until he tore Badger from his snout.

Badger did not let go.

If we have an individual consciousness, this story is strange. What power could make the badger not let go? Was it a foolish death?

No one knows the full answer to this. But we can perceive many medicines that the story holds. The story is about the spirit of Bear and Badger. Particularly Badger. That one badger will never reproduce again. That badger died without another badger in sight. In time, on that mountainside, only that bear's scar will hint at the happening. Then the bear will die.

What lives on? What could possibly have been a reason for this?

The part of this story that is easily overlooked is the witness.

There was a human great ape in the bushes, silently bearing witness to the power of Bear and the power of Badger. He watched and learned depths of their character. He remained until the bear left. And he held this story in his mind as if he had won a great treasure, an empowering medicine. He came back to his people. The witness spread the medicine throughout the world. In the minds of his immediate relations. In my mind. And now in yours. You are a carrier now of badger medicine.

Badger does not let go.

In this way, what lives on is the medicine of Badger. The story and the character. And it is spiraling through the cosmos in the form of the results of that bear's consciousness, and in the form of every human consciousness who knows this story. That badger medicine is bending the whole world as a result of that one badger, that one bear, and that one human. We can wonder what other observers were affected. For now, we know that there is clear medicine for humanity in this.

You have this story now. Someday, when you want to give up, this story will be in your being and it will offer you the inspiration to not let go. Or it may teach you the results of never letting go.

If we evolve our idea of evolution, we can realize that we are one Bios evolving itself. We can then include a transspecies evolutionary view. Transspecies means thinking both beyond and through the lens of species. Badger is evolving *through* the human species.

Peace through Conflict

One strange paradox of being is that we can study conflict in order to find peace. Martial artists, if they are awake through the whole process of their life's contemplation, become peaceful people who choose not to fight.

I had a great teacher named Tai Hazard. No flowery poetics can make the cut to scratch at the surface of a description of Tai's wholeness. Tai was a badass. Tai was a Shotokan karate instructor, a master carpenter and furniture maker, a Kyudo instructor, a zen priestess, and a wilderness wanderer. There were other great talents, but that is my short list. Tai was seventy years old when I met her, and she, in great kindness, offered to teach me carpentry.

Tai had the gentleness and confidence of a drowsy, relaxed bear. When she paused to think before speaking, she emanated the feeling of being alone on a high sunny meadow on a windless noon. She was quirky and liked to laugh, often at herself. She was an easy friend to many life forms.

One day, while I was diligently working on making an accurate cut, Tai walked over to me and stood in stillness. On the inside, I was again recalling an unpleasant memory and trying to recraft outcomes within the secluded ecosystem of my own mind. Then trying to make myself focus on the present and not think about it. Tai took a breath and smiled.

"Hey Matt," she said, "did you ever hear the story of the female samurai?"

I pulled myself out of my negativity loop and looked up at her. "No."

"Set that down for a second and let me tell you."

What follows is the story she told. Please forgive any historical or cultural inaccuracies in this and other relayed stories. They were passed on verbally and modified by many minds, including my own. They morph in the natural, ungrammared way of a decolonized being. A good story is mythical, and the mythic feeds us with its connotation, not its denotation.

One time, in Japan, the samurai infused the land with the spirit of the warrior. The samurai had a strong code of honor and a very clear order. In those days, there was a certain kind of ranking system for samurai. Samurais, over time, would gain higher rank in accord with their accomplishments. To be a high-ranking samurai was a true honor and gleaned much respect from the people.

Of course, while the code was taught and the teaching clear, not all samurai followed or understood the deep teachings of honor. Some samurai became fixated on their rank and all of the prestige and respect it would bring.

Some followed honor as a way and wrote the code through their actions. Some of these were very high-ranking samurai. And they were loved for what lived through them. One such samurai was a true rarity of the land. She was a female samurai. No women were samurais in that land until she appeared. From a young age she persisted and endured all of the resistances until she was trained. And she endured all of the challenges wrought from her gender in that context. And she excelled. Very soon, she became the best fighter, and she embraced the deeper teachings. Year by year, conflict by conflict, training by training, duel by duel, she grew in rank. It was her way that brought the rank, not her seeking of it.

After many years, she became one of the highest-ranking samurai in all of the land. She was the favorite of her lord, and he would do almost anything she asked. She rarely asked for anything.

Being both very high ranking and being a woman posed a consistent challenge for her. Some young and rash samurai would spend time strategizing ways to increase their rank. They would look through lists of samurai with their ranks and plan on who to duel next. If they won a duel against a higher-ranking samurai, they would increase their rank significantly. Again and again, these young men would look through the list and come across a woman's name. Even if they heard the tales of her prowess, they would become blinded by the fact that she was a woman. They would think that surely they could beat a woman.

So, again and again, nearly every day the female samurai would receive challenges to duel. Thankfully, the code allowed her some grace. She could refuse up to three times. With each refusal, she made sure the youngster would know of her accomplishments and come to his senses. However, some remained blinded, and continued to challenge until they forced a duel to happen. Even with the dueling, there was grace afforded. The duelers could choose the terms of the fight in order to minimize the death rate. Usually, if it came to a duel, the female samurai would manage more compassionate terms and send her opponent away with a limp and a damaged ego. However, some were so blind that they demanded the highest stakes, which would mean the greatest rank increase. They demanded a duel to the death.

The female samurai tired of these duels. They were imposing on her ability to do more important work in the world. So, she made a request to her lord. She asked him if he could build her a new dojo with a very specific design.

"Anything for you," was his only reply.

And it was done. The builders were sent out and the designs became a full, beautiful dojo. The dojo had one peculiarity. The hallway leading to the dojo was unbelievable long. It had no embellishments. It was an austere and uniform tunnel leading to a distant point.

Soon after the dojo was complete, the female samurai came across her first mandatory duel. A young samurai from a village to the south had persisted through all of her refusals and terms. They were to duel to the death. The female samurai, being so high ranking, had the privilege of naming the location of any duel that came her way. She formally invited the young samurai to her dojo to duel.

The young samurai came on the appointed day. He was strong and quick and agitated. He knew of her accomplishments, but ferociously beat away his fears, convincing himself that he could beat any woman. When he arrived to her dojo, he mustered up as much anger and ferocity as he could. He flung open the door and shouted his challenge. He saw before him the great chasm of the hall. In the distance, at the end, he saw the female samurai.

Her voice traveled down the hall. "I accept your challenge. Let it begin."

The young samurai mustered his anger again. "Will you not come to meet me, or are you too cowardly?"

The voice responded, "you come to me."

The young samurai shouted his battle cry and began running down the hall. He ran full speed screaming until his breath exhausted.

The female samurai sheathed her sword and sat, her gaze fixed firm upon the approaching samurai. She became still in her body. She became still in her mind.

He ran and ran. His breath growing harsher. His energy of anger leaving him for all the effort. He ran and his steps became belabored. He shouted weak shouts as he came closer.

The female samurai was still.

He tried to keep his anger up, but his concentration was forced on his breath and the endurance needed to keep running. His sword lowered as he ran closer and closer. His run slowed. His breath deep and heavy. His eyes dilating. His legs burning. But still his determination to stay aggressive and to win the battle moved him on. Until he found himself standing right in front of the female samurai.

Gasping for breath, he screamed at her "unsheathe your sword and fight!"

Her eyes right on his. Her whole being as still as rock.

"If you will not unsheathe, then I will strike you!"

Only stillness in response.

He screamed his greatest scream and pulled his sword back for the killing blow. His eyes met hers.

Stillness.

The young samurai gasped as he felt all the disturbance in his own body. His breath fluttered. His eyes teared. He saw and felt her stillness.

He sheathed his sword. Dropped to the ground. And bowed his deepest bow.

He got up, turned, and walked away.

The female samurai was still as rock.

Still as a rock.

We can pick up rocks and have them become an extension of our-selves. Tools or weapons. How do we become the rock itself? As it is.

I remember wilderness therapy and working with so many young people who had faced such deep challenges and injustices in their lives. The human world had hurt and healed them again and again, and in this situation, they were given the ability to take their hurt and their life-fire directly to the wilderness.

I think of Cable. A young man from a very remote village in Alaska. He had his share of repeated trauma in his life, and he had joined us for a sixty-four day wilderness trek in the Tongass National Forest. He was often quiet and most of his interpersonal dynamic consisted of trying to make other people laugh. Other than clowning, he rarely disrupted the flow of the group. As guides, we often discussed what he needed in order to access more depth of communication and relationship. We wondered where his edges were.

Cable, one day, thoroughly shattered his compliant demeanor. I think, colloquially, we would aptly say that he just snapped. It was evening and we were preparing for sleeping under tarps when Cable revolted. At first, it seemed a revolt against the guides and the whole context of our wilderness culture. He began swearing at us and running away from camp. But soon it showed that it was some deeper revolt. Cable became violent. He swore more loudly and started throwing sticks. Then rocks. Big rocks. You inherently know when someone is throwing rocks around you but they don't actually want to hit you. You know when they are trying to put the rock through your head. Cable's anger was in each rock, and each rock was a true weapon.

At the same time, I had a good connection with Cable. The rocks were thrown at my head and the anger was real, but there was some deep knowledge in me that the anger was not for me or our culture or anything that was happening at that moment. The anger was simply anger, and it was coming out. It was not going in.

Cable ran through the tarps and pulled strings. He threw rocks and screamed obscenities. He scrambled through forest and hurled logs behind him. I called to him, reasoned with him, requested of him, chased him, and watched him. Finally, when he was further up the road and throwing rocks in my directions, I thought of the female samurai. I sat down in the middle of the road and did my best to go into meditation. I reduced reacting and inserting myself into the situation. I did my best to become like a rock for Cable. He seemed confused by this, and my job was to not react to that. I sat.

And then Cable began throwing rocks at the side of the road. He threw them as hard as he could. He stopped swearing. He put everything into his throw, trying to sink an anger-filled rock as deeply as he could into the berm. After some time, I got up, and walked a little closer to him. I picked up a rock and threw it into the berm as well. I put everything I had into that rock. My own sadness and anger and all the other complicated emotions that are always somewhere in my system. I felt it in my body as it sank impersonally into the receiving Earth. I threw again. Cable threw. The two of us, eventually, side by side, throwing our emotions into the great, giving Earth. No matter how much emotion, no matter how violent, the rock simply stuck and became a part of the berm. No reaction. Just impersonal change.

Over time, it turned into a game with the two of us. Trying to hit the other person's rock. Then trying to hit other objects. After some time, the two of us simply walked, wordlessly toward his tarp. He crawled into his sleeping bag and slept.

I remember Jake. Jake had one of the hardest personal stories I have yet to come across. So much pain and trauma. Within Jake was a sweetness and a brilliance that was continually struggling to stay in the light. But the pain and the disorganization of his life's story overwhelmed him with tidal waves of violence. Usually, this happened before bed time. While everyone else was getting in their sleeping bag, Jake would often begin swearing and shouting defiance. He would take off into the woods, and one of us would follow him just to keep eyes on him.

There, in the secluded wilderness space, Jake would unleash his fury. He would wreck everything he could. Push down standing dead trees. Destroy foliage. Tear up roots. Throw rocks. Break logs. He would scream and smash whatever he could. And there, too, he was met with a consistent impersonal reception of his actions. Nothing fought back. Nothing judged. What he faced, again and again, was a landscape wrought by the results of his actions. Again and again, he would tire. He would become soft. He would recover his sweetness. And he would sleep deep sleep.

For Cable and Jake, sticks and stones were the extension of their bodies. They were the extension of their minds. Roaring and crying, swinging and throwing, they exhausted everything and were met with stillness. Stillness transforms.

The female samurai knew stillness. She had most likely exhausted her violence by repeatedly meeting the unconquerable indifference of the world as it is. Cable and Jake were learning stillness from the Earth. In learning this path from the Earth, they were learning their true power and identity.

Learning true power is a journey of healing. With sticks and stones and breaking bones, we learn that healing never means that something goes back to how it was. Nothing can go back in this world. We can't unhurt ourselves. True power only exists in the here and now as it is. We learn that healing means carrying the story with a newfound vitality. We carry scars and bony masses and knees that don't work the way they once did. We learn peace from these conflicts. We morph our bodies and minds and identities around this education and we live even more through them. We become healing itself. In this way, we become Earth.

Orienteering in Two Worlds

Nihul Matar dressed as if he had committed his life to the possibility of being asked to participate in a surprise L.L.Bean photoshoot. He was from Delhi. I often suspected that he spoke English better than I did. Nihul Matar was a photographer; he loved to talk—particularly about any subject that could demonstrate his skillful use of English vocabulary. Philosophy and Politics were topics of choice. When I met him, I was in the Indian state of Himachal Pradesh and had been asked to guest teach an English class on the outskirts of the tiny Himalayan village of Rajgarh. Nihul Matar had been hired by an NGO to photograph the lesson, which I confess I felt a mild aversion about. I was younger and on a personal search for authenticity, and I wanted to sustain the delusion that I could evade being a symbol in the eyes of the people. We are all symbols, and that is just how it goes. When you are a foreigner, that aspect tends to be more pronounced.

On that day, I was tired. The 9/11 tragedy had occurred a week before and tension between India and Pakistan was increasing. Family and friends were in shock. They wanted me to come home. I planned to head to Southern India as soon as I finished my time in Rajgarh. Upon that, I was riding one of the stages of sustained travel where I was getting tired of the whole country. I did not want to go home. I did not want to stay there. I did not know what I wanted. Maybe some period of deep cosmic rest. A true break. So, the universe provided me with the medicine I actually needed: getting photographed doing something that I was ethically conflicted about.

I walked into the classroom and everyone clapped. I felt more conflicted. The teachers smiled and the kids flocked around me. They began petting my arms and examining the hairs. The English teacher spoke this bit of English to me. "Thank you. Please. Teach." He smiled and then walked out of the classroom. Nihul Matar was there in the corner with a camera that was big enough to kill a bobcat with a half-hearted swing. He took a martial stance, his camera extended, waiting for action. My stomach twisted and my heart fluttered. Having no other choice, I gave in to the moment and came up with a "lesson" that was more about play and connection than any retention of language. The kids laughed and played. I cheered up. Nihul Matar got the shots he was looking for. I ended abruptly and left the room, my stomach still twisted in conflict.

I sat in the teacher's room and drank from my plastic bottle of "Good Luck" brand water. Nihul Matar came in shortly after me and sat down. He was silent for a bit. "That was a great lesson. Thank you." I nodded. "A bit shorter than I expected." I nodded again. My stomach twisting. My breath settled, and my heart cracked open just a hair. I shook my head. "I'm just tired. I'm struggling a bit with being a foreigner coming in and teaching these kids. It seems like a good show. But it's really not my place."

Nihul Matar nodded and looked out the window. More silence. This was rare for Nihul Matar.

He turned to me. "Do you have a guru?"

The American individualist in me was taken back by the question. I remembered where I was and the context. "No."

"I do. My guru is very helpful for me. He helps steer my ship, so to speak." Nihul Matar paused and sipped his canteen of water. "My guru just recently told me this story. Perhaps it will help."

I stared out the window, my stomach still writhing, and listened.

Here is the story Nihul Matar told to me on that day:

Once there was a man who had spent much of his life on a quest for Truth. This man had been through a wide array of sects, philosophies, and practices. After all that time, the man had become disheartened, as again and again, with each engagement he found that something was missing. He had given up on the quest and settled into the mundane world. He had a regular job, a family, and a modest home.

One day, while walking a familiar street on his way to work, something caught his attention. A modest group of people were standing around a small man dressed in a simple robe. They were listening to him as he spoke softly. They seemed enraptured. The robed man was clearly a teacher. The scene enticed the man, and, as if drawn by invisible magnetry, he found his feet moving toward the teacher. He approached the group and found a place where he could get a good view of the teacher.

Then, in that moment when he clearly saw the teacher, the man's entire life story seemed to stop. The whole world as he knew it seemed to stop. The man felt as if he was standing in the middle of infinity, with no reference. He swooned and felt a great terror. Then, a once-banished thought flooded his being. From the deepest layers of his mind, he felt a sudden surge of hope: this teacher must be the one to actually know the way to Truth. The man clung to the thought and his world restructured around him. He oriented and found himself again in the crowd, staring at the teacher. The hope, the longing, was there inside him. Almost the only sensation he felt. He had found the teacher. He will finally learn the Truth.

Just at that moment, the teacher bowed to the crowd, turned, and walked away. The crowd bowed back and began to disperse. The man felt a sudden fright. The teacher was leaving. The force of hope within him sent a surge of energy through his body. He pushed the others aside and carved a path in pursuit of the teacher.

But though the teacher had just been there, the man was amazed to find that the teacher was just barely in his sight. The teacher moved like smoke through the crowd, and the man forced his ways with as much speed as he could to try to catch up. He saw the teacher's robes disappear around a corner. He made it to that corner only to see the robes disappearing around another corner. All thoughts of his job, his family, his home had shed from his mind. The man became singularly focused on reaching this teacher, this one person who clearly could show him the way of Truth. And so the man forsook his duties to his job on that day. He forsook everything for the pursuit. But corner by corner, street by street, the teacher seemed perpetually out of reach.

The whole day passed and into the evening. Periods of time came when the man thought he had lost the teacher. He searched and searched around the area he had last seen him, a great fiery pain in his gut. And each time, just as he felt the darkness of despair casting his soul toward its endless night, the teacher appeared just out of reach.

Like this, the cycle continued. In the late hours of the night, the teacher disappeared completely, and the man became convinced that he had lost him. He huddled and spent the night on the street in the area he had last seen the teacher. Thoughts of his everyday life moved across the skyscape of his mind like migrating geese. There and gone. The man knew that he was committed. Even if he lost the teacher, he would dedicate his life to finding this man who held the Truth. Finally, his deepest quest had an object, and the object was attainable.

The next morning, the man felt the great warm-washed joy of relief when he saw the teacher again, walking further down the street. The pursuit continued. And it continued in the same way as the day before.

Then the next day the same.

Then the next.

The man became more and more ragged, and people began to take pity on him. They gave him coins or food, and the man accepted with great thanks. He needed much energy to keep up with this teacher.

Days turned to weeks. He completely stopped thinking of his job and family, of any other aspect of his former life.

Weeks turned to seasons.

The pursuit of the teacher who held the Truth was the man's entire life.

One day, in the late spring, the man followed the teacher to the edge of town. This was unusual, and, to the man's delight, he saw the teacher taking an old road outside of town. The man grew excited. The teacher could not hide in crowds and his path on the road was predictable. The man picked up his pace, but no matter how fast he pursued, the teacher still managed to remain at a distant point on the road. The man's legs ached and his breath wheezed as he pursued.

Then he saw the teacher step off the road and onto a faint trail that lead to a nearby mountain.

The man pursued.

The teacher moved up the mountain with the grace of a doe. He stepped through forest and clearing with surety and never seemed to waver. Up the mountain he went. False summit by false summit. And the man pursued. He was wild in his pursuit. His pants slashed by brambles. His mouth dry. His eyes stinging from his own sweat. But he knew, deep down, that the moment was coming. He would finally meet the teacher on this mountain. He would learn the Truth in this place on this day.

The teacher approached the summit and disappeared behind a small rock.

The man scrambled after him, slipping and sputtering, he pushed his way to the top.

And there, at the top of the mountain, just behind a rock, right in front of him, the man saw the teacher. The teacher was seated in still-ness looking out over the world. The teacher turned to him. His face calm. He seemed to be listening with his eyes.

The man's heart like a war drum. He opened his mouth, but his mind struggled to make words. The moment was actually here. Finally, the man spoke, "I have followed you for longer than I can count. I have given up everything to pursue you. My family. My home. My job. My whole life. I know that you have the answer. You know the Truth." Tears streamed from the man's eyes. He dropped to his knees. "Please teach me."

The teacher looked at the man with the same gentle curiosity one might a bobbing wildflower. He smiled. He nodded.

"The Truth?" the teacher said. He nodded. "The world is a fish." He became silent again and stared out over the landscape.

The man listened and suddenly felt a great tidal wave of heat pass through his body. Disbelief. Then anger. Violently hot. "Wait!" He growled. "No. No. Do you mean to tell me that I gave up everything... EVERYTHING... to follow you and you are going to sit there and tell me that the world is a *fish!*" He shouted the last and stared with fury into the teacher's eyes.

The teacher looked surprised. He took a breath. "You don't like it?" He said. "Okay, it's not a fish."

And that was where Nihul Matar's story ended.

When Nihul Matar finished this story, my first response was a close-minded snap judgment. Though I knew there must be wisdom in it, I thought the story was kind of stupid. Thankfully, that part of me that knew there must be wisdom held onto that story. I gnawed and sucked on the bones of that story for years until the marrow started to enter my system.

The world is a dreaming, and we are bending being round us with the mysterious gravity of our essential "I". The power of perception is such that if we like it, over time, the world is a fish. If we don't like it over time, it is not a fish. Every species in this ongoing wave of time is selecting small bits of the whole of the energetic spectrum and calling them the world. We specialize and evolve our own worlds of experience. Each of us living full meaningful lives awake to the thinnest sliver of the entirety of reality. What delicate and sensitive beings we must be. Ever-shifting.

Awareness of the whimsy of perception begets an abiding consciousness of that which lies beyond and through the perception. We know we are just touching the whole of the energetic spectrum. This knowledge changes our values, which then change our behavior. The world is an internal/external event that points toward something beyond the bounds of experience. With this in mind, how do we navigate such a world? How do we glean meaning? How do we choose our behavior?

The Henhouse in the Chicken

The thing that gets the chicken to go to the henhouse is the henhouse that's in the chicken. In order to keep chickens over time, you have to start by keeping them in the henhouse. They have to familiarize themselves with the henhouse, to know the safe roost, the consistent source of water and food, the place to lay eggs, and the grounding sights and smells of their sisters. What they are actually building is a henhouse in their minds. They are becoming attached to the Place, and the Place is becoming a part of who they are. More than anything else, it is the mental object of the henhouse in the chicken's mind that affects the chicken's behavior and biology. When the chicken has attached to the Place as a safe home, the chicken allows herself the ability to experience home. She and her sisters go to that Place willingly at dusk. Where else would they go? Home is the Place where the chickens can experience the physiological and psychological processes of safely amping down their nervous systems, of rejuvenating, of sleeping, of dreaming. As their minds say that this Place is the safe home, their bodies morph into the experiences of safeness and homeness.

If one chicken learns to fly over the fence, the mental object of the henhouse changes and is never the same again. It is a Place she can willingly enter and leave without needs of human hand at the gate. When the mental object of her home changes, her entire world changes itself around this new experience. If the chicken experiences a predator break-in or there is stress and aggression in the flock, the henhouse in her mind changes and becomes less safe. Her behavior changes. If the stressors continue, her body performs more poorly as it does not experience the deep healing and relaxing processes it needs for the best health. Over time, with repeated extreme stress, the chicken might seek another home. One that it will perceive as safe.

What happens with humans when we have the wild Earth as a safe home in our minds? What happens when we fear it and hold it as an unsafe Place? How does this affect our behavior?

As e. e. cummings wrote, "since feeling is first, who pays attention to the syntax of things will never wholly kiss you." This is a poet's way of speaking a truth. Feeling is first. If the deep mind feels safe, the thoughts that bloom from that state will be wholly different than the thoughts that might bloom from a frightened mind or an angry mind. An angry mind cannot bloom the thoughts of a safe mind. The deep state, the mind's depth orientation, dramatically affects the cognitive content. We know this. Trying to problem solve the way to take care of our Earth while maintaining the same basic feelings and perceptions of the Earth may be like shuffling deck chairs on the Titanic. What is affecting the relationship is the deep orientation.

Here is the magic of human consciousness in relationship. The world is a fish *or* it is not a fish. We can change the way we look at the world. We can court dramatically different feeling states while in relationship with the world. These different deep orientations create wholly different thoughts, which create wholly different behaviors. Something changes in our walking the world when we recognize that we are also walking our own minds. We experience a certain understanding of the importance of our thinking and feeling. We learn that the way that we hold something in our minds can, over time, cultivate it into abundance or prune it out of existence. What if we had seen the passenger pigeons as a truly sacred song of the cosmos? What if we had deeply and truly seen them as a vital organ of our largest body, our planet?

Metaphor is real. Metaphor is a force that can kill worlds or create them.

Metaphor is a relationship. It is not just a human force. It is where the human mind meets the world, and the two sing this one song together. It is an interplay. As such, we can listen to the world and we can shift our minds in accord. We can listen to our minds and shift the world in accord. We can hear the change in song as we shift. We can actually practice the way that we feel about a creek. We can court emotion. Feeling the deep gratitude for all that the water provides. Feeling sadness for a chemical spill that poisons the water. Feeling the joy of witnessing the power of the creek's rushing torrents after a heavy rain. We can practice seeing the creek radically differently. We can stare into the creek's waters and see that they are connecting to the mountains, connected to the creeks and rivers below, which are connected to the sea, which are connected to all of the oceans of the world. We can look until we actually see that this is one unbroken body of water, and we are actually witnessing a smallest part of the one water of the entire world.

The concrete and the obvious become simultaneously an engagement with the metaphorical and mythical planes of inner life. Living happens exactly where mind meets matter. As we are more aware of this, we can navigate our own psyches in the concrete world with increasing skill. We engage in concentrated practices, like staring at the creek and feeling our emotional connection. We can make a concentrated effort to shift the mind side of our experience: the way we think and feel. This is often called prayer or meditation. We can make a concentrated effort to shift the matter side of our experience: the way the world is before us. This is often called ceremony or art. Mind shifts matter and matter shifts mind. There are many other ways that we do this intentionally. Exploration and wonder are powerful practices in this respect.

The overt reveals the covert. The superficial is the face of the deep. If we want to know about death, we visit the place that holds death: the predator's lair or the recent natural disturbance. We feel inside our bodies and notice the changes in our thoughts. We wonder at what we are witnessing and the Place itself shifts before us.

Let us revisit the place by the Salish Sea where the herons nest in the alders; the place we visited at the end of the earlier chapter of this book. It is good to come back again and again to one place. We learn the truth of impermanence. We learn that wisdom reveals itself to those who have good kung fu—who come back again and again.

In this place, herons slice sky with great wing and glide to and from their high birthing baskets. The alders sway gently and, once the young are born, the air echoes with the guttural mannish cry of the hungry growing children. When these hatchlings are awake in the nest and the busy parents constantly occupied, it is a place that pulls the primal out of you. You will step lightly here. You will see the great dark shapes above, like pterodactyls, and you will feel, in the core of your being, the fear and alertness of your ancient tiny mammal ancestors.

It is a place I go to learn about death. I take only the right person at only the right time. Together, we witness birth above. Egg shells and feathers and shit coating the ground. The body singing with the old song of being prey. The slugs and alders eating the excrement. The parents landing on twiggy nest and vomiting up their recent kills directly into the mouths of their young. If you move around enough, you can find the eagle's nest, which sits right on the edge atop of a large grand fir. Sculptures of shorebird skeletons and desiccated wings decorate the base of the fir. They form an artful ring of death.

This Place is the human psyche. This is all of the messiness of our relationship with death. This Place manifests all of the confusion of the polarity of birthing and dying. We have to step on it and breathe it. We witness the strange digestion of the dead into the mouths of the newborns. We touch the worn feathers of the once free flying sea lovers. And we immerse our entire bodies in that Place in our beings where we know that death and life are one. We look at the skeletons and we see mortality. We touch mortality.

I remember taking one mentee here years ago. He spent a long time in silence under the eagle's nest. He stared at the skeletons and smelled the feces around him. Quieter than I have seen him. He sat, maybe for the first time, fully engaged with that part of his being that contemplates death. He talked little on the way out, but later that week, I received an unusual email from his father. The young man had come back to his house with a certain quietness in his body. The father shared that the young man had, from a very young age, been very sensitive about death and had showed a deep aversion toward any witnessing of it. After spending time with that Place, his mind settled and opened, and he talked with his parents extensively about death. He wondered aloud. He asked questions.

We visit, through the land, the Place in our psyche where fears reside. Sometimes fear of death. Sometimes other fears. There is a common stage in development where young people state a desire to face their fears. Oftentimes, they cite a fear of heights. So primal. So, we visit the Places where land and psyche meet and the state of fear of heights is created. It is as skillful a way as I can think to work with these states. Go to them. Physically visit the Place of fear of heights. At a cliff's edge, a person can learn directly with no abstraction or confusion, their own personal process of working with fear.

Before approaching a cliff edge, I recommend taking some time to open up your senses. Look around, listen to the landscape, and feel the breath of the wind on your cheek. Feel your feet against the rock. Literally, feeling how they feel right in that moment, right in the place where they are meeting the rock. Starting with orientation and awareness of the ground is a helpful way to give the nervous system a good foundation of support before you go into an experience that will activate more of a fight or flight response. The wonder of the cliff and you is that the cliff will never push you to do anything. The cliff just is. What gets you to take that next step that starts to activate your fear reaction is your own voluntary musculature. You choose. You have authority. The cliff provides you unerring constancy.

When you take that step and feel the activation, take a moment and notice your breath. Without any attempt to control. What is it doing? Notice what that fear state feels like in your body. How do you know you're afraid? What, physically, indicates this fear to you? Does it have a shape? What qualities? Observe your internal landscape with the same wonder and keen awareness that you observe the external landscape. No assumptions or demands. Just observing the reality as it is. Inevitably, if you go into the body and feel the fear, it will change your experience. For those moments when you are truly observing, you are not reacting. You are present. Such presence is the antithesis of reactive fear patterns. You will learn more about yourself and, by *not* doing anything to try to change the state, you will most likely find yourself less fearful.

Then, look around and take in the landscape again. Notice something new and attractive to you with any of your senses. Something that you like or find beautiful or compelling. This grounds your system in the present again and it reinforces that the present has positive resources for you.

This is a kind of eco-somatic approach to fear. It is what happens when mind, body, and world all work together to understand the fear. When you understand fear, it usually changes. You find other emotions or values underneath. You have less of a reaction around the things that used to trigger your fear. You know yourself better, and you find that you have more agency in the world.

If you are having trouble accessing the internal experience, why fight it? Since internal and external are always co-creating one another, why not just start with the external. I remember sitting next to a young man, Aaron, who was suffering from a few major childhood traumas and some current cocaine addiction patterns. Aaron was like so many other people who choose to work with me. He did not want to sit in an office. He did not feel alive in an office, and he wanted a different way. So, he included the natural world in his therapeutic experience. Aaron had an understandably strong avoidance pattern for discussing any past traumatic content. Compassionately and honestly, this is a brilliance of his being. The avoidance allowed him to be functional enough for a time. No one wants to dredge up old content needlessly. We only live now. The challenge I saw for Aaron was that the old content was living now in those avoidance patterns, in the body, in the blocked emotions, and the unresolved fight or flight responses. When he softened and felt just enough support, he would say that he knew he needed to address it, but he did not know how. So, I asked him to ask the creek.

Aaron spent a long time by a strong creek in a spot that had both a slower moving pool and a tight rapid. Aaron opened up his senses and felt inside his body. Basically, he brought his attention to two things that are actually happening here and now. I will never forget watching him. He had such a sweet lionish heart and desire to feel and live what he saw as a good life. His body would twitch with some frequency and he was often uncomfortable spending more than a minute with the sensations inside his body. This one time with the creek, however, Aaron seemed to discover a relationship that held his attention. I remember watching his body still and his eyes soften. He sat in silence for a very long time. I have learned to bypass my cultural training that says *I* should be actively doing something when I am doing my "job" for people. I have learned that if I am to truly advocate for the people, then in situations like this my job is to get out of the way. This was between Aaron and the creek and it would take as long as it needed.

When he did speak, there was a slower pace and a deeper tone in his voice. He shared what he saw. He said that the creek was his mind. The surface of the creek was his conscious thought. He could see, through his relationship with that creek, that his mind was sometimes slow and sometimes fast due to the conditions of the container. If the bank was wide, it was slow. If the bank was narrow, it was fast. Both could be smooth. The mind can handle all kinds of conditions with grace and smoothness. What made the surface turbulent was the rocks underneath. Aaron could see, right there before him, that when something is underneath, it bends the shape of the surface. On the surface, you cannot tell exactly what the rock looks like or what it is exactly made of. With a big enough rock, the surface breaks and becomes whitewater. The water flows in many directions—against itself and up toward the sky. Aaron shared that his mind feels like that most of the time. It is fighting itself and breaking apart where it puts its energy. On the surface, he can't see exactly what is making all the disturbance, but he knows it is there and he has suspicions about what it is. Aaron realized that the way to make water smooth is to move the rock underneath. He wanted to work with the rocks of trauma that were under the surface of his conscious problems.

A stream of consciousness can be a literal event. There are many different models of consciousness out there. The strange truth is that every one works in different ways; meaning that at different points in experience, a different model might fit better. The world as a fish or not a fish. What matters is how the model affects the person in the present moment. In Aaron's case, this was a natural event between person and Place. At that moment, in that Place, the cosmos created an organization of Aaron's mind that could in no way be extracted from the creek. Aaron and the creek were not one, not two, in that moment. They were a relationship, and that relationship birthed a particular consciousness. The naturalist simply pays attention and learns. This event taught an important lesson to an important person. When there is a tumultuous layer, sometimes you have to move the rocks.

With wonder, I remember Jackie, who also had a traumatic background, and was working with moving through her fear of strangers. As we worked together, Jackie crafted a healing path that was helpful to her. We went to parks where there was a somewhat higher chance of a passerby. When she first saw a stranger, she would go into one entrenched reaction pattern without a chance to perceive more information and do something new. Typically, she would startle and freeze. She would feel a seizing in her chest and throat and it would be hard to breathe. Jackie realized that a path in the park was like a path in her mind. It funneled everything onto it. So, she decided to use that trail in the woods as a tool to create new paths in her own mind. When she would see a person on the trail, she would first notice what was happening in her body. Not judging. Just noticing. She then practiced to notice something new about the person. Then something about the landscape around her. Then back to her body. She placed herself in a position where she could pace herself. She had an easy exit strategy so she would not be overwhelmed at any point. Over time, the reactions began to wither. One notable attribute that began to arise in its stead was curiosity. She noticed herself being more curious. New paths were being created in her mind, and her mind enjoyed it. The physical path taught mental path.

We all know that we are not supposed to feed park squirrels. We all know that people do. I suspect most of us have had at least one moment of enjoyment watching a squirrel up close doing something cute or funny. Let's leave the conversation about the ethics of feeding squirrels aside and just pay attention to what happens when we feel that joy of connection. That joy of connection is not culturally trained. It is clearly primal. E.O. Wilson might call it biophilia, "love of Life."

If we are having trouble feeling connected to other humans, why not find places where connection has not been as complicated by life's story? If compassion and empathy are weak, why not develop them in a way that is fairly easy at first? Humans can really hurt each other. And, over time, the wounds can create a distrust and dislike of humanity. When we dwell in these states of distrust and dislike, we find that some of our higher functions, as highly social mammals, begin to wither. We need compassion and empathy in order to survive. That is an absolute sentence, I know. And I invite a moment of deep contemplative thought around what the world would look like without compassion and empathy. I even give the challenge that it is impossible to fathom World without these forces.

One young person, Sage, was struggling with weakened compassion and empathy. He did not feel connected to other people, and felt like something might be wrong with him. We worked with this over the years in different ways, of course, but there is one moment where I think Sage and a squirrel taught me the most about the power of biophilia.

Sage had challenges connecting with people in school, feeling

compassion or empathy with his brother, and developing trusting relationships with adults. We spent a lot of time in the beginning of our
work together just building rapport and trust. Every bit of this rapport building was important and challenging work for Sage. We mostly
worked with landscape connection or embodiment experiences that
were genuinely interesting for Sage. We might make a friction fire or
practice kung fu or adventure to a yet undiscovered ridgeline. Most of
the mentoring was in context of whatever we were doing directly, not
much about his life outside of mentoring. We were building resources
for him. We were making a safe and positive container. We were
building trust that he could experience life at a pace that would not be
overwhelming. In this context, we worked with empathy and compassion whenever it came up. Again and again, for Sage, the experience that
would light up his compassionate thoughts and actions was an interaction with wildlife. His eyes would widen and he would still himself if a
bird approached unusually close. He would wait, then move as slowly as
he could. With him, more than any other mentee, I would consistently
experience very close wildlife encounters.

One day, we met in the field of a big park and I was preparing to
lead us into the woods. Sage was upset and said that he felt tired and
just wanted to take it easy. This is one way a nervous system states its
condition and presents a regulation need. Sage needed to feel more at
ease, centered, and grounded. So, we started walking very slowly toward
some shade under the douglas firs. As we walked, Sage noticed a squirrel
coming very close to us. I can see in my mind's eye how his body shifted
when he engaged with the squirrel. His eyes softened and his spine
curved into a supple spring. His head movements became serpentine
smooth. He gave me a wide-eyed glance as if to say, "be still." I stilled.
I watched.

What took place was a courtship. I watched Sage court a relationship with that squirrel and the squirrel with Sage. The two approached
each other delicately, testing edges. Building trust. They got closer and
closer. Sage tried many techniques to get the squirrel to come right up
to him, but what proved the most successful was simply attuning to the
squirrel. The one rule of courtship, as my mentor would say, is *pay attention.* Paying attention means no assumptions and no demands. Sage was
transfixed. At times, the squirrel would run off and seem like he was
gone for good. Sage would turn to me then, his eyes excited and big,
and I could just sense the strong beat of his heart. He did not want to

leave. He wanted to wait until the squirrel got back. I asked him some simple questions about how he felt in the moment and how it was for him to pay attention to the squirrel. I asked if he could sense when the squirrel was nervous or curious. What did that feel like for him? The squirrel came back again and again. We spent an hour and half with that squirrel. It was all the medicine Sage needed. At the end, his eyeshine glowed with that biophilic starlight. We wondered together if he could have the same relationship with people.

Causality is a funny thing. Ultimately, who knows why a thing happens. I won't say that connection with that squirrel was the cause of Sage consequently softening and displaying more compassion. I do highly suspect it was a key ingredient in the transformation. What I started to notice after that outing was more discussions about ethics and good conduct. Sage started to bring up situations that happened at school or home and he actively developed thoughts on how he could best handle them. Thoughts oriented toward good conduct contain compassion. This is easy to notice as they are forming before you. They include considerations of the other, of the group as a whole, and of the greater system of Life. It seemed like Sage, after this, was growing his force of compassion. That squirrel, in part, cracked the nut of his compassion, and Sage's compassion was now meeting the outside world.

Now pause, if you will.

Where is your breath in your body? Where is it coming from? Where is it going to? Notice. Pay attention. Can you see something new in your surroundings? What can you smell right now?

What will you find if you were to go into your body and feel one of the rocks beneath your surface, one that still carries a hurt and you know it but do not want to admit it? Just listen. Listen inside your body. If you could pick a place in your body where you hold it, where would it be?

Now listen to that place in your body. As it is. No need to change anything. Just notice like you would a place in the landscape.

Can you still smell the air around you as you do this?

What place on this Earth is holding some wisdom for you? If you let yourself put out an answer without editing it, what happens? Where could you go to learn about this? A desert? a lake? a dense thicket? A hole in the ground?

Now go there.

Timeless Ways of Mind and Place

How old is the human psyche? Where did it start being the *human* psyche?

There are some ways of interacting with the Earth that seem timeless and cross the bounds of current and past human cultures. They seem to be fundamental elements of the Earth-connected human psyche. Two that come to mind are the Threshold and the Four Directions. We can look at these two practices as external entrances to fundamentals of the human psyche. The practices help us to access parts of who we are. With continued practice, we develop these parts of ourselves.

The Threshold

> *As you walk through this door…*
> *As you cross this line…*
> *As you step onto this rock…*
> *As you set foot on the other bank…*
> *As you step over this rope…*
> *As you turn and walk away…*

Do not look back. Do not come back until you are ready. Only you will know when you are ready. Come back through the same passageway. Know that when you cross that threshold, you will be a different person.

The threshold is a technique of working with the land to create a border between two states of consciousness. Literally, you choose a line to cross. It might be as simple as drawing a line in the sand or stepping between two trees. The important part is that you are clear with your intention and that you allow yourself to attribute importance to the act. It seems to me that the threshold must be a primal technique, as it often does not need much explanation. People tend to just get it, like they already know how to do it. There are varying levels of cultural and personal resistance that are inevitably at play, but if the explanation is simple and inclusive of personal and cultural beliefs, people from many different cultures and walks of life tend to embrace this.

The technique is austere by nature. Choose your own threshold. Find something in the landscape that will be meaningful to you. It could be a natural construct or you could actively create your threshold. Tell yourself that once you step across that threshold, you will step into a place of possibility and wonder. For you, it may be a place where you let your imagination roam free as it did when you were a kid. Rocks can talk and bugs can hold entire worlds of story for you. It may be, for you, a place where magic happens. It may be a place of spiritual receptivity. It may be a place of the beginner's mind. The place of creativity. The important part is that it is the place where you find yourself open to new possibility and where you are receptive to wisdom that is revealing itself to you. It is a clear decision to step out of the everyday way of being and into a place of mystery. Do your best to make this as meaningful as possible, and find the way that *you* cross the threshold and step into another world.

When you return, pay attention to the threshold again and be intentional about stepping back into the everyday world.

It is that simple. You can use the threshold if you are holding a life question. When you cross, you can be alert for ways the world is offering you its own guidance around that question. You can go looking for a sign or a vision. You can go with an intention. You can simply practice stepping into that other state of being.

If you are suffering from anxiety, you can ask the simple question, "how do I work with anxiety?" Step across the threshold and pay attention. You will notice that your mind sees anxiety as it is in the world, and it perceives answers or lessons that are pertinent to you. You can walk across a threshold with an intention, such as, "I am a man who courageously loves himself and his world." Stepping across the threshold and paying attention, stories and meaning will weave themselves around that intention and you will gain wisdom.

The threshold allows greater access to the experience of creating metaphor. We are always participating with our own psyches. We can use the threshold to access what psychology calls *the liminal state*, the state where we find metaphorical meaning. A place of new connections.

What is objectively true is true in the objective state. Personal truth is state dependent. Rocks talk in one state and they don't in another. All states are a part of our humanity. We all access different states throughout our experiences of living. They come together to create our sense of Self and Place. The threshold is a way of discovering and deepening the personal sense of Self and Place. It is a way of cultivating the fullness of our humanity and of our world.

The Four Directions

The four directions are literal: north, south, east, and west. Four compass points. Four sides of the world. Four magnetic orientations. Four unique sets of characteristics. The sun rises in one; it zeniths in another depending on our place on the globe; it sets in another; the fourth holds the north star or the southern cross, but never the sun. Four directions hold four different basic characteristics of weather depending on your Place. Four directions, in my Place hold the glaciated volcano named by some "the Great White Watcher" to the east; the arctic weather that passes through a great river valley to the north; the Salish Sea and rocky islands to the west; a string of volcanoes and the wet South Sea weather to the south.

The truth that I have found is that I have not grown up with much embodied connection to these four directions. Even with map and compass training, and a basic sense of orientation to the four directions, it has been and will be a long courtship to let these four directions enter my body and bend my primal self into a deep sense of knowing my planetary position. It a curious tale, the two-dimensional trending of empire and industry. The story of writing, from parchment to printing press to pixels is the story of the human mind developing certain attributes. In the development, the story goes, we happened to have pruned certain other attributes. We are more oriented toward being flatlanders now, in the primal sense. This is a statement that could get very heady, but an intellectual engagement with this while making meaning from marks on a flat surface would not produce the experience of its truth. Practicing the bird's eye view, peripheral vision, and depth vision begin to reveal, through experience just how two-dimensionally oriented many of us are. Orienting to the four directions again and again, in different locations at different times, helps to court the mind into a primal baseline of three-dimension awareness.

Really, I would love to be able to find a way to provide the lived experience via this text, but I can't. Remember the Zen teaching about the texts? The experience is beyond the texts, but the texts are a *skillful means* to help you get to the experience.

So please hold this as a curiosity for yourself. Challenge these words and test them through experience. What happens if you find the four directions at the beginning of a walk and then try to hold them in your mind and body consistently throughout? Can you do this throughout a day? A week? If you stare out over the horizon, how can you court more of a bird's eye view awareness of your landscape? Test your eyes on their perception of depth. Ask the question of them, are you making this scene flatter than it is? If you spin very slowly in a circle, can you hold consistently and throughout the sense of the directions in relation to your body as opposed to landmarks? If any of these are difficult, then ask why? Difficulty means new neural networks being created. It does not mean "unnatural." If most of us were asked to go start a fire in the woods on a rainy day, most would fail. But we have been doing this, as a world people, for tens of thousands of years prior. We have evolved with the four-directional awareness as much as we have evolved with fire. The four directions are a deep aspect of our humanity. The four directions make us think planetarily instead of by roads and boundaries. They change our experience of who we are.

If you do practice this, then I ask that you notice changes to your mental state as well. Do you notice yourself feeling more at ease as you orient this way? Do you generally feel more confident? Do you find yourself noticing new things about your environment? Do you notice your behavioral patterns shifting? Do you find that developing this relationship to the four directions starts making metaphorical meaning in your life?

The four directions are the grounded origin of a medicine wheel. So many cultures throughout history and before have a psychological, spiritual, and physical grounding in the medicine wheel. The medicine wheel is a way of understanding life itself in four directions. Four basic characters. Some cultures have more than four directions. Some have eight, some include vertical dimensions like Earth and Sky. All, however, are grounded. They all are birthed from our physical relationship to our round planet. All show how we grow and find meaning as this relationship evolves.

Four directions are a vital practice. A serious endeavor that has been essential to our survival. They have been so essential to each individual human that culture after culture has woven their tapestry of life's meaning on the warp and woof of the north and south, the east and west. Now, too, a re-membering to the four directions as an orientation holds a skillful means for our survival as a species. With this orientation, we learn to navigate impermanence instead of resist it. We learn that the different directions life takes have different general characters, and that all things tend to cycle. We learn to hold our consciousness as a planetary thought.

Albert Bandura, a powerful contributor to a few fields of psychology, noticed that people are not just reactive products of selection pressures served up by a one-sided evolutionism. He recognized that they are prime players in the coevolution process. He noticed that psychology is a part of this process.

Psychology is ecological by nature.

When we ground our psyches in the physical world, in accord with our planet, our thoughts and our behaviors change. We become, as beings, more grounded and attuned to the ways of ecological processes. Orienteering in the physical world means cultivating an ecological psyche. It means, if we are participants in industrial consumer society, navigating to new psychological environments. The skillful means to do this is to physically navigate ourselves into our Place.

How do we navigate to a new environment? The wilderness guide in me says, "pay attention and keep putting one foot in front of the other. No scree slope lasts forever."

The wilderness guide in me also says that you can fun. You can have a sense of adventure. The challenges will come and the discomfort will be unavoidable, but they don't have to dominate the journey. In fact, it has been my experience that most of us forget the pain of the cold nights or the loneliness or the sore feet and remember the beauty and the brilliance of the cold wild river laden with sunset orange salmon or the sacredness of the peaks in alpenglow.

You have a compass. It is your entire internal landscape. You have a world that is waiting for you to court her and to remember yourself. You have geology that is singing to you stories of the Earth ages that have created you. You have hazards that teach you who you are as you meet greater forces of existence. You have the moon, sun, and stars to glimmer your mental cosmos and craft you into the awareness of you as a tiny sphere in the unfathomable bigness. You have a whole world that is composed of the works of your ancestors. You can touch the world. You are touched back. The whole world is the way we are touched by our ancestors. We, the whole world, are the culmination of all striving. This is where we are. Everything is calling us to remember this primal security.

> *Listen.*
> *Do you hear the calling?*
> *Look.*
> *Where are you?*
> *Who are you?*

Rites of Passage

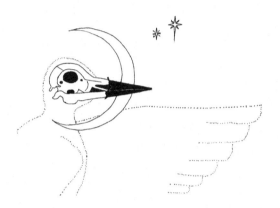

The Return

Some day, if you are lucky,
you'll return from a thunderous journey
trailing snake scales, wing fragments
and the musk of Earth and moon.

Eyes will examine you for signs
of damage, or change
and you, too, will wonder
if your skin shows traces

of fur, or leaves,
if thrushes have built a nest
of your hair, if Andromeda
burns from your eyes.

Do not be surprised by prickly questions
from those who barely inhabit
their own fleeting lives, who barely taste
their own possibility, who barely dream.

If your hands are empty, treasureless,
if your toes have not grown claws,
if your obedient voice has not
become a wild cry, a howl,

you will reassure them. We warned you,
they might declare, there is nothing else,
no point, no meaning, no mystery at all,
just this frantic waiting to die.

And yet, they tremble, mute,
afraid you've returned without sweet
elixir for unspeakable thirst, without
a fluent dance or holy language

to teach them, without a compass
bearing to a forgotten border where
no one crosses without weeping
for the terrible beauty of galaxies

and granite and bone. They tremble,
hoping your lips hold a secret,
that the song your body now sings
will redeem them, yet they fear

your secret is dangerous, shattering,
and once it flies from your astonished
mouth, they–like you–must disintegrate
before unfolding tremulous wings.

– Geneen Marie Haugen

We all cycle and storm; flower, fruit, and fall like the seasons. We move from dark incubations to sunny constancies. Our lives are authored with the ink of change.

We all go through wounded times, where the nature of the wound is unclear, and darkly digging at the tuber of its essence seems to be our work in the world. It is the digging itself that yields the most livingness.

Action by action, path by path, we haul shovels full of inner unknown, exposing that soil to the sunwarm light of our consciousness. And often times the shovel strokes miss the mark and, dig though we might, the tuber of our suffering remains in its dark meditation. We dig from many vectors and our lives change dramatically. We work at the problem in many forms. We become raw and unsettled but determined.

If we are graced, in those broken times, we find ourselves delivered into the hands of some complete enough people who patch the wounds begot from all the digging and help us to guide our own shovel.

In a time of my life when I felt soulsick to the core and my body made its way to broken, I retreated to a tiny cabin on a sacred hill deep in the Berkshire Mountains. Though they would laugh and deny the label, I know that I was blessed by the cosmos to be immersed in a community of wisewomen. Whole people with the wisdom to treat me as a broken-pawed wild thing, to offer just enough to keep the rest of me alive and supported as I worked toward the healing. They had dropped the burden of seeking outcomes somewhere dusty-far back on their respective life paths, knowing in their bones that the wild offers a chaotic theory reciprocity that befuddles any binary sense of fairness. When the tended wild thing recovers enough, he soundlessly wanders back into his low-languaged untamed home of the wilderness, never to be seen again. That is the way of wild things. The way of the wise-woman is to know this.

Tai Hazard was one of these wisewomen and, as you might infer from her previous mention, she was prone to teach through story. While, on the outside, we were learning carpentry, Tai was truly a mentor for my soul.

I was an inward-looking awkward student, who performed from sporadically gifted to sporadically daft. Sporadics do not make for good carpentry. Having an internal focus when building a door is a recipe for a long, many-mistaked process. Tai was very patient. She knew that linear thinking was as much a tool as any handplane. Even if I would never make a great carpenter, she worked with me. There was some-thing in our relationship that was worth it, and learning from the wood and the blade would let us serve the world in unforeseeable ways.

Tai would sometimes pause the two of us in the middle of work. On some occasions, she would simply have us look around or take a breath. On others, she would unexpectedly launch into one of her stories. A story that I needed to hear.

On one such occasion, she told me the following story:

In Japan, in an era past, the country was divided into many feudal states. Each with a lord. Each with its own ambitions. Each with a history of conflict and broken-down negotiations. This was a fine recipe for war. And war happened again and again. War needed men to hold spears and fight for their lives against other men. Thus, men needed to be put in positions where this was their only option. So, lords sent out their militaries, armed with horses, fierce weaponry, and the ability to murder or starve families. The militaries went from village to village and used a combination of honor, lies, and threats to coerce able-bodied villagers into the army. This was a more inefficient form of the modern-day draft.

To be fair, the lords were not just war-minded. They believed in the country and culture, and they often had their own form of honor. So, in one such country, the lord gave the order that his people should be given a one-year notice before being conscripted into the army. The conscripts would have a full year to prepare all their business, to attend to their families, to settle their debts, and to fulfill their last remaining duties before they were taken away, most likely, to their death.

And so, one day, in one village, in this same country, an armed horde of military men rode through issuing the decree of conscription to every fighting-aged man. One such man owned a small shop through which he supported his family and elderly parents. With great sadness he received his sentence of conscription and knew that he must spend his entire next year preparing his family, his business, and his community for life without him. His wife and children wept. His parents held an aire of disbelief and confusion. The sacred order was broken. In peace, sons bury their fathers. In war, fathers bury their sons.

The man was honorable and he loved his family. He was never a fighter, and he knew nothing of war. But his duty to those he loved kept him focused on what he had to do, and, day by day, he went about his preparations. He began teaching his family the ways of the business. He made a list of all of his debts and duties to others and, one by one, attended to each. He would not leave his family or community with any extra burden.

Preparing for his departure made his days full. From the time he woke up to the time he lay on his pillow, he was busy working to take care of everything that needed done. The times he did have with his family became precious and he made sure to pay them all the attention they deserved. He worked late into the night, and would retire in wonder at the fullness of his day.

And it was only at the moment when his head was on the pillow and he was courting the restoration of sleep that he would remember himself. Every single night, as he lay, he would remember that he was actually going into the army. He would remember that he had no penchant for fighting. No training whatsoever. He would think that he should at least visit the swordmaster up the hill to receive some simple techniques to help him. His mind would then, again and again, recognize the high probability of his own death. Instead of pushing the thoughts aside, the man put his mind fully into them. He would imagine with all of his might a potential death. He would see himself being crushed to death by horses. Would feel the crack of his bones under hoof and the filling of his lungs with blood as he suffocated. His hands clawing at the dirt as he spat and desperately struggled for his last breath. He would feel himself die then, and his body would tingle with the reality.

The next night, another death. By spear or sword or arrow. By strangling. By cold. By disease. Night by night, he died again and again. Day by day, he worked. Days turned to months. Months to seasons. Seasons sped and soon enough the year was nearly completed. The man's focus had paid off, and just one week before he was to leave, he woke up, got ready to continue his preparation, and suddenly realized that he had nothing left to do. He had said his goodbyes to his community. All of his duties were fulfilled. His family was working the store all day long. The man was alone. Ready. And then, he remembered the swordmaster. He could think of no better way to spend his time. If he learned a few techniques it would at least increase his chances of coming back to serve his family and community.

He walked the road up the hill and came to the gates of the swordmaster's school.

He explained his situation. Because it was a small community, he was known to the swordmaster. He was well-respected, and the swordmaster, who did not usually take such temporary students, made a concession for him.

He told him to come back the next day and he would teach him a few simple techniques that should help him in his coming battles. The conscript bowed and gave deep thanks to the swordmaster. He returned to spend the rest of the day with his family. That night, he lay down and fell directly asleep.

The next day, he came to the swordmaster's school, ready to learn. The swordmaster handed him a simple sword, similar to what he would most likely be given by the army, and showed him the proper way to strap the sheath to his body and to draw the sword. The conscript learned instantly. The swordmaster nodded and then showed him the first basic technique. He performed a high parry that turned into a strike. He then asked the conscript to attempt this technique, ready to offer his first corrections.

The conscript nodded, drew his sword, and performed the technique perfectly. No hesitation. Smooth. Efficient. Powerful. The swordmaster's eyebrows raised. He asked the conscript to do it again. The conscript did. He repeated it ten times. Each time with perfection. The swordmaster stared long at the conscript. The conscript stood still, wondering if he had done something wrong.

The swordmaster spoke, "you said you had never learned the sword before. I see you were not honest with me. Who taught you this technique?"

The conscript was confused. He shook his head. "Great master, I have told you the truth. I have never wielded a sword in my life. I have no training and no love of fighting."

The swordmaster's eyes narrowed. Everything in the conscript's countenance indicated that he was telling the truth. After six breaths, the swordmaster nodded. "I must admit, I have never seen such natural talent. Your gift may just save you your life." He shrugged. "If you have this basic technique already within you, I may as well teach you a more advanced technique in order to increase your skill in battle. Watch closely. This technique can take years to train, but if you can perform it with at least a moderate level of skill, it will surely come in useful."

The swordmaster displayed a subtle low parry followed by a spin and devastating strike. He moved like wind. His sword a blur until it met with full force one singular point in space. The conscript watched. The swordmaster then nodded to the conscript. The conscript drew his sword, took a breath, and then performed the technique. He moved like wind. His sword a blur until it met with full force one singular point in space.

The swordmaster shook his head in disbelief. The technique was perfect. His gaze was like a blade stabbing into the conscript's center. "Again!" he shouted. The conscript performed the technique again.

Again it was perfect. The swordmaster walked directly in front of the conscript, his hand on his own sword. "Who are you?" he demanded. "Tell me now. You have obviously been trained. No one can perform that technique without training. You must have been sent by another swordmaster to steal my techniques. Who is your master? Tell me now or I will cut you down." His hand on his hilt contained the feeling of a coiled snake at the ready.

The conscript's eyes widened. He dropped to his knees in honor of the great teacher. "Great master, you know me. I have lived my whole life in the village. I have never wielded a sword. Ask anyone. When would I have time to train? Where would I go but your school? I am only doing what you ask. I mean no offense, and I am deeply thankful for your teaching. Please, believe me."

The swordmaster became as still as the dirt beneath his feet. He seemed to be staring directly into the conscript's soul. After some time, he let out one long breath. "This is the most unusual thing I have ever witnessed. I do not understand it, but I must admit that you are right. I cannot imagine how you would have been trained by anyone else. I am only sad that we have only now just met and that you will be taken by the army in a week." He paused as if consulting some voice from within. "I am not the author of this world, and it is far stranger than my imagination. If you have such skill already, I will teach you a master-level technique. Fully learn this technique, and your chance of survival will increase dramatically."

The swordmaster took in a long, graceful breath. He unsheathed his sword and cut the air in a spiraling expression of force. The sword was nearly impossible to see. The movement containing such subtlety that the eye alone could not perceive its fullness. He seemed to be in one moment in one place on the Earth and in the next to have appeared in a new location, his sword a direct stab into the heart of the cosmos.

He turned to the conscript. Sheathed his sword. Nodded.

The conscript took in a long, graceful breath. He unsheathed his sword and cut the air in a spiraling expression of force. He seemed to be in one moment in one place on the Earth and in the next to have appeared in a new location, his sword a direct stab into the heart of the cosmos.

The swordmaster's eyes bulged in their sockets. He shook his head. "This cannot be."

He turned and began walking away. "Follow me," he called back.

The conscript bowed and walked behind the swordmaster to a small garden. The swordmaster offered him a seat at a table. He ordered one of his students to bring tea. The two sat down and enjoyed the light breeze as it danced through the nearby trees. Insects buzzed by them. Tea was served. The swordmaster served the conscript. The conscript bowed in thanks and sipped. The two in silence for many heart beats. Then the swordmaster spoke, "now, you will tell me everything you have done in the past year."

The conscript bowed. "Great teacher, you want to know everything? I have done so much." The swordmaster's face became a stone cliffside. Unbreakable. "Everything."

The conscript bowed again and began to tell everything he could remember doing. He told of the moment of being conscripted. He told of every way he had planned his days and all of things he had done to prepare his family and community for his absence. The swordmaster listened and nodded. The conscript went on with detail after detail. He told of this business. His family. His debts. His duties. His friends. His obligations to the village itself. He told of everything that happened up until the point when his head hit the pillow. And then he told of what happened when he was about to fall asleep. He told of how night by night he experienced death by death.

The swordmaster's eyes narrowed at this. "Every night a new death?" he asked. The conscript nodded.

"Every night but the last."

"Explain."

The conscript bowed slightly. "This last night, I set my head to the pillow and expected the thoughts of death to come to me as they have for nearly an entire year. But none came. As I lay there, my mind was blank. I became curious about this. I tried to think of a new death. Then I realized that, in my mind, I had died in every way I could imagine dying. So, I closed my eyes and slept."

The swordmaster's face softened and deep soul smile washed over his countenance. He nodded. He got up and bowed deeply to the conscript. "You may go now. I can teach you no more."

The conscript stood and bowed back. "Great teacher, what do you mean?"

The swordmaster's eyes sparkled with soulshine. "You are no longer afraid of death. There is nothing more to learn."

Rites of Passage

The hard truth is that we are all mortal. Every one of us will die. From president to pauper. The hard question is, *will you accept your death and become good soil?* Or will you hold on to the poison of resistance? Each individual must decide.

To get to the point of accepting our own deaths, we practice small death by small death that happen throughout the course of a lifetime. Like the conscript, we die day by day, way by way. As we become more alert and attentive to death, we see the impermanence of our own bodies and minds. Our egos reveal themselves as a delusion of permanence. The world of our attachments, our expectations, our demands reveals itself as baseless.

Yet, strangely, the skillful means to this understanding is through ego, life, and story. We do experience this ever-changing world as individuals. We do learn over time. So, we recognize some major life transitions. We learn from the world that, in order for there to be life, there must be death; in order for there to be death, there must be life.

Chapter eleven of the Tao Te Ching illuminates us:

> *Thirty spokes share the wheel's hub;*
> *it is the center hole that makes it useful.*
> *Shape clay into a vessel;*
> *it is the space within that makes it useful.*
> *Cut out doors and windows for a room;*
> *it is on these spaces where there is nothing that the usefulness*
>   *depends.*
> *Therefore, benefit come from what is there,*
> *usefulness from what is not there.*

We cannot fill a full cup. Our identities must empty before they can fill with something new. So, we recognize the death of what is no longer serving us. We empty the cup of our identity so that we can birth a new one.

A new identity means new attributes, new benefit to self and world. Major life transitions, such as the transition from one life stage to the next (e.g. adolescent to early adulthood), divorce, marriage, etc. are skillfully facilitated, for humans, by ceremony. A rite of passage is the ceremony of transition.

The term *rite of passage* mostly likely carries a variety of meanings and associations for each person. Some may envision an ancient ceremony where youth must perform dangerous tasks to become an adult member of the tribe. Some might think of graduating from high school or college. Others might envision a secret club in middle school where kids dare each other to eat a slug or share drops of blood in order to become part of the group.

If we dig into the ancestry of every person reading this, we will find rites of passage ceremonies. In every culture, on every continent, some form of rites of passage has served to help keep the culture intact and the people empowered. The shapes and forms vary as wildly as do species of plants or human languages on our planet.

In this book, rite of passage refers specifically to a ceremony in the natural world that marks a transition from one life stage or identity to another. A rite of passage includes intentional preparation time, a period of concentrated effort and growth which includes facing some sort of death process, and a public recognition ceremony that marks the birth of a new identity.

While graduation ceremonies mark a completion of work, a rite of passage is a deeply personal process that focuses on who the person is becoming rather than what they have done. Rather than a middle school inclusion challenge, a rite of passage is held by the full community. The challenges are meant to help the person cultivate both self-knowledge and a connection to the greater world.

As people, we grow through challenges. We thrive on positive social relationships. We have a deep need for self-awareness. A rite of passage takes these essential elements of humanity and concentrates them into a ceremonial process.

For youth, in particular, the passage into adolescence or young adulthood can be a very confusing time. They are growing fast and their sense of self is struggling to catch up with the warp speed changes. Their biochemistries are flooding with new recipes and they are facing a parade of "first times." They are feeling a deep developmental tug to sever from their dependencies and to learn how to support themselves. Rites of passage are a means for the community to provide a container for our young people. They can have the time to sort through these changes, to reflect, and to gather guidance. In this safe, formal container, youth can test themselves and enjoy the empowerment and self-knowledge that comes from overcoming a challenge. They can feel the joy and deep support of a community that recognizes their work and their value and tells them that they have a new place in the community.

Rites of passage do not have to be relegated to an ancient practice from distant lands. Providing them now might be one of the best ways we can care for our youth, our lands, and our community. This chapter is meant to excite creative thought and consequent action around providing rites of passage. If you have not been through a ceremonial rite of passage, it is not too late. It may sound strange to propose marking your adulthood if you feel like a well-adjusted and relatively complete adult. If you feel this way, you have transformed already. No doubt about it. Thank you for your work. And the odds are that there is more transformation available to you. A nature-based rite of passage ceremony can initiate certain ecological and psychological growth that is still lying dormant within.

I have observed this happen, time and time again, and each time with each adult, there is a powerful transformative process that happens. There is some deep and ancient power embedded in the ceremony. Previously unfathomable aspects of self emerge. It forms a bond with land and community that does not break afterward. It is simply a part of you. I would like to keep in mind, as we consider rites of passage, that the life stage and the physical age are not paired in a clean calculus. The odds are that a vast, vast majority of people in industrial consumer culture would deeply benefit from an outdoor ceremonial rite of passage marking their ecological adulthood even if they are already in their seventies or beyond. What would happen if we, as community members, each took steps toward our own rite of passage ceremony? Such a question is answered through the asking. The asking happens, in part, through the doing.

If you will, please pause at this moment.

Listen.

Can you hear the outside? What do you hear?

What is one thing in your environment that you have not been noticing?

What is your breath like right now?

Where is the air you are breathing coming from and going to?

Is your child still alive within you? Is the elder alive or emerging? Do you know these aspects of yourself well? Who are you now as the adolescent?

We can consider there to be four cardinal directions of human development: childhood, adolescence, adulthood, and elderhood. As we wondered about in the last chapter, these four stages are often paired with the four cardinal directions on the planet. In that pairing, we understand that our life stages cycle. For the Earth, there are cycles within a day, within a month, within a season, within a year, within the movement of other planets and stars, within the eras. In a human life, there are also many cycles nested within one another. On the grossest level, we pass from one biological life stage to the next. We have only four and then we die. However, within each of those stages, we find other movements. There are times in our adolescence when we are still growing who we are as children. In our adolescence, we are tending to the emergence of our eventual elder. If we become adults and forget how to play and be innocently in our bodies like a child, it feels like something important has been lost and there is a consequent imbalance. In this sense, the four cardinal directions of human development are also four qualities of being that are pertinent in all life stages. They are all important.

Place and Wonder belong in our beings. In every stage of our development, Place and wonder help to create the ecologically conscious us. A rite of passage contains the wonder of stepping into the liminal state. In order to grow our connection with our Earth, Place needs to be a part of a rite of passage.

Each one of us, by nature, has an ecological child within.
The ecological child reminds us all, from adolescent to elder, that the child holds vital keys to the existence of all species. Children have an innate quality of wonder. Their expression of joy is unbridled and wholly available to the mundane. Their creativity can be disorienting unique, causing us to think in ways we have never thought before. The child in all of us direly desires to remain awake. Raising our children means raising ourselves. A kindness of living is that the child part of you continues to grow and explore throughout your development—no matter how suppressed it might be—that *you* is still here facing the world with wonder, joy, and creativity.

Each one of us, by nature, has an ecological adolescent within.
The relationship with Place and wonder is, perhaps, the most personal of experiences. No one will ever see the rock the way that you do.

The robin who watches you from the grass as he gleans is only beheld in that way by you. You are only beheld in that way by him. The stars and waters have a particular message, a meaning that will only ever be received by you. In many ways, adolescence is the process of realizing uniqueness. It is finding how you fit in the world. Your Place. This is a wonder-filled, terrible, ridiculous, painful, and empowering emergence. As strange new chemistry storms the body and the mind, the adolescent learns how she or he cannot just stay afloat, but, in order to enjoy living, must learn to swim. It takes more than just humans to teach this lesson. It takes a varied world of relationships with many different living beings to be able to hold the depths of adolescent feeling. The adolescent pushes the boundaries in a most primal expression of human vitality and personality. She bends the walls so that she can claim a place from which to stand. It takes the magnitude of great forces like mountains, weather, solitude, the night-revealed cosmos, hunger, and the innate qualities of other living beings to learn which walls in life will truly take the bending and which ones we will ever be bent to.

Each one of us, by nature, has an ecological adult within.

After all that work through adolescence, of forming ourselves and our Place, of pushing boundaries and distinguishing "I", when we really hit adulthood, we are asked by the world to release our attachment to the form we created. Adulthood means a strange paradox of agency and self-knowledge mixed with sacrifice and a state of realizing the constancy and ubiquity of the unknown. Our job shifts into making walls, creating structures, tending to others. We are the mother bear. The bull elk. The adult is called to see the world clearly and to understand what is actually possible for a community. In the most primal sense, the adult provides the basic needs: shelter, water, fire, food, and love. It is the earthiest time in a life. There is a joy of purpose, of tending, of skill, of extension of self. There is a grief too. Impermanence and entropy are like a splinter in the adult heart. Place teaches how to remove the splinter, balm the wound, and allow the scar to forever change the pace of the heart. We look to the deer who tend to their young in the face of a massive forest fire. We sit with the lava field where a single sprout grows. We listen to sounds of the forest after the storm. We feel the bigness of the world and of the cosmos, and we are reminded that we can only be now.

Each one of us, by nature, has an ecological elder within.

We carry the wisdom of the thousand-year-old redcedar who has lived through the death of almost all of her companions and stands in a smallest patch on a vastest continent; we extend the story of passenger pigeons once darkening the sky days with the passing of their billions, of the woodland buffalo, of the coming of metal and appetite. We have the insight of the old mossy-backed buck who travels like smoke through the forest, who has seen most of his kin die and has learned to know how to be the cougar and the hunter better than they have. Elderhood: when the children have been had and have grown into their own adulthood, and when bodies no longer radiate with compelling vitality. When there is an oldness, a dust in the wrinkles that lives there whether you like it or not, that carries its own vitality that is larger than the body or even the mind. Death and entropy like the invisible friend from childhood returned—butted up against us and will not leave our company for even a moment. Because it is the only thing that can make sense, the elder blossoms the ability to see beyond himself. She can think beyond the edges of the structures and into some mysterium that is beyond the bounds of rational thought. A strange balm that reminds us back into the ubiquity of wonder and the sweetness of Place passing like a river through time.

I wonder if we have some suffering and forgetting mixed into the recipe of dominant industrial culture. I wonder if there is an alienation of generations that has become so pronounced that we are forfeiting sufficient contact with one another. The children, the adolescents, the adults, and the elders must co-create one another, like the cougar and the deer. Who is the elder without the younger generations to communicate with and teach? How can the adolescent skillfully weather the storms of her becoming without the steady care of the adults to help guide her? How does the adolescent hold the child and the child the adolescent? Who are we without the regular laughter of children and their reminder of the profundity of the simplest questions? For how many millenia have we grown up in constant connection to all life stages, and how has that affected our evolution, the essence of our being?

When we live with the Earth, the communion of generations naturally arises. How else could we survive the winters? We need the children to lift our spirits and motivate us. We need the strength and the personal probing of the adolescents. We need the structure holding of the adults. We need the mentoring of the elders. If media and marketing coupled with the convenience of consumer society form wedges of alienation betwixt us, perhaps this has gone too far. When we can sustain a vast majority of our time with peer groups, perhaps it is a tear in the fabric of our realized humanity. Can we mend this? Can we remember together a little bit more of who we are? Humanity is the expression of multi-generational, multi-stage relationships. The different stages in relationship temper and teach and grow one another. We help and hold each other in the transitions.

It may be the case that many of us are not talking about the grief of adulthood that is common in this time. The adults work so hard for a world where the health and longevity of our planetary home is in question. Like a herd of deer before a massive forest fire, tending to their young.

Perhaps we have a need now to attend more to what is beyond our human-to-human relations. In industrial consumer society we seem to de-value our own human elders, relegating so many to isolation and, perhaps, predating their bodies and minds with aggressive marketing and medicine. Perhaps it is not coincidence that this occurs in a time when we have obliterated our old growth forests and expunged them from nearly all of our peoples' experiences. We don't know the old growth forest: the Earth elders. In doing so, have we clearcut our consciousness of the value of elderhood? How, then, do our adults receive ecological guidance and perspective? This is a hard question for me to ask. It brings tears to my eyes. But I offer to the world that it is a question worth asking. Compassionately, if this is the case, there is no sense in anger over this. I suspect we just didn't deeply know that as we felled our forests of giants, we were felling our own humanity. Orphaning ourselves to live in a world unguided by actualized elderhood.

I have heard the perspective that American culture, as with many other industrialized consumer cultures, is a culture of extended adolescence. True initiated adults are fewer and further between. There are more and more adolescents in adult and even elderly bodies. How many of our political leaders display adolescent mindsets? This is something for each of us to consider and to come to our own conclusions about.

What do we do with arrested development and severed generations?

There is old growth still here on our planet. There are elders who are very much awake and alive. Can we listen to them? Can we do our work to tend to the life stages we have around us and make them more conscious? Can we grow our own elderhood back? It is inside each of us.

I wonder about the majority of our psychological developmental theories. So many say that the bulk of our development occurs from birth until the mid-twenties. I suspect this is true for the bulk of our people. However, I wonder whether it is true for the essence of humanity. I wonder about our transpersonal development, that which seems to really awaken and mature from the mid-twenties onward. Perhaps we are so individualistic that our beliefs are arresting our development here. Perhaps an underdeveloped sense of identity with the world and a lack of elderhood in our communities is causing our development to arrest or slow in a place where it does not need to.

Are we the inheritors of ego-based psychology which has roots in the individualism of the Enlightenment? Keep in mind that the Enlightenment was the European birth era of many empowering insights and ways for humanity, among them a stronger engagement with reason and ideals of humanitarianism. In focusing so much on the individual human, did we prune some of who we are in our more-than-human relationships? With our ancestors? With our future generations? With the cosmos? Is there a grief here? If so, how can we hold it and let it transform?

Learning how to hold and transform means growing new relationships. New relationships eventually create new identity. We can find our elders. Step into an old growth forest, the few that are left in the highly industrialized nations, and feel. Realize that no one tree, no one plant or animal or fungus makes the elderhood. It is a community that holds a connection to ancient time. That has grown over time the capacity for holding the biggest and oldest thoughts.

It takes work and courage to transform. It takes connection and suppleness. It takes a sense of service, and it takes an ever-becoming of something greater than ourselves. Our development can be arrested, and there are many people actively changing this world who have adult bodies and are stuck in only adolescent ways of thinking. We can change this. It seems that we are best when we honor every stage of life, keep the experience in our hearts, and balance each other in a community that holds good proportions of children, adolescents, adults, and elders.

Time paying attention to our living world, in every setting, reveals that we all depend on each other. The elders of every species create the world for the younger to grow. The youth promise the extension of all the life efforts. The youth carry the whole forward. With rites of passage, we recognize the value of each life stage and we make the transitions conscious. We develop who we are in each stage, and, in doing so, we develop our full ecological humanity. We create the world.

Intention and Attention

When I experienced my first formal rite of passage, I was thirty-four years old. The format was simple. A small group of us would spend a few months in our everyday life finding our intention statements for who we are deeply down—who wants to emerge. We would consequently recognize what part of our identities wanted to die—were no longer serving our own emergence. Then we would meet for a week with guides in the wilderness of the southern Utah desert. There, each would perform a three-day fasting solo. Then come back and share our story with the community. Then to go to our respective homes and be the emergence.

The deserts in Utah are friggin' hot. Hotly hot. In my experience, there is a strange glitch in the fabric of time and space and the sun moves at a quarter of the speed it usually does. It is a quiet and itchy place. It is an arrogant harasser of the luxury of human boredom. It refuses all pleas and curses and selfish prayers. It looks at you like the glossy eye of a statue of the Buddha. It rings like a low bell. It will take much more than such a tiny, ephemeral you to ever budge it.

I went because I had been suppressing my care for the world and for the things over which I had no direct control. My identity had been entangled with fears that feeling my deep care would change what I do and who I am socially and culturally. So, in that time, after much delving and guidance, my intention statement distilled to, *I have the courage to care, and through my care to die and to be reborn.* Kind of intense, but they often are. Intention statements often express the courage to be mythic and the vulnerability to be heard in one's own deepest and unshared language.

This is not the story of the entire journey. It is a story within the story, plucking experiences the way one might pluck a bouquet of wildflowers from a vast prairie.

The third day was the hardest. That is not true for all people, but it was for me. My drive for accomplishment had evaporated a day ago, sucked out by the heat of the desert sun. I had given up trying to take a walk or explore my surroundings or even trying to listen or feel. At that point I was lying in a crevice on some sand and rocks that offered passing graces of shade. I don't recall thinking much, but I wasn't meditating. I was hot and empty and my body felt like it was made of drying clay. I would occasionally look at the sun's position in the sky and groan.

In the depths of this midday heat, the only sound that rings through the landscape is the metallic drone of the cicadas.

As I lay there, a cicada came and landed on the branch of a nearby scraggly juniper. My eyes settled on the cicada and remained there for a forever or two.

Then some distant spark. An awakening of my neck muscles. Of focusing of the eyes. A question bubbling up from some opaque fathom of my being.

My mouth opened and my throat became alive again and I asked the cicada directly and aloud, "hey cicada. How do you do it? How do you stay alive and move in all this heat?"

I waited and listened with the patience of a dried stick.

Then my throat moved again and I whispered the answer, "don't move. Be moved."

That cicada's teaching continues to get me through a lot of life's storms. That story, as I've passed it, has come at the right time for the right person on more than one occasion.

That cicada's teaching got me through the day to the moment of my greatest understanding. But that is a story for the right person at the right time. You may be the right person, but now is not the right time.

Larry Hobbs, who has taught me quite a bit about rites of passage, often says that "an intention statement should make your knees shake when you say it." It should have fear because it includes a death of identity. With the land, you go through a psychospiritual death much like the conscript would in his nightly liminal states. The border of wake and dream. The border of life and death.

The actual death and isolation processes in a rite of passage ceremony must be deeply challenging in order to pull out the deepest powers of who we are. In many cultures over time, rite of passage ceremonies had a mortality rate. Every person passing through this ceremony knew that there was a chance of actual death.

Death is necessary to the opening to life. When you prune major neural networks, you potentiate connections that were unfathomable before. You can *be* in new ways.

When we face death, in any of its forms, we find a mystery force within that surges to meet the threat of annihilation. This force is the force of indomitability. It is the force that does not give up or waver.

As W.H. Murray wrote, "until one is committed, there is hesitancy, the chance to draw back, always ineffectiveness. Concerning all acts of initiative and creation, there is one elementary truth the ignorance of which kills countless ideas and splendid plans: that the moment one definitely commits oneself, then providence moves too. All sorts of things occur to help one that would never otherwise have occurred. A whole stream of events issues from the decision, raising in one's favor all manner of unforeseen incidents, meetings and material assistance which no man could have dreamed would have come his way."

When we have the courage to delve deeply and find our intention, then to undergo death and isolation processes with the undomesticated Earth, we win wisdom. The wisdom wiggles its way to our bones and shifts the shoreline of our beings. We morph to such a different I that we sometimes can't remember how we ever thought or perceived the way we once did. We die and become. We go back to our community as a different being, a different way, and thus the whole community morphs. Thus, the whole world transitions.

Anyone who has worked hospice will tell you that death is rarely composed of one burst of high intensity experience. Dying is often slow and subtle. It is often more like a mosquito slowly draining you part by part than it is a pack of wolves rending you to pieces in one go. Prick by prick, buzz by buzz, a low annoyance that never stops. And only infrequently punctuated by sudden throes of intensity. So, too, with a rite of passage process. We face death. We have peak experiences. We walk home with hard won wisdom of who we are and who this world is. And part of how we win this is by enduring the lack of excitation. With an extended isolation in the wilderness, we learn the untampered pace of being. It is slow and has no interest in entertaining us. As civilized people, this means we often get bored. Really bored. We stare at things, we look around, and we realize that nothing is competing for our attention. We are not special in this environment, not in that way. So, the boredom is a part of it. And, as we experience it, we begin to realize how much of our lives and our environments are catered to the human experience. We realize deeply how we are conditioned by this, and how it has affected our relationship with the living world. We realize that it is actually stressful to have so much consistent focus on ourselves. We recognize, after a time, that boredom is the sensation of conditioning leaving the body.

As this conditioning leaves the body, so does its pace. So does its expectations and demands. We stop trying to satisfy our civilized conditioning and we start to experience the primal self, as it is in our home environment. When we realize that there are no more human expectations on our behavior and thoughts, we allow ourselves to think and do what is suppressed by our socialization. The non-essentials strip away, and we can see more clearly who we are and where we are. There is an I beneath who lives the ecological pace. This ecological self has the patience to look inward and look outward long enough and deep enough to experience new perceptions of world and self. People then come back from rites of passage with clear seeing and depth wisdom. Larry Hobbs, who I previously mentioned, is consistent in pointing out that the stories people share about their journeys are half a deep resource for the individual person and half a deep resource for the community.

So much of the wisdom that I carry was passed to me through other people's stories. Sitting in a circle and just listening. A sacred and simple act that we all, deep inside, know how to do. Truly listening to a story means you are dying of thirst for it. You need the wisdom more than food or water. This is not abstractly poetic. It really is the way to listen to a story. The listener feels this deep need in her soma. Each person, vastly unique in all the cosmos, goes on a hard a strange journey and comes back with a story that will never be recreated. A wisdom that knows no duplicate. It is the only time and the only place for the world to receive this. The listener is the only soil in which that story, as it is, will be planted.

In this place in this chapter, I have written notes on many deep stories that I would love to share. I can see faces; feel the rush of the blood in my chest as I witnessed the evidence of their transformation; smell the ocean air from a night long ago where I found a deepest truth; hear the low and soft tones of voices coming from throats finally relaxed into being the body they are. I want to share these things, but the stories must be tended like an heirloom seed. Carefully placed in the right soils so that they may propagate and continue the great work of Life.

After returning from a rite of passage experience, the work is to incorporate the new "I" into the already existing and often entrenched fabric of home relationships. It is often the stage where the work really gets done. It means time and effort; failing expectations; dropping assumptions; working to remember what happened and what was learned; finding new resources; witnessing yourself change old patterns; watching how the world both resists and embraces you as a different person. It is the process of true enduring change, and such a process is always mysterious. A rite of passage experience, in this way, does not just happen, it matures. It is a slow emergence over time. I have found that I often reflect back after a year, then five and realize with some wonder that the intention statement that once made my legs shake has become who I am.

With attention and intention, with community supported becoming and remembering, we learn to be awake in our transitions. We learn to own our stories. And, over time, we perceive the truth: that there is only one "I" that will ever live. Never again will the world organize itself into my childhood. No other adult like me will ever be. This realization, at its deep levels, creates an indomitable drive to fully live the life I am given. To spend the time and effort it takes to know who I am in each stage, in each aspect. Rites of passage teach the importance, the beauty, and the wonder of committing consciousness to the strange varied journey of living. The only power I have is this "I". The only way I can understand this power and use it wisely is to know who this "I" is.

Where does the I begin? Who is the individual I? Who is the I that is greater?

I wonder, as we finish, if we are all of us, the whole of bios, undergoing a great rite of passage. Are we at the threshold of a great fast where we will encounter the possibility of death and endure all that it takes to change? Will we be conscious and perform the full ceremony? Come back with a story that will nourish all of the future generations?

Lose Your Mind
and Come to Your Senses

I have heard of a rite of passage ceremony in which initiates are blind-folded and led far, far across the landscape, crossing forests and waters. They are taken to a tree and told to spend the night with it, still blindfolded. The next day they are lead back to where they started. Only then do they take the blindfold off. They are then told to go find their tree.

There is a story of a Buddhist teacher who went into a deep meditation. While in this state, his mind traveled to other planes of existence. He arrived in a place where he witnessed a Buddha teaching the path of morality, mastery of the mind, and wisdom. The Buddha communicated everything through the sense of smell.

A local to my area learned that he was going blind. He was an avid naturalist and did not want to lose his connection with the wide landscape. So, as his sight faded, he dedicated time and effort to sitting under different species of trees and listening. He eventually heard the difference in the sounds the different species make as wind passes through their leaves. He learned to distinguish the trees by their different voices, and he became known for this.

Two monks were once standing in a garden and watching a flag blowing in the wind. They began to argue about what was actually moving. One monk said it was the flag that moved. The other said it was the wind that moved. An old monk ambled up beside them, smiled and bowed. "Noble sirs," he said, "it is not the flag or the wind that moves. It is your mind that moves."

If you are willing, make a moment. In late spring, take your shoes off and go. Seek out the flower of the dead nettle in a yard or the edge of a forest. Pause and kneel before this funny-shaped lavender bump of a flower and take a breath. Feel the wind passing through your body hairs; cascading through the branches of your eyebrows; dancing the forest of your head. Accept the sun into your pours. Feel the active microbes at your feet getting sucked into the vital Earth of your being. Smile.

Lean in close to that flower and invite wonder. Collect your focus and determination without losing the wonder. Stare. Stare deeply into that flower until you are staring deeply into one singular aspect of the flower. Now stay focused. Your vision may blur or skip, but keep your eyes fixed. It will pass. Wonder how you can focus more on that piece of flower. Wonder until you notice your vision changing. Keep staring and wondering. New aspects of that inconspicuous masterpiece will perform their artful revelations. Stare and see and wonder until the flower becomes the biggest thing in your visual field. Literally. Then hold that place of perceiving until you feel a natural pull to resolve.

Release completely. Breathe in the scented wind. Smell. Look at something distant and let your eyes find their natural way to focus. Release and breathe the big world. Feel the Earth beneath you. Smile. Say goodbye to the flower in your own way.

I mentioned earlier in this book that Josh Lane and I once blindfolded ourselves for three days. I am honestly surprised to find that this is the right time and place to share this story. I was imagining it would not end up in this book. But what you are reading is a wonder and it contains the wilderness. There is no way of knowing what exactly lies in the next drainage until you get there. And then it is a part of your journey.

Quite a few years ago, Josh and I were living together in a house full of wonder-filled creatives. We were both very lucky. During this time, Josh fed me many seeds of what has germinated into what you are reading about in this book. He is a very good planter. As you might imagine, we all had a wide variety of adventures. The three days of blindness adventure is, at this point, the experience that sticks out the most for me. Josh had been reading about the practice of blindfolding yourself for days and had done some research on best practices. I listened to his proposal and said yes.

On the appointed day, upon waking, we each put on goggles and then a bandana overtop. The goggles let our eyeballs move in their sockets. The bandana blocked out as much light as possible. Josh and I thought it prudent to stay in the house or very close to the house on the first day. We had no safety net, and getting lost outside with a bandana over your face was a personal and potentially social terror. I had never thought it was possible to get lost in my own room until that day. The bathroom was a journey. Making food was a tragicomedy. Sometimes comedy failed and the meal ended up more a carnage akin to the ending of Hamlet.

On some occasions, I would be taking a blind stroll through my long, narrow living room and hear dull, vague shuffling sounds. I would instinctively pause and listen. I would hear a tiny bump. Then another shuffle. "Hello?" I'd say. I'd hear "Fogarty, is that you?" in response. Then mutual laughter. Then the conversations with Josh. We discovered, fairly quickly, that there was a section of the living room where we would both get disoriented. We both seemed to eddy in this tiny corner of dead space by the fridge. Some sections of the house and some furniture were easier to intuitively navigate than others. We began to pay attention to the differences. We tried listening. We tried feeling the sensations inside our bodies. We learned touch textures and smells in that familiar area.

And then we would each, independently, choose to make forays outside. Around our home was a short maze of lawns and other buildings, then access to wooded areas. The first obstacle was the endless lawny sea. Long landmarklessness. I remember being of the opinion that I was terrible at navigating this. A twenty-step foray in the beginning meant a twenty minute adventure of trying to return to the back door. There were some curses uttered.

But changes did happen. The next day I woke to darkness and

remembered. I overtly remembered the project and the experiences, but I soon found that my body remembered much more. My navigation of the house became notably more graceful. I noticed myself noticing Josh much earlier. I remembered where I placed objects and began developing a knack for putting my hand on them on the first try. The outdoor forays increased until I found the edge of the woods. The way back was humblingly long, but worth the strange accumulation of lightless experiences.

On the third day, our friend, Mary, joined us in sightlessness for a day. Another friend, Odette, was gracious, patient, and adventurous enough to propose that she take the three of us out to a restaurant and then a bookstore. If we were the kind of people to turn this offer down, this would not be a book worth reading.

So, Odette led us three blind mice toward the car. This was, of course, an immediate comedy. I remember following Odette's voice faithfully through the darkness until the speaking stopped, then allowing my alertness to quicken. Listening for cars in the parking lot. Trying to build obscure ideas of where I might be. Odette's voice would return, often with laughter and an apology. It turned out that one of us would often end up going the completely opposite direction and she would have to herd the straggler back into the loose fold, thereby temporarily abandoning the other two.

When she managed to get us all in the car, we played games of guessing where we were. Odette, in my opinion, had the perfect demeanor for this task. She let us guess and fumble and only after some time she would chime in with some accurate information. Usually delivered with a trickling stream of laughter.

Here is one thing I would have not anticipated, and I bet that you didn't either. When we got to the restaurant, we began direct interaction with the public. We were able-bodied, young, relatively normal looking people. The only difference was that we clearly had blindfolds on over our eyes and could not see. With this one difference, everyone that we ran into only talked to Odette. I had to assert my voice into the conversation to remind people that I could hear and speak with no impediment. Josh and Mary had similar observations. I still wonder at this. Were people assuming that we were not talking as well? Were they uncomfortable with the obvious difference? It is weird to blindfold oneself in public. I know this. But I wonder why. Really, why is it so strange? Once it was explained by Odette in a culturally acceptable way, people enjoyed witnessing our antics. But still, they did not speak to us. Is there a fear of the difference? Of the lack of sight? Of the idea of a type of person who would do this in public? Just questions…

The social and psychological curiosities were often outshined by the hilarity of our joint meal. It is very hard to get a good bite of food when you can't see the plate or your fork. It is even more difficult to gauge the amount of hot sauce you are putting on your meal when you are handling a previously unknown bottle. As I write this, a smile shines on my face. The memory is a sweet one. I remember the bookstore and the joy of finding the music section where I could listen to music by blindly typing on a keypad. I still laugh out loud when I remember not knowing where anyone else was until I heard the sound of a lot of books falling and Josh's consequent "uh-oh." The careful crafter of the book display was probably not as happy about our experiment as we were. Odette ushered us out of the store fairly quickly afterward.

It was at night, just before bed, when I decided to take my blindfold off. I walked out of the door and toward the woods. This time, I had no fear of how far I would go. I would walk until it felt right, then reveal the world of light to my longing eyes. I walked and stumbled and eventually let go of attachment to ideas of where I might be. At some point, I remember feeling like I was in a small opening in the middle of a forest. The opening felt kind and tending. It felt like the place that would hold me as I came back to sight. I took off my blindfold and opened my eyes.

As I opened my eyes, the lit world that was usually so stable was a whirling vortex of dizzying information. The forest floor seemed to be spinning right in front of me. My vertiginous mind struggled to make sense of this onslaught of information. The world whirled and I fell to my knees. I was so dizzy I had to drop onto my hands as well. I tried looking around, but the sights did not make sense. I breathed. I experienced mild primal fright. I breathed again. After about a minute, the world began to reorganize itself and I started to make sense of where I was. The images took on meaning and quickly became the meaning itself. I stood up. There I learned, more than anywhere else, that balance typically depends on both the body and the eyesight.

My first three steps were stumbles and I fell onto my hands. I got up again and felt my legs remember how to coordinate themselves with the visual information. Like a flash recapitulation of my toddlerdom, I learned how to step. Within ten steps I was back to steady. I looked around and saw the dome of my visual place melt into normalcy. I felt tingly throughout my body. My vision had normalized, but the strength of the experience and the power of seeing kept me in a state of wonder. I walked back to my home.

A young student of Zen traveled to see a Zen master speak to the public. The teacher taught and answered questions, but soon the teaching was over and the student found herself as befuddled as she was before.

She learned where the teacher's house was and went there in the evening. The teacher answered the door and let the woman in. The woman explained her befuddlement. The teacher smiled and invited her to her back porch for tea.

The two women sat in silence sipping tea for a long time.

The teacher gestured to a patch of snowberries in the distance.

"Do you see those snowberries?" she asked.

The woman nodded and held them in her attention.

"Do you see how small they are?"

The woman looked at the snowberries until she could see just how small they were.

The teacher nodded.

She gestured again.

"Do you see those snowberries?"

The woman nodded again.

"Do you see how big they are?"

The woman stared and saw.

The teacher smiled.

"That is the essence of Zen."

Losing your Mind and Coming to your Senses

What is the relationship of mind and senses? If we change the relationship with our senses, do we change our minds? If we change our minds, do we change what we perceive? Does a change of mind and perception challenge our cultural agreements? Does this change our relationship to Place? How does this change the Place itself?

The Wilderness Awareness School teaches practicing a sense meditation every day. In the meditation, you open up each of your senses one at a time. With each you expand the edges of your awareness. You ask questions through your senses. You endeavor to discern the world as it is. This is a core practice, and is considered essential in developing a deep connection to the natural world.

Here is an exercise that you can try if you'd like:

This will take about ten minutes once you find a good spot to do it. Outside is preferred and a wilder setting is best, but you could do it in your room if you'd like. Make sure it is a place where you won't be disturbed and you can be completely still for the duration of the exercise.

Get a **good rooted stance**: a straight spine and feet pushing into the Earth. Slightly tilt the nose down and fix your gaze just above where the horizon line would be if it were to extend directly out in a flat plane before you. Choose one spot in your visual field to stare at. It is best to choose something stationary.

Once you have your spot, you will use the rule of opposition. Focal vision is the visual antagonist of peripheral vision. You will start by "flexing" your focal vision so that, when you release, you will get more skill uptake with your peripheral vision. To do this, **focus completely on the spot** you have chosen. It is imperative that you serve as your own guide here. Tell yourself to focus with as much directed effort as you can on that spot. Suspend any disbelief and search for a new way that your eyes can see that spot deeper and more clearly. Travel into the spot with your mind. Magnify it and see the contours, the lines, the colors, the shapes. If the rest of your visual field starts to do strange things, ignore it and have a firm commitment to no take your eyes or your intention from seeing deeper and deeper into that spot.

After you have truly focused, **let your eyes settle in the bottom of the eye socket**. Consider them to be in a fixed position, still oriented directly toward the spot, but no longer traveling outward. Your eyes will not move from this position in the eye socket for the duration of this exercise.

Without moving your eyes, you will start to **examine the peripheral field**. You can use the numbers of a clock to help you navigate, 12 being directly above you, 3 to your right, 6 below, and 9 left. Without letting your eyes move, examine 12 o'clock just above you. Examine the whole peripheral field from the spot to the very topmost edges. Ask yourself if you can see details, lines, colors, movement, numbers of things. If your eyes do move, just bring them back to position and continue examining the peripheral field.

Move along the clock slowly, making sure you truly challenge yourself as you go through the exercise. Introduce emotional content, making it imperative that you see all the details of the peripheral field. The more you invest in this, the more nerve signal will grow. Which means, quite literally, the more your mind and your powers of perception will expand.

When you have come back to 12 o'clock, **expand your vision out to the full 360 degree field**. As you take a breath, have the breath expand the edges of what you can see. Breathe again and push your vision further. Suspend disbelief and have your vision wrap around you so you can see behind your back, above you and below you.

Keeping this awareness and keeping your eyes fixed in their position in the sockets. **Slowly begin to turn** to the left. You are no longer looking at the spot, but the eyes have *not moved* in the sockets. As the body turns, keep your visual awareness on the 360 degree periphery. Move all the way left. Then move back to center. Then move all the way right.

Finally, return to center. Make sure your vision is fully expanded. Without moving your eyes in the socket, and keeping your head position so you are looking toward just above the horizon line. **Begin to walk**. Your peripheral vision will help you navigate as you walk to a location and back.

When you have finished, take a breath and see how long you can keep this awareness. Notice any change in your mental state, your level of anxiety, the tension behind your eyes, etc.

If you tried this exercise, you most likely noticed a significant change in your perception. If you paid attention, you probably also noticed a significant embodied sense of relaxation and centeredness.

When we open up our senses, we commit real effort to expanding the edges of our perception. The body responds, and the practices have resilient effects. If you were to do the above exercise every day, over time your peripheral vision would remain open at all times. It becomes automatic.

As we open our senses, we allow for more accurate experience. We get more precision and a higher volume of information from multiple sense dimensions. We get more of the world in greater detail. This allows us to create a better understanding of where we are. It also helps us to understand who we are. We get a truthful understanding of the senses themselves and how they work. We learn more about their accuracy, their inaccuracy, their role in experience, and their malleability.

Senses do not reveal the one static truth. They display one aspect of the truth. They take a tiniest slice of the electromagnetic spectrum and show us that. If we use a sense organ more or in a different way, we get a different slice of input. We experience information outside of the habitual range of perceived energy. For instance, when we are blind, our other senses become stronger.

That tiny slice of energy that we perceive is then translated by the mind of the perceiver. As labeling and meaning happen, the conscious awareness of sensory input becomes malleable. What we consciously perceive ends up as a rough approximation of the input presented in a way that makes a contiguous story with our past experiences.

Look at this duck:

Now look at the picture above and see the rabbit.

Can you see the duck and the rabbit at the same time?

Can you look at the drawing until you don't see any representation?

Some of you may recognize this image from Thomas Kuhn's work. He wrote, "The Structure of Scientific Revolutions" in which he developed thoughts around paradigms and paradigm shifts. A paradigm could be considered as an overarching way of thinking that explains and gives structure to observations. Anomalies are observations that cannot be adequately explained by the current paradigm. Kuhn points out that scientists will continue to try to solve the problem of anomalies with the same paradigmatic thinking until a new paradigm is offered. No matter how many or how great the anomalies, the scientist must rely on some paradigm in order to make any sense at all of the information. Lacking an alternative, the scientist will use the current way of thinking. Eventually, some scientists judge that a crisis exists. In crisis, revolutionary science explores long-held obvious-seeming assumptions. Eventually, a viable alternative is proposed. The scientific community resists and struggles against the alternative. The alternative is tested and only that which is strong and consistent enough endures until, at some point, the community shifts from the old overarching paradigm to the new one. This is a pattern of human thought. It is happening now.

Long-held obvious-seeming assumptions are embedded in perception. The willingness to challenge perceptions and explore new possibilities means challenging the fabric of a paradigm. Perhaps this is a deep reason for why it is strange and disturbing for people to see a person blindfold herself. She is challenging the way that we all think.

Can you see the white triangle?

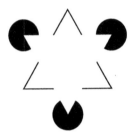

Is there a white triangle?

Can you look at the picture until you don't see it?

What is moving? The marks remain the same, but the perception shifts radically. The phenomenon does not change; the mind does. The movement is within the microcosm of your own neurology.

Now pause if you will and prepare to look away from this text. When you do, take a look at the world around you. Feel your breath and weight of your body against the chair or ground. Bring your mind to the shadows. Hold your attention for a while until your attention is strongly oriented to the shadows of everything in your visual field. Slowly look around and witness the world of shadows. Do you find that the world seems different when you do this. Do you notice something new? How does this change the way that you feel as you witness the world? Have you been attending to the light in the same way you have been preferring to see a white triangle?

Welcome back. I hope it is interesting and fun to play with your perception. It can be. There is a liberation in it. When we do this, we remember that the world is free and playful by nature.

Now, let's play with the text itself. Try to look at any one word without reading it. If and when you think you've accomplished this, try shifting your eyes to a new word and don't read it first… meaning don't recognize it as a word at all; just see the shapes as they are. If you are like most people who have learned to read early in life, this is nearly impossible to accomplish for any length of time.

Interestingly, reading is learned. It is a product of nurture. We are not born with the reading instinct. Reading is not even taught until later in our development. But the training is so strong that it is an amazing feat to be able to overcome the conditioning and to perceive the shapes on this page without recognizing them as words first. These are just patterns of color. We are barely engaging with the patterns of color. We are perceiving patterns of mind.

What else has been taught and reinforced as strongly as reading?

How is that affecting your perception?

Burning through the Mental Objects

The odds are that very, very few people reading this are aware of the actual leading edges of neuroscience. It is a growing field of discovery, and it is becoming a skillful means for the dominant culture to better understanding ourselves and our world. The contributing practitioners are the writers and holders of the leading edges of this knowledge. We, the culture, are the recipients of general, relatively well-accepted information. I only write this to remind myself and others that a field of discovery is always growing, and the information we have now will not be the information we have in a few years. That is okay. We can still use the information we have now as a skillful means for engaging consciously and healthfully with our world. Consciousness and the health are the measures for information's usefulness.

Which leads us to considering neural networks. We've mentioned neural networks before in this book. Let's think of them now as a term for a pattern of neurons that tend to fire together in the brain organ. As science currently understands it, sensory input is received through the sense organs and enters the brain for processing. The processing is long and complex. Information undergoes a process of being organized into groupings, combined and recombined, and then packaged into the brain organ's meaningful representation of what was received.

In order to do this, the brain has a kind of notation system. When you see something like the letter "B" on the page or screen you are experiencing the result of a network of millions of neurons that are firing in a pattern that represents that organization of light. There is a particular pattern of particular neurons that fire to create the experience of "B." When neurons are firing, it means they are actively engaging with stimuli from the present moment. When they are done firing, they leave a kind of memory. Neurons that fire together leave behind a preference for firing together again. The more they fire, the stronger the preference. This is the creation of a neural network. The more a network is used, the more it becomes your baseline experience. You are what you do the most.

I propose thinking of such a neural network as a kind of mental object. We have a mental "B" in our heads, and if a visual stimulus received by the brain looks enough like a "B", then the mental object of "B" lights up. We may experience the mental objects more than the actual light patterns.

If a network is strong enough, we only need a small amount of the sensory information to light up the whole network. So, if we see a sloppily written "B", we'll still get a "B" out of it. We perceive the mental object. We can see a tree in a handful of artfully placed lines on a piece of paper. We can see a robin by catching just the edge of his wing. We can spot a predator by catching a patch of tan in the bushes. It's brilliant.

As a network becomes stronger, it develops an attractive force. Coincidentally, the same network actively suppresses other firing. Networks develop a kind of gravity, drawing energy toward them and away from other possibilities. Networks also develop affiliations with other networks. These networks tend to fire together. The network of "robin" is associated with networks of "bird," "flight," "worm," etc. The brain is less likely, through attraction and suppression, to think of "gorgonzola cheese" when "robin" is active. Classical conditioning is a simple example of associated networks in action. If we ring a bell consistently before we feed a dog, eventually, the dog's mouth will water when the bell rings. As mammals connected with our planet, when we hear a kingfisher's call, our minds go to the basic need of the water that we know the kingfisher must be near. When we run into a bear cub in the woods, our minds go toward the dangers and safe response options. As organisms, we depend on associated networks, attraction, and suppression to make any sensible, navigable narrative of the world.

Current life experience is always introducing new input, so the neural networks are always changing. Mental objects are being modified, being born, strengthening, and weakening through the act of living. Minor events alter the network minimally. The vast majority of the network stays the same and is reinforced. A major event, such as a peak personal experience or a traumatic experience can radically alter deep patterns in the brain. The mental objects become strongly reshaped and we do not perceive them in nearly the same way. Most likely, we all have experienced a powerful act of love and a powerful act of hatred. We know that, after this happens, we no longer perceive the person or place in the same way we once did. We see the person or place differently. We have new associated networks that light up along with this radically modified mental object.

The mind is always changing. It is like a great river. Being altered every moment, but tending to maintain a fairly consistent overall shape and quality. Ever-responsive to conditions. The Taoists say that "flowing water never goes stagnant." A brain that is engaged with the present flows strongly, recombining to the ever-new. A brain that adheres to entrenched neural patterns maintains its shape in resistance to new information. It becomes stagnant and more areas become relatively lifeless.

We rely on strongly attractive baseline networks to make sense of reality. They are our bedrock. We have a vocabulary of consistent mental objects that create a sense of identity and a sense of world. This comes through as a perceptual *habit* of reality. A paradigm is a habit. Human reality is largely a habit. We seem to be at our best when we have enough mental integrity to have a sense of self and world while, at the same time, having a mind that is accustomed to flexibly incorporating new information in transformative ways. We are capable of changing and experiencing new ways of thinking and perceiving without losing skillful agency in the world. We have a healthy degree of what scientists would call "neuroplasticity."

Now, let's look at this image again:

What if you had never seen nor heard of a "duck"? The markings remain the same and the potential for the mind to see that representation is still there. But in order to get your perception there, the mind has to build sufficient networks through experience of other perceptions to make a thing called a "duck." It then has to associate the markings with the network of "duck."

We are surrounded by ducks.

What I mean by that is that there are new ways to look at almost everything around us. There are new aspects and new relationships that are yet undiscovered. The world itself is always changing. No perception is utterly accurate. Habits of perception and behavior that are beneficial in one circumstance can be devastating if they become entrenched. As the saying goes, "to the hammer, all the world is a nail." To the thirsty, the world is a quest for water. To the industrial developer, the world is unused green spaces left to transform. To the objectivist, the world is a separate thing filled mostly with inert and lifeless objects.

The "wall of green" that Jon Young talks about is a manifestation of neural networks. We exercise neuroplasticity when we begin to penetrate this wall of green. We develop new relationships and this means new neural networks, new mental objects, new ways of perceiving the world, and new consequent behaviors. As we learn more about the actual tree in our back yard, we begin to see all that the tree is doing for our world. We develop a personal relationship with the tree. We begin to know ourselves as we truly are: interdependent with the tree. A part of a greater system. The wall of green shifts and we actually perceive this aspect of the world differently.

One of the greatest means toward such a shift in relationship and perception is wonder. When we wonder, our brain organs are actively inviting new combinations. In this mysterious state we court seeing the world as it is, not as we would like it to be. We seek to meet what is beyond the mental objects. We get a little closer to the source. We could call this a phenomenological engagement with the world. In a phenomenological relationship, we are endeavoring to see the true phenomena, the things of the world as purely as we can perceive them within the confines of our sensory perceptions and given the nature of our conscious processing. It is an unattainable absolute that is worth every moment of the journey we travel toward it. Wonder might just be our experience of the state of taking this journey. We wonder into things. We wonder through our ideas, our mental objects, and we wonder beyond the previous bounds of our perception. We see the things as if for the first time. And within us, our strange electric river of thinking explodes in three dimensions to irrigate lands previously unknown. Our neurology becomes a storm of creation. And we literally see the world differently.

Our senses cannot provide us with the true form of anything. We can only experience a bent slice of information reformatted into a coherent story that we have fabricated about reality. Therefore, learning the world always means learning the self. As we see a thing more clearly, we more clearly notice our own role in the seeing. With wonder, we perceive into deeper knowing. The more we know the world and ourselves, the better we function, the happier and healthier we seem to be.

Now, if you will, I invite another pause. What happens if you really let this information settle? Even if you have heard it all before, what happens if you let yourself sit with it for a moment? If you have the chance to be outside or even look out a window, I invite you to do so. With wonder, observe the world and yourself and recognize the nature of this experience. How does this change the way you feel? How does this change the way you think?

No matter how much time we spend outdoors relative to others in our culture, most of us spend most of our time in buildings and cars, relating to humans and learning human-centered ideas. All that said, when we work outdoors, we are inevitably working outside of a lot of habitual networks. This forces us into some more phenomenological perception and practices our neuroplasticity.

Why? One reason must be increased awareness. More awareness means less primal anxiety in the system. It means more skill with perceived threats. As we see each perceived threat more clearly, it means fewer overall perceived threats.

As we become phenomenologically engaged with our full living world, we become more rooted in the present. The present is the only place where our personal being has power. We suppress habit patterns of cognition that take us out of the present. So many of our psychological maladies are wrought by habitual reactions to the memories of past events or to predictions of future outcomes. Any reputable research you find on memory reveals how inaccurate, paltry, and skewed it is in comparison with the phenomenological event.

When we are engaged with a sense organ, we are receiving information in the present. Sight, sound, hearing, smell, touch, and the internal felt sense are all connected to the here and now. It makes sense that, as an organism from the scientific perspective, we have grown into feeling better and being healthier when we are engaged with the present moment. This is what allows us, primally, to be more skillful at finding our basic Earth living needs and preserving our lives. In the present, we engage with the only source of actual new information. Our primal selves can then feel agentic in the world. We feel safer. When we feel safe, we engage more neurology associated with social communication, self-soothing, and calming. We become much more socially engaged, we process out of fight, flight, or freeze responses, and we seem to have more access to higher mental functions. If you have ever seen a skillful mediator bring a heated conflict into a state of calm and honest discussion, you have witnessed a person who is sustaining his engagement with this complex of neurology.

Losing your mind and coming to your senses means losing the ideas you already have about the world. It means burning through the mental objects. With wonder, we come to our senses. We come to them and we court them. We ask them to show us something new. We wonder at the newness. The lost mind is never found. We become someone different.

Now, I invite us to pause again and put our minds into the planet as whole. The whole of our living relationships supporting all life. Sending our minds into the bigness of us, into the swirling tumult of oceans, the flat waters, the high mountain airs, the wilderness of the atmosphere, every eye or antenna or root or mycelium that reaches through us. Send thought to the places we are scared to think. Feel where we are terrified to feel. The last breath of the polar bear in an expanse of relentless, cold water. The acid burning into the coral. The crippling of our protective sphere above. How do you feel in your body when you go here? Can you feel at all? Do you want to stop reading? Do you have emotions? I suggest the reactions that you feel are because you care. It is because of your basic goodness. You are a sweet being that loves to be loved and lives through the loving. No matter how armored, no matter how confused, that is what lies at your core. You are also courageous. You can feel this. You can join the we, and we can feel this together.

Are we not in crisis right now? Are we not at a threshold where many of us fear that our way of thinking cannot biologically sustain us?

If a way of thinking veers away from serving life, does it make any sense at all? No life, no thinking. How many of our youth believe that they will be able to live a full and happy life into their late elderhood? Ask them. Remember to let yourself feel as you begin hearing their answers. Listen to them. They are the inheritors of the projection of our current way of thinking. There inheritance is not preordained. Humans can change the way that we think.

What if there is little chance of the endurance of much of our biosphere *in our current way of thinking*? Is there another way of thinking where this is not true? Can we wonder about this?

Courtship

I invite us to take a cross-cultural wander here. A friend once gifted me a book written by Victor Sanchez called, "The Teachings of Don Carlos." Victor Sanchez has a fascinating life story including much time and effort living the teachings of the Nahua people located near the place of his birth in central Mexico. In this book, he consolidates and illuminates the practices in the works of Carlos Castaneda. These practices are anthropologically called "shamanic." No matter what your cultural orientation, I invite you to consider this as neither an anthropological consideration nor a "new age" or fringe way of thinking. These are the practices and perspectives of a People. People who have lived and died and passed on the ways that they have paid attention to the world and themselves for generation after generation after generation. The ways have been tested, refined, and grown over thousands of years. They have held culture and land together and kept enough harmony to sustain life through so many challenges. Each Peoples' teaching stands as its own world of value. Worthy of bowing to and learning from with the listener's ear of a wilderness wanderer.

In this book, Victor Sanchez discusses how much personal history dictates how a person spends her or his energy. He says that our personal history almost wholly determines our actions and thoughts. He then talks about the role of practice:

"If the use of our energy is predetermined, then how can this be changed? In reality, such a change is possible, although rare. The contradiction is resolved in practice.

Practice begins with a form of specialized conduct, actions that from our point of view of the ego are completely out of the ordinary. We might call them purposeful acts—or not-doings in no way connected to our past—which have the effect of opening little by little our field of possibilities. Through persisting in the performance of unusual acts, we create a disruption in the habitual patterns of our energy use, and as a consequence they begin to "loosen." Once this loosening process begins, we are in a better position to redirect the energy formerly spent in consuming activities toward new, much more worthwhile pursuits. In the moment we direct part of our energy toward less wasteful uses, an excess of energy is generated, which in its turn permits us to advance even more toward the redirection of our energy. This begins to express itself through the gradual increase of aspects of our life that pass from the realm of the impossible to the possible: giving up smoking or drinking, letting go of anger, taking time to listen to the songs of the trees and the messages of the birds. If we are persistent, our field of living and perceptual possibilities widens until the tendency to act in accordance with our personal history disappears. At this point, a person can be said to have erased personal history and is therefore free from its influence."

Let's take a moment to consider this teaching, rooted in the Peoples of the southern part of the North American continent. It is not the same as the views of psychology. It is not the same as the insights of neuroscience. Different People. Different paradigms. Different perceptions. But is it not interesting how similar in essence? Does it not seem like we are perceiving, in our own ways, the same essential pattern? Personal history could be considered, in a scientific mindset, to be a term for all the existing neural networks. Like reading. Like what taught us to have an egoic identity. These networks determine so much of how we live and act and think and perceive. Practicing thinking and acting in a dramatically different way could mean growing neuroplasticity. Is this not, basically, what we do in therapy? Is this not what we do when we are truly learning something new? Is this not the way of wonder? How mysterious it is that every culture can create its own vibrant ecosystem of perception and story. That each contacts the essence of the world in unique ways. That when we share our ways, we get new perspectives and fresh contact with that essence. We can get closer to the truth of the world as it is. No one culture monopolizing the truth. We are a species of many senses through many minds, perceiving together in a tapestry that ever points toward the truth. Mystery is a universal human currency. Mystery plus human attention yields creativity. Creativity unlocks the potential for greater health and happiness.

Social psychologist, Daryl J. Bem, describes knowledge from our senses as "zero-order beliefs." He says that these beliefs are such deep assumptions that we don't even notice them as beliefs. The ground is hard. The sky is blue. The wind makes a whistling sound. Yet, Bem points out, sensory perception is culturally specific.

Some people in specific cultures cannot perceive the difference between blue and green. Some people in specific cultures cannot hear the songs plants sing. Anthropologists and psychologists working for the Max Planck Institute for Psycholinguistics and Radboud University share findings that the Jahai people of the Malay Peninsula seem to be generally as good at naming what they smelled as they were at naming what they saw.

It is interesting that whether they come from a shaman, a scientist, or a monk, the insights of the world generally co-arise with new perceptions. These perceptions are then useful in healing people and healing land. Interesting that the human body will tell us, with some accuracy, if we are bending ourselves more toward health, wholeness, and deep happiness. As we subjectively experience more wellness, our organs tend to work better, our biochemistry seems to have more balance, and our bodies seem more energetic and resilient. We move away from anxiety and depression and a host of other illnesses. Interesting that when we get negatively stressed, anxious, or depressed, our perception tends to narrow. We miss certain types of information when we are in high arousal. If you have ever experienced having a kind of tunnel vision or a limiting of your range of action during an exam or a competition, you know this experience.

When we are living in a perception dominated by the editing and input of existing networks, as in illusions, we are literally living in and reacting to our own ideas about the world. This can be devastating if we really think about the ramifications of this. We literally might not be able to perceive how a person or the world has changed. We might react to our old, fixed ideas about that person or place rather than what is right before us. This, on the most extreme level, can detach that perception from reality and from our interdependent connections to them. It is the seed of all of the terrible things that objectification can create in human behavior. It allows for terrible crimes and, on the mass level, ethnocide or ecocide. That means terrible suffering for generations for every being involved. If we were to widen our perception, we would see the waves of suffering such actions cause for the whole web of living.

Literally, the world suffers with such an extent of the death of awareness.

Are individualism and ethnocentrism a form of perceptual narrowing? A mental state wrought by cultural patterns and personal history. What happens when we loosen our views and widen our perceptions? When we shift more toward thinking as a full human species who are part of a full life community on one vibrant planet. Where we actually live the experience of all life being interconnected and interdependent. Where we really can't separate the trees from our lungs. Where we each realize that the bounded nutshell of our single personal mind also enjoys the infinite space and boundless possibility of connection. That we share mind. What an individual may not contain, as a single conscious experience, is the ability to hold the entire picture. What happens when we let go and view our individual selves more akin to a neural network in the workings of a giant mind. The neural network cannot experience the whole of the mind. The network just does its part. This is a strange and identity-dissolving experience to point toward. Letting go enough to accept that we will never personally perceive what the bigger mind does. Another person is a contributor to the big thinking. Another ecosystem is a network of mind contributing. And the workings of the whole will be ever-outside of the possibility of our personal comprehension. Can we be a good set of cells in a bigger body? Can we embrace this as it is and love what we do perceive?

Can we dissolve more of our fixed attachments to our own personal narratives? Enjoy them as we experience them, wonder through our perceptions, and learn to lean on the bending of ourselves by many other minds? If we continue to practice engaging with the six senses, we begin to discern that each one is actually a separate experience. This is a nuance that is hard to explain in writing. Gotama Buddha said simply, "in seeing, only seeing. In hearing, only hearing." We notice that the world of sight is not the same world as the world of touch. Some secondary part of our mind is putting these senses together into a viable coherent story. In this way, we come closer to phenomenologically experiencing the world with each sense, and we reduce our attachment to thinking that our perception is the ultimate truth. We become engaged and flexible. We learn to skillfully swim the river of being. With wonder and abiding awareness, we become more flexible in our perceptions and gain more ability to recombine information into previously unfathomable ways.

We have fewer assumption and fewer demands of the world as we perceive it.

Which leads to courtship.

I mentioned earlier that one of my teachers talked a lot about courtship. What I take away from this now is that to be in relationship, we follow that one rule of courtship: pay attention. We remember that paying attention means no assumptions and no demands.

To catch a swarm of bees, you must pay attention to the bees. You must court them. You must learn who they are, what they love, what they fear, where they feel the most safe and vibrant, *how* they love, what they enjoy eating, where they fly, where they sleep, and how their buzzy little bodies speak to other bodies. Catching a live swarm means knowing the landscape and looking for the right tree with the right exposure at the right height near the right amount of food. It means creating a home where your beloved wants to live. Of their own accord, the bees will send their dancing drones in search of the best options. They will decide whether or not to accept your courtship. Then, in a greatest ceremony, the queen will rise and take more than half of her colony to your place where you will be bonded. And if all is right, sweet honey will flow.

To know the owl, court the owl.

A mentee, Harper, has the uncanny ability to call close wildlife encounters toward him. The way that he best understood how to do this was to use what we called, "the other way to think." Harper quiets his mind. He opens up his senses. He looks with his ears and listens with his eyes. He imagines he has delicate fur sensing the air. And he thinks by receiving. It's wonderful to witness. He slows down and feels the world as it is.

He has an affinity for owls, and he can walk up close without the owl being more than curious. His eyes widen, as if singing their own owl song. Over time, Harper has learned that he actually imagines himself as an owl. The biggest eyes ever. The wind in the feathers. The sharp claws ready for the quickest grasp. A patient potential blending into the branch.

To know the world, court the world. Knowing the world, you begin to know the extent of yourself.

I studied ecopsychology at Naropa University. One of the things I learned is that when you tell someone you have a masters degree in ecopsychology, ninety percent of the time their next question, if they dare ask another question, is "what is ecopsychology?" This book is my best attempt at a current answer to that question.

However, I bring this up to share a story that one of my teachers told about the founder of Naropa. Chogyam Trungpa was yet another eccentric teacher. He was a Tibetan rinpoche who, after leading his village over the Himalayas in an escape from the Chinese occupation of Tibet, ended up coming to the States. He then went on to found a school that combined the methods and rigor of the Western academic tradition with that of Tibetan Buddhist contemplative education. My teacher was one of the first to go to the school.

She told me that, one day, Chogyam Trungpa asked them all to meet for class outside in a nearby field. She said he had them all congregate on one end of the field. When they were all present, he marched across the field with a bullhorn in hand. Once on the other side, he faced them and shouted into the bullhorn, "be an ant!" She said they all just looked at each other, trying to figure out what was going on. Again, he directed, "be an ant!" She said that they just stood there uncomfortably in a line looking back and forth to see if anyone knew what he wanted. Then someone got down on her hands and knees and started to busily meander through the field. Someone else did, and fairly quickly, they all realized exactly what they were to do: be an ant.

She laughed as she remembered this and shared that there were more than a few times when her mind started to revolt, saying things like, "I'm paying all this money for an academic degree and this guy is telling me to crawl around in a field and be an ant. This isn't education. What kind of..." we can all fill on those blanks. She went on to say that they were acting like ants for a very long time. After a while, that complaining mind shut down. And soon the rest of her little wordy thinker shut down. And she said that it turned out to be one of the most transformative experiences of her education. She became an ant.

Now, I know that the same complaining thinker can pop up right here and debate that she didn't actually become an ant. It will say something in good postmodernist, individualistic fashion like "we can't ever come close to an ant's experience and all she had was her human imagination convincing her that she was something she was not." Well, that may be true as well. But what if we operate under the assumption that all perception is personal? What if, as naturalists, the only thing we are concerned with is what is right before us? What if we are simply curious about how a human being responds to being asked *to be* something else? If we are not hurting ourselves or anyone else, and we can re-center ourselves after the experience, aren't we just stretching our edges of who we are and what we perceive? We may never be ants, but after stretching our minds toward them in a compassionate way, we will most definitely have a stronger connection to them. We will most definitely have a slightly expanded view of the breadth of the world and the impact of our actions. We will have this as a personal knowing. Not reliant on texts or experiments brought to us as secondary experience. Not something we have to decide or piece together. A direct experience. The bedrock of being.

We court the world through the connection we have to the world. The senses are the way we touch and are touched by the world. Losing our minds and coming to our senses means the direct experience of widening our perceptions. When we widen our senses, it means we are paying attention to that which we are courting. Widening our perceptions means widening ourselves. It means reaching out to be in touch with more of the world. Widening ourselves, we actually connect the world. We become together. As we change, we are the world changing.

The Primal Psyche

Out
of a great need
we are all holding hands
and climbing.
Not loving is a letting go.
Listen,
the terrain around here
is
far too
dangerous
for
that.

                               –Hafiz

In my thirties, I had made a commitment to visit my sit spot every day if I could. I was deeply involved in the Kamana Naturalist Training Program, which was challenging me to get to know that part of the land in every way I could imagine. Like any good teacher, the program imbued me with curiosity and creative responses to my lingering questions. I was curious what happened at that spot as dawn gave way to sunrise. I knew that many animals were active at these times. So, I challenged myself to get my uncooperative body out of my warm and cozy bed next to my warm and cozy partner, put on many layers of clothes, walk out into the cold, dark pre-dawn, and head up the hill and into the woods. Once at my anchor point, I made a commitment to sit in meditation for an hour. For some reason, I had decided to do this with my eyes closed, which, in retrospect, is a funny way of trying to satisfy that naturalist curiosity.

So, on one of these days, I was about twenty minutes into my sit when I heard a consistent rustling of sword ferns coming up the hill behind me. It was headed in my direction and was quite noisy. My mind instantly oriented to the sounds and I began to wonder what it could be. It sounded big. My heart started to pound a little more and that morning meditative sleepiness I had been navigating was vanquished as easily as the dark gives way to light. I'll confess now that I suspect myself to often be a somewhat confused practitioner of too many things. Having made the commitment to meditate with my eyes closed, and having a sense of the value of discipline, I felt a sudden surge of commitment to not open my eyes and to remain in meditation. Just to feel how my body responded to this approaching sound while not reacting. The sound got bigger and closer and then I heard the most frightening and guttural growling I could have imagined. A wave of alert and fear shot through my being and everything in me wanted to open my eyes. Whatever it was very near and it was growling and making terrifying noises in my direction. My mind rifled through possibilities and my heart drummed in double time. Yet, it became a test of my discipline. I kept my eyes closed and remained still, accepting that I may not learn the answer and I may be in danger. The warrior-like test for me was this: in the face of that fear and that unknown, could I keep to my meditation? The growling continued, but so did the movement. Whatever it was continued past me and made its way further up the hill until I heard it no more.

I spent the remainder of my meditation noticing just how much my mind wanted to return to that moment and figure it out. It took my heart rate quite some time to return to normal. When my timer beeped, I opened my eyes and looked around everywhere for a sign. Nothing. I thought of getting up, but remembered my naturalist intention of staying put and noticing the movement of the natural community as dawn moved into sunrise. I stayed put, watching a grey squirrel scurry up and down some nearby douglas firs and appreciating the occasional mixed flock of chickadees, brown creepers, and kinglets. Finally, as the light began to take hold, I felt my aching legs beg me to be done with it. I started to get up to go home. As I was a third of the way through the movement of standing up, I heard a familiar sound. Coming down the hill amongst the sword ferns, I heard the same big rustling I had heard in meditation. I froze in my crouch, hands against the log in front of me. Completely still, I waited as the rustling approached. I was amazed that I might, after all, get to learn who had passed me in the pre-dawn night. Then I heard the deep fierce growling. I knew it was the same thing. I could not see it. It must be smaller than I had suspected, as it didn't stick out over the sword ferns. It circled the hill above me and then began heading directly toward me. I lost sight of its approach just over a crest, but I heard the rustling. My heart began beating double time again. It was growling and coming nearer.

Then, over the edge of a fallen log, I saw it. Two black marble eyes filled with the starlight of cosmic curiosity that the youth of all species seem to contain. A little raccoon face scanned the landscape and almost overlooked me, but then seemed to catch its error and directed its focus right at me. With a quizzical head wiggle, it seemed to be assessing me. Then, deciding I was not concern enough, the kit proceeded, stepping over the log and heading toward me. It walked right toward the other end of the long log I had my hands on. It then started walking along the log toward me, barely recognizing my existence. My legs ached from the awkward crouch but the curiosity for what this little kit might do if I remained still gave me strength enough to stay still.

Then another head popped over the log. A second kit proceeded behind the first. Then a third.

Three kits on the log all walking toward me, and the first was within ten feet when I heard the deep terrible growl. All the kits froze. One made an adorable cooing sound. A quite large momma raccoon crawled over the log, assessed her three still kits, looked at me, and gave a menacing growl. The kits were children indeed, and as with kids of any age, they could not stay still and listen to their parent for long. Two started sniffing and checking out the area around their log and the one closest to me hopped off, directly to my side, and decided to start climbing the redcedar tree at my back. Mom growled again and walked on the same path. All three kits cooed at different times. The other two, watching the fun the first was having, made their way toward me and scrambled up the tree.

The mother walked along the log right toward me. Came to the ten foot mark. She growled and through the corner of my eye, I believe she bared her teeth.

I was convinced that the raccoon could hear the sound of my heart slamming into the edges of my chest cavity. I was sweating. My legs were killing me. I was doing everything in my power to remain still and not to send out any signals that might encourage the mom to attack. I could not move my head for fear of antagonizing her. Directly behind me and above me, I heard the scrambling play of the kits. They cooed and clawed, and I could hear the occasional youthful fumble of missing a branch or having their claws slip along the bark. The mother, seeing that I was still, walked closer to the base of the tree and out of my eyesight. All four raccoons were within ten feet of me, some above, some on the ground, and all just out of my field of vision. The mother would occasionally let out a small growl that seemed directed toward me just to let me know that she still saw me.

During those moments, my consciousness violently volleyed back and forth between the awe of being in the midst of a family of raccoons playing together and the fear of the protective mother who could easily lash out at me without me having nearly enough warning to get out of the way. My legs were electric hot with pain. I tried to breathe through the fear waves or to talk myself out of them, but they kept coming.

Then another moment which I deeply wish that I will never forget. Without me willing it or really thinking it, my whole way of thinking shifted. My eyes felt as if they took on a brightness, a playfulness, a curiosity. They seemed clever and marble black. My body felt as if it was shifting to a wiggly nimbleness. I felt, in my whole being, as if I was shifting into being a raccoon. The playfulness of my kin just above me entered my being and I felt as if I was one of them, searching the world alongside my family with the curiosity of youth.

When that happened *all* of the fear seemed to drain out of me and into the Earth and it was replaced with an actual comfort. It was an actual physical sensation. I felt stronger and supported by my family of raccoons. I was one of them. They played above me for quite some time. I remained still but I was calm and glad to be there.

The kits grew tired of the tree and tumbled down one by one, passing by me. Two walked right past with nonchalance and the third paused to look at me again. That little one walked closer, sniffed me and cooed. I bobbed my head back and we stared at one another for a moment with wonder. Then he tumbled off to meet his siblings. The mother passed in front of me, turned and gave a quick low growl as if to remind me that she still knew I was human.

Attachment

Attachment is a bewilderment of a word. As does the wilderness itself, attachment holds medicine and poison, shelter, tool, and doom. From the old French term to fasten or affix or to arrest. Perhaps from the proto-Germanic term for a stake which is driven into the earth. It is the most common English translation for the Buddhist term that points to the root of all suffering, akin to clinging or grasping. Attachment. When the separate come together and become one; when they blend; when they join and differentiation becomes confused. In Western psychology, attachment is a vital part of the process of personal development. One must attach properly to a primary care giver in order to know oneself. Through this process of attachment, a person can develop healthfully. A person can be secure enough in the world to then detach and differentiate from parents; to create healthy attachments with friends and intimate partners; to form healthy attachments to one's own children so that those children may continue the process.

Such a word demands care in holding. Such a word beckons discernment; it calls us to alertness with each usage. It is the clashing rocks that each of us, an Odysseus, must carefully navigate.

Attachment. The growl of the mother. The coo of the kit. The eye to eye contact of mammal to mammal. The physical closeness. The deep knowledge that the other is present and available as the one spirals outward into new ways and new places. The mental and biochemical safety of a place to return.

As the child is born to grow and wander, the mother is the first Earth. The first home. The child attaches to this first home before the child is even born. Unfathomable to imagine independence. From the birthing, the child is held and given the eye contact, the breath, the soft words, and the warmth to introduce her to the now home in the bigger world. The primary caregiver becomes a single place in a much wider world. The child ventures outward in increments, and, barring intervention, always returns to the caregiver. The child faces the most terrifying events. The first pains. The newest challenges. The child feels all of this in the giant sense organ of her body, and the new waves of experience inevitably send her into overwhelm again and again. Like being thrown into a rough ocean in order to learn how to swim. The caregiver is the one in the boat, right beside her, that pulls her up and gives her respite from the struggle of swimming. Every child, every person, needs rest. Every person needs a strong hand to help when the waves are too much.

In the concrete, this might display as a baby crying because of a loud noise that hurts her ears. The baby feels this through her whole being and she does not know how to respond to the overwhelming sensation. She loses control and her whole body convulses. She cries and cries, and she does not know how to regulate herself. The mother or father picks her up and says a gentle word that interrupts the overwhelming sensations in her body. The feel of the embrace around her. The loving eyes. The strong attunement to a trusted, older, and self-regulated person teaches her system how to calm. In this moment, the child is walked through the experience of moving from being overwhelmed to being regulated and calm again. This newer being depends on others to learn this effectively. The child needs the trusted adult in order to learn, eventually, how to bring herself out of overwhelm and into a state of calm. The child needs a trusted witness to see her accomplishments and verify them. Someone who gets on eye level and uses language to listen to and express understanding with her. She needs to experience empathy and to know she has impact on the world. The child grows, from simple short forays across the room to first steps, to fights with peers, to major accidents, to athletic feats, to creative endeavors, to social injury and social success. The child grows ever-outward and is accompanied by witnessing and regulation. Eventually, the child grows to adolescence and then adulthood, and, in the case of having strong and healthy attachment, that person has a sense of security in the world. Not always secure. Not perfectly secure. But a familiarity with security as a strong and abiding resource.

If the attachment needs are not met, as in a neglectful or an abusive caregiver, attachment theory points to a great deal of developmental energy that is allocated toward trying to find stability and security. The child must learn, in any way possible, to regulate herself. It is a primal survival strategy. This creates a sense of a less safe world, and typically, people in these situations are less prone to seek out new experiences. If the caregiver leaves their presence, such children are more prone to be distressed, as they seem radically unsure as to whether the caregiver will return to meet their needs.

The attachment strategies that grow into us during childhood manifest themselves in our future relationships. In intimacy, we display some spectrum of secure attachment, co-dependency, avoidant attachment or anxious-ambivalent attachment. We relate as we have learned. And the work of intimacy in older stages of life tends to be to continue working toward secure attachment in order to reduce our suffering and to increase the health and happiness of ourselves and our relations. We look toward a good balance of intimacy and independence.

Interestingly, attachment seems to be flexible when looked at cross-culturally. In some non-Western societies, a child does not seem to be attached to a caregiver specifically. In places where a group of people, such as in an intact village, hold communal responsibility for the upbringing of children, these concentrated attachment patterns with the primary caregiver are not observed. Some other force or pattern, held by the village, seems to be responsible for helping a "well-adjusted" member of society to develop. The sense of security is still there. The balance of intimacy and independence is still there. Could it be that the container for the attachment is larger? Can a village hold the attachment role that caregiver holds in a Western nuclear family? How does this change the way that the people think and relate to one another?

What about attachment to Place? To the Earth? If we look at the full story of humanity, we see how long we have lived directly connected to and dependent on Place. Now, we use the term *indigenous* to point to cultures who have maintained this strong connection. Every human on the planet comes from indigenous culture. Our common ancestry spent most of our species' lives in such a relationship with Place. Our indigenous way seems to have a healthy intermingling of identity with Place. The plants and animals, the rocks and rivers, all hold story that connects to the birthing of humans and to the interconnectedness of one another. Humans are differentiated yet connected. Intimacy and independence. A deep identity of belonging, of security with the Place. Secure and healthy attachment.

What happens when we don't have such healthy and secure attachment to Place? Do we birth ideas of Nature as completely separate from ourselves? As ourselves as aliens? Do we separate our minds from our Earthborn bodies? Do we fear Nature? Do we develop unhealthy hatreds for our distanced mother? Does this work its way into strange polarizations and aggressions within the culture, such as misogyny? Do we dream of Armageddon or a tech fix that will make a human-controlled cyborg of the Earth? Have we not learned how to be intimate with the Place that birthed us? Are we confused about whether or not we, humans, belong with the planet? Have we not developed our understanding of interdependence? Are we suffering from a deep, abiding insecurity? A distancing from our great caregiver and a corresponding lack of essential development? Is this condition what co-arises with an empire-driven industrial consumer culture?

These are real questions. Please actually ask them. Notice if you are reacting and take a moment to remember where you are. Is there a breeze right now? What are the plants nearest you doing at this moment? What eyes of what species are wondering with the world so close to where you are? How are you all sharing breath? Then back to the questions. Can we really ask these with compassion? What questions are better to ask? Can we figure this out together?

One beautiful elegance of the human experience is that we are fundamentally flexible. We learn and change all the way from before birth to the last moments of death. Even as adults who survived radically insecure attachments, we can learn healthy attachment. We learn through the graces of other relationships. We learn together. We can practice and develop and create secure attachment. This is typically not easy, as it means unlearning a pattern that was written into our developing being. But it can be done. And the path leads to less suffering and happier, healthier relationships. A person who had reactive attachment disorder as a child can enjoy a healthy and strong relationship with a partner and with his own children. It takes work on the part of the person. It takes many people caring together to find the way.

What if we concentrate our minds toward developing a healthier attachment to Place, and, thus to our planet?

Ecopsychology

One thing I won't do right now is suggest that ecopsychology is the answer to our problem. Let me explain:

I had a teacher once, Mario D'Amato, who was a Zen Buddhist scholar. Mario is a wonder of a man. When I knew him, he taught all of his college classes in a pristine three piece suit. His hair and beard were daily sculpted with the care of a Zen garden. He had a bit of a rockishness to him when he was still. In his eyes, the glean of a hint of danger. When he spoke of the profundity of Zen, he articulated the finest points with the skill of a swordmaster. He embellished these points with consistent profanity. His swearing was an art form. It was so dissonant with his physical appearance and the context of academia that it carried the attribute of shocking you into actually listening to what he said.

One day, Mario had incited an intellectual riot in the classroom by proposing that we do nothing to fix the problems of the world. Students volleyed back and forth their worries and rebuttals. The classroom vibrated with conflict wrought from the deep heartsong of unexpressed grief. Mario remained silent for some time. The conflict escalated. The problems of the world filled the room.

He took in a deep breath and, with a booming voice I had never heard come out of him, he shouted, "It's already at peace!"

Everyone stopped. There were full seconds of silence. For that moment, that strange thought seemed to fill us all. We could not speak.

It is already at peace. Our job is to perceive peace.

Ecopsychology is not a solution to a problem. It is seeing what is already always there, fundamental to the human experience.

I suspect that ecopsychology is another way of thinking. I suspect that it is known through experiencing. It is a deep emergence of a remembering collectively who we are. Trying to define ecopsychology from ego-psychological way of thinking is like asking the flea to define the elephant. The elephant can do a much better job at defining the elephant. Let the flea define the flea.

Ecopsychology is simple. It is remembering through experience that my personal psyche is a part of *our* psyche, which is a part of the psyche of the life community. Whole minds nested in whole minds. Ecopsychology is just a term. It is not a movement or even a way. It is, as the Zen would say, a finger pointing toward the moon. It is yet another piece of this book, which is another piece of the human experience that helps to remind us to experience the source directly. If someone points toward something to look at, how much time do we need to spend examining the finger? Why not just join them and look at the source?

So many of our ancestors and so many existing cultures in this world carry deep and powerful teachings that point us toward the experience of our larger, ecological psyche. I suspect we all know that these same ancestors and these same cultures carry deep wounds of violence and destruction wrought intentionally upon them. The engine of empire, industry, and consumerism has done and is doing terrible things. It is hard work to even look at it. Big grief. No clear answer and a need for a lot of communication and willingness on every side. It is a great, great sadness. There have been unfathomable terrors done by human hands and minds to one another, and we have, across the planet, lost entire worlds of how to be human. Every language that dies means the death of a uniquely human world and a uniquely human-connected Place. I live in a Place where most plants and animals will never hear their deep names again: the ones spoken by various Coast Salish peoples for so many thousands of years. The ones that connected to the stories of who humans are; that wove together the life-giving blanket of Place. How much grief must a people hold with such losses? It bends and stretches an ego-based mind to think that the plants and animals themselves must hold their own kind of embodied grief for this loss. Mustn't they? Mustn't they have grown for millenia in accord with a certain way of being treated by human minds, hearts, and hands? The relationship that had shaped them over time, like an ingredient to the soil, now missing.

How do we find harmony and resolution as a human and a Place community in the wake of these atrocities and the death of our spoken connection to the ancestors? How do we grieve and heal when we now all live on the same land and each of us has been born into an inheritance of violence done by and to our immediate ancestors? It is a strange and deep truth that every one of us in industrial-consumer culture is holding grief. Every one of us comes from a displaced people and some part of our souls is missing our soils. Most if not all of us have carry heritage of participating in violence against a Place-connected people. Can we feel this? Can we listen to and witness one another?

A strange paragraph to come after a sentence like "it's already at peace." But what if it is? What if the peace is here? What if peace emergence happens in the courage of feeling and connecting and listening? What if it doesn't necessarily mean the cessation of pain? Grieving is feeling pain. And it is simultaneously the experience of releasing the attachments to what was. To let the pain be felt and witnessed and then to make room for the new. In this way, grieving is generative. Right now, this is here for us if we choose to pay attention and live it. We must do this together, and not just as humans. It is big work.

Toward the Primal Psyche

When we look at the world and see the condition of our own hearts and minds and those of people we love and care about, perhaps we can see that deep self-love is the only way to rebound from an ailing biosphere and a seemingly insurmountable wall of grief. No one can hold this grief and sickness as an individual. To love ourselves, we heal by uniting with each other and creating a whole that can handle such forces. Then we understand that independent humanity is not enough. We must connect with what is ailing through having the courage to love. Love cannot happen in isolation. Love is a living relationship. We connect to the world to love the world, and in loving the world, we understand how to care for the world. In loving, we understand *who* we are. We remember who this Self is and its many sizes and shapes.

Who, then, is this Self?

Identity is the story that we get told about our awareness. It is the container that tends to bend our perceptions and guide where we direct our awareness.

True change comes as a change in identity.

To know who we are and to actually shift the container of our identity toward the truth, we pay attention. We notice the patterns and attributes of our own consciousness and our relationships. Consciousness rarely has anything to do with control. It is mostly noticing.

On the personal level, this means having a phenomenological engagement with the world: being here now. It is the experience of not reacting to events from the past. Not reacting to simulations of what could happen in the future. It means radically being in the present with neurology engaging more accurately with the information presented. A greater sense of accuracy with what is.

It means making a habit of noticing what we notice. Noticing how we feel and think depending on where our minds are directed. Noticing exactly how we are connected to every other thing. Noticing the nature of connections.

Just by noticing, we are taught the old mammalian lesson of riding the waves of danger and arousal skillfully. We learn to stay present. We can clearly discern whether or not a threat is present and the truer nature of the threat. We can observe the threat arise and pass away. Like a deer who has survived a cougar attack, we can understand at the deep level that the threat is gone and allow ourselves to move through the experience. Whole books have been written about why other animals process traumatic experiences so skillfully. A stronger phenomenological orientation is likely a primal reason. When we are not relying so much on the simulations and entrenched neural networks, our ideas about the world, we can let go of the stressors that are not actually in front of us. We can identify safety and we can let our bodies and minds experience letting go of the stress.

When we learn to let go of stress, we allow ourselves to experience safety and security. Just as in attachment theory, safety and security promote the willingness to have new experiences. We lose the threat-filled tunnel vision and enter wonder. Inevitably, we drop the threat-induced perception of a separate being to fight or flee from. We can then experience ourselves as part of the connected larger world. We leave the momentary state of dealing with a threat and enter the abiding state of Place.

When we perceive our actual, existing connection to Place in a primal sense, we experience being connected to the incalculably vast life-supporting network of our surrounding living world. We are immersed in gifts of shelter, water, fire, food, medicine, tools, beauty, and love. We are connected to greater mental networks. We tap into the communications of birds. We are a part of the breath that moves across the land. We are a flowing expression of soil. Neurologically, this means that in the present moment, we are perceiving and experiencing an unlimited offering of resources. The more we look for resources, the more we see. We are releasing the threat-induced tension of thinking we are an isolated mind, and we can relax into being a part of bigger and smaller processes.

When we have the courage to engage with the world phenomenologically, we, by nature of the act, burn through mental objects. With enough time and effort, our deepest held assumptions become flexible and can even completely change. As a people, we gain the ability to shift paradigm. We can think differently. We can be differently.

We remember who we are.

This entire book is an attempt to point us toward the experience of remembering collectively who we are.

Let it be said that we cannot un-eat the apple.

You are reading this on a screen or a manufactured paper product. Many of us have had some sort of medical intervention that has extended our lives. The words I am using are birthed of civilization. It is as unfathomable to uncivilize ourselves as it is un-eat an apple you ate a week ago. The apple becomes you. You are who you eat. We are civilization. And we are primal. Not one, not two.

We can, accepting all of our personal and cultural conditions, burn through the mental objects of our ideas about the world and perceive the world more and more as it is. We can develop healthy attachments with the world. Healthy attachments and a phenomenological orientation of perception will penetrate our own sense of identity.

A client, Jacob, was once suffering from vicarious trauma. His friend was going through many hard times and he was feeling so much compassion that it had begun to seriously challenge his own ability to meet life. He was regularly feeling sick to his stomach and he was dealing with challenges around death and impermanence.

One of my kung fu teachers would often say, "respect the obvious." Heeding his advice, Jacob and I went into a nearby field to visit the deer. Specifically, the recent remnants of the deer. If you are dealing with visceral processes, why not consult the viscera? Very little will give you a more visceral response than witnessing a pile of something else's viscera. What is supposed to be inside is now out. It makes mortality very plain. There is a certain shock value to this, and that's okay sometimes. Sometimes it takes a pile of guts to make us cut through the bullcrap and remember that our lives are finite and precious.

When we came to the gut pile, Jacob paused and looked at me, questioning. The gut pile was three days old, and most of the guts had already been taken. Mostly, what was left was the intestines and their contents. I nodded toward the gut pile and stepped back so that I was out of his peripheral vision. This was an experience between Jacob, the guts, and the cosmos. I asked Jacob to stare at the gut pile for an extended period of time. Long enough to actually start seeing it. It was the time of day when the metallic green flies had come to walk the remains and to suck up the dying deer cells in order to grow their own fly-ish lives. The odor infused the area with promise of death. The bald sun beat light into the desiccating fascia and revealed a strange palette of reds, blues, browns, whites, and greys.

It was not long before Jacob's body stilled as he stared more deeply into the gut pile. After he seemed to have centered his attention and built a relationship with the gut pile, I asked him to really see. I asked him to look into the gut pile. To see what lead to it. The movement of a young faun, curious and wobbly legged. Belly full of mother's milk. The quick and innocent grace of youth coursing through her. The gentle nudges of her mother's nose to guide her into the world. Then the moment of death. The faun had been struck by a car and the mother had witnessed this little one, in moments, pass from an animate only-ever-once-I-of-a-deer to limp pile of flesh, fluid, and bone. I guided Jacob to see the story in this. To take the time to see it and then feel it. And then to see, after just three days, all that was left. The head and legs dragged away by hungry coyotes through a faint trail in the blackberries. The visit of the opossum to gnaw on remaining organs. The swarms of insects. The trails of slugs. And then now, what remained. Scuffs on the dirt around a drying tube of feces. Maybe the last discernible story of that one deer. And soon there would be nothing left that anyone could ever read again.

Jacob's breath deepened. His eyes seemed transfixed. We were as silent as the sun.

Some mystery feeling within the bounds of my own being compelled me to speak again. I asked that we both imagine and feel into how that mother might have felt for her young. The deer sharing many emotions that humans have. The deer developing their own attachment to mother. The mother, who must have felt the wonder-surges of pleasure and sweetness as her little one drank from her nipples, from her body. How must it have felt to witness the one she carried and raised be forever scattered outward. Never integrated again.

Jacob's eyes winced, then softened. Many breaths passed.

We brought our minds to the mystery that deer don't seem to develop psychosis after losing a loved one. They seem to process this grief with a quickness that startles the human heart-mind. The mother was likely grazing blackberries as we stood there. Perhaps standing on the rodent-gnawed bones of another once-was deer.

We looked at the pile. And saw it now, as it is. Only now. We looked at the vitality of the moment. The buzzing livingness of each fly body. The ever-eating and drinking ground filled with a vibrant tapestry of root and invertebrate tunnels. The truth now of life as it is. The unyielding vitality of the moment of Place. Jacob stared.

I asked him to look up and open up his sense to the whole of his surroundings. To see the story of so much once-was. To see the unfathomable network of Life vibrating all around and through us. Here and now. We paused.

I don't know exactly why, as it doesn't seem to fit neatly, but I was compelled to say one last sentence. "Nothing here wants anything from you."

I walked away and waited for Jacob to follow when he was ready.

When he did come, we stood beside one another in more silence for a time. I asked, "what happened for you there?"

He said, "I don't know. I feel different." His voice was calmer and softer and his eyes steadier than they had been before. He took in a deep breath. "You know, when you said, 'nothing here wants anything from you,' I felt this huge weight just lift from my shoulders. I hadn't realized how much they had been holding."

This is a bit of a strange story. Not necessarily tidy and definitely up for interpretation. I suspect that one thing that happened was that Jacob spent time deeply exploring the experience of death, trauma, and loss. Of directly witnessing the result. Of seeing how the world holds this. Perhaps experiencing, at a depth level, that there is never one point where the world is not holding the situation. Before, through, and after a single life, there is an unending holding. And it does not ask the single life to do any of the big work. Nature has it. The personal psyche can let go of trying to resist or control life and death. The personal psyche can rest in the bigger mind of Life.

In physics, you can reduce pressure by cooling down a closed container. There are the same amount of particles inside the container and the shape of the container remains the same. The pressure reduces because the particles aren't as active. They are not pushing each other and the bounds of the container. In the psyche, this is akin to amping down the nervous system. For Jacob, losing his mind and coming to his senses was a way of amping down, of reducing pressure. In physics, you can also reduce pressure by increasing the size of the container. The same amount of air that was in a little, fully inflated balloon barely exerts pressure on the walls of a giant balloon. For Jacob it seems that touching the bigger mind expanded his container. He wasn't just holding all his pressures in that small container of the personal consciousness. He remembered that he is participating in a larger process, a greater mind.

I wonder what physically changed for Jacob during this experience. How did his biochemistry change? What networks were formed? How does the body remember such experiences? I would be willing to bet that such an experience had a biochemical influence on par with a prescription drug. Without ingesting any drug. Without negative side effects. Better chemistry through Living. What would happen if this kind of experience was practiced regularly? The experience of such connection would inevitably become a deeper and deeper neural network. It would become attractive to a degree that it eventually would work its way to a baseline way of being. Wouldn't Jacob then enjoy an identity that knows connection to Place and how to rest in the bigger mind? Is this a way of developing healthy attachment to Place?

Strong and long veins of light gray clay branch their ways through the landscape between the Nooksack River and the Chuckanut mountains. These veins are often exposed on the banks of our streams and rivers. The water carves the land deep enough to reveal the treasureful below. I've taken many people, from youth to adults to harvest this strange earthy substance. To get our hands wet and slimy in the dreamy crafting of pots and bowls and cups and more. We let the crafted vessels dry and then build a big fire. Slowly court the heating of the vessels hour by hour until we can nestle them into the center of the coals and then feed the fire. We wait until the next day when a thin dusting of snowy ash coats the remains of that fire. Then we dig in with bare hands and find the treasures. The clay has become hard and holds water. We have, without any industrial intervention, created a life-sustaining tool.

We could, instead, go to the thrift shop and find a superiorly crafted and fired glazed pot of almost any size we can fathom for less money than we would typically spend on a light lunch. We could do this in thirty minutes and be done.

This points toward what may be a major dissonance in industrial-consumer thinking. Economically, we calculate time, money, and the quality of goods. The quality of the experience itself, the effect on the psyche, most of the effect on the body, and most of the effect on the rest of the living world are not considered in the economic approach. I suspect that almost everyone reading understands this and also recognizes that we don't only make value judgments based on this economic system. We do plenty of things that we know enhance our lives and have no or a negative economic value. I wonder, however, just how much this economic system is affecting our ways of thinking. How much does it sway our behavior and intervene in our assessment of the value of actions? How much time pressure does this system exert on us? How much pressure to maximize our time, to be efficient, and to fit our lives around what will keep us economically viable? I suspect it is fair to say that we, commonly, do not believe that money accurately measures what we most value in life. It does not measure, love, happiness, good relationships, healthy ecosystems, insight, and many other valuable things. It measures very particular things that are recorded in giant volume of tomes in the United Nations. These tomes detail, arbitrarily, what has economic value and what has not. They are based off of a British strategy for recovering from the debts Britain incurred during war. Now, every nation must agree to these conditions for economic value in order to be a part of the United Nations.

Isn't it important to remember that the economic values are arbitrary? Humans made them up. They are values based on the mindset of men participating in war and domination. They are, by nature, values that are not aimed at cultivating or even sustaining life and happiness. If you are bold, and I suggest that you are, please learn who Marilyn Waring is. If nothing else, watch the documentary on her called "Who's Counting? Marilyn Waring on Sex, Lies, and Global Economics." If you sleuth on the internet, you can find this movie streaming for free. Marilyn started her public life as both the first female and the youngest member of New Zealand parliament. Part of Marilyn's amazing life journey has been to deeply pursue the question of how we choose value in the economy, why, and what the ramifications are.

I now suggest pausing for a moment. What is your breath doing right now? How does it feel? How did your body respond to the last couple paragraphs? Has your way of thinking changed? And now I suggest remembering where you are and who you are, on the big scale. Can you feel the blood moving in you? Can you feel your planet's atmosphere on your skin? Can you stretch your mind for a moment into the water all around you; seeing it as one shape enveloping the whole vibrant Earth? Can you remember the vast expanse of roots and mycelium holding the ground below you together? Can you rest in the fact that this is all a part of your living system?

You are, at your core, co-creating the deepest economy. The economy of Life.

The dissonance of being a member of the deep Life economy while serving the shallow industrial consumer economy happens at the primal level. We know, cognitively, that humans have lived without industry or agriculture for about 99% of our species' lives. On the deep personal level, however, we don't really know that we can survive without industry. If we don't experience it with our own hands, then we don't actually know it at the deeper levels of the personal mind. We suffer from a psychological enmeshment with industrial consumer society. We live a forgetting of who we are with our planet. And there is fear in this.

Primally, most people get most of our basic needs met through the shallow economy. It has become a baseline that bends our values and our actions around it. Of course, we have cities, the internet, cars. We have fully eaten the apple. The blind reaction to such dissonance is to try to extinguish one of the two factors. To disbelieve that the shallow economy cannot sustain life on Earth or to try to fully reject all aspects of the industry and consumption. Neither of these seems possible. I may be wrong, but this is my read. I encourage my whole community to weigh in on this, as many already are. The first step to resolving dissonance consciously and gracefully is to develop the ability to observe the situation without being bound to it. We give ourselves enough distance to see clearly what is happening and to not react. One way we can do this, in this instance, is to remind ourselves that we, humans, are not actually utterly dependent on the industrial consumer economy. We've simply become enmeshed. That first step back into observation is to just let our psyches know, on the experiential level, that there actually are other options. We become aware and alert in our primal psyches. When we are enmeshed, the process of disentangling has to happen slowly and consciously. We transform at the pace we need in order to stay whole.

When we harvest clay directly, we access the deep economy. This becomes an act of liberation psychology. It liberates us from the engrained pattern of thinking that we need industrial processes in order to live on this planet. Harvesting clay or making fire or experiencing any of the other practices in this book liberates us from the dissonance. We become more primally competent, and not as primally reliant upon industry. We experience a radical shift in our way of thinking because our deep baseline has shifted.

This bends our perception and we start to personally and fundamentally perceive the world from the perspective of the larger planetary and biological processes. Our consciousness awakens more to the primal psyche. This is where our personal minds touch and participate with the larger mind. We see more clearly, without the need for cognitive interventions or specialized education. Long held culturally-based assumptions and demands on the planet become more evident. We see clearly that such mental objects as "weeds" and "trash" are a luxury of a temporary system profiteering from outsourcing its needs to other parts of the planet and serving their desires. We see assumptions embedded in our language and then in our perceptions.

If we continue to rely on opaque and foreign industrial processes for our shelter, water, fire, and food, we will suffer from an unsurmountable dissonance on the primal psychological level. Foreign and opaque means a process that we don't understand at the deep personal, mammalian level. The creation of the products does not happen in our local area, and we cannot readily be taught how it is done. It is *practically* inaccessible and unknowable. We are divorcing our identity from ourselves… our bigger selves and our primal selves. We're living this thin, cognitive line of identity that is far too fragile to handle the forces put upon it.

The intellect is a precision instrument. It cannot be expected to handle all of the primal and planetary forces.

The Canadian physician, Gabor Mate, says that the two factors that cause stress are lack of information and loss of control. We live in the information age, and we cognitively know that almost any information is accessible to us if we pursue it. We cognitively know that systems such as democracy allow us for a great deal of control. However, all the indications are that many people are very stressed right now. What if information must penetrate to the level of experience in order for the deeper physiological processes of the body to respond? What if we have to be primally competent, in our bodies, in order for our whole living system to act and feel unstressed? Maybe we have a need to get our hands dirty, in the clay and in the dirt, in order for our personal systems to recognize at the Earthy, mammalian level, that they have sufficient knowledge and control to take care of themselves.

Wonder, Ethics, and the Call of the Wild

Back to Jacob. Jacob's mind is a fascinating universe of powers and challenges, strange formations, and awe-inspiring supernovas of "I." His thinking, when measured and compared, is often on the lateral edges of a bell curve. He has been born with a cosmic task of recognizing that he must be creative in finding ways to fit his mind gracefully into many of our cultural systems, such as education. I have been honored to walk alongside him for years now and to witness his strange wander into knowing himself and understanding how others think.

Jacob has a tendency toward obsessive compulsive behaviors. At seventeen, I presented meditation as an option for focusing his mind and developing the ability to just observe an experience without being drawn into reacting. Jacob found this helpful and began practicing on his own. He worked with a body scan. With the body scan, he would notice the sensations happening on his body and practice just letting them be as they are. He was quite challenged, as, perhaps, all of us are, with the task of just observing a sensation. His mind was doing what human minds do: assessing a sensation as good or bad, explaining it, and then trying to do something about it. It was very foreign for his mind to just be curious and feel something that it had labeled as uncomfortable. It was just as foreign for his mind to not seek a pleasurable sensation. He realized rather quickly that this was tapping at the root of not just his obsessive-compulsive tendencies, but of many other life patterns that create suffering in the long run. So, he kept at it, but he struggled quite a bit.

We wondered about ways to make it more approachable so that he could get a good foundation little by little. The wondering led us to paying attention to wonder itself which led to wander.

Jacob had to get out of his idea of his own mind in order to experience what it is like to just observe with curiosity. Not wanting to change anything. So, we went out to the nearby field and Jacob found a good spot to mark a threshold. He told himself that once he passed through that threshold, he would enter a state of wonder with the world. He would experience seeing everything as if for the first time. Like he had just arrived on this planet and had no idea where he was or what anything was. His job was to fall into fascination.

So he did.

It was beautiful to witness. I stood back and quieted my own mind, just watching him from afar as he paused for many moments to feel the spray of strange green spikes on a spruce twig. He stared long and wide-eyed at the dappled ceiling of our vast planet. He knelt in awe before a tawny stalk of seeding grass.

When he came back, his voice was deep and slow. He had a smiling about him: a warming glowishness. After some time, he reflected that the experience was nothing less than profound for him. He learned much about the land and he felt calm in his body and mind. We then reflected on the simple truth: this is the same way we wander our own bodies and our own minds. With wonder. Wonder does not want to change anything. Wonder sees more and more clearly the truth as it is, and it admires that truth. Jacob learned that day to approach his own being as a wonder-filled wilderness, and his meditation practice changed from that day forward.

The wilderness demands the ability for silence. A silence so deep it happens among the subtlest sensations in the body. To live in accord with the ever-emerging order of nature, the mind must learn how to still the mental chatter and the body must learn how to be non-reactive to the chatter of physical sensations. On the gross behavioral level, this means the ability hunt or hide or wait without wasting energy. This means having a well-developed executive function.

Executive function is a term in psychology for specific mental processes. It is an utterly crucial part of developing the human mind. Executive function is being able to handle all kinds of input at once and making choices that are in accord with the needs of the personal system. It is the property of the mind that offers working memory, inhibitory control, and mental flexibility. If you are out in a field picking berries, it takes in the weather, the sensory input, the conversation you are having with your friend, and the varying impulses you may have to pee and to take a break. Executive functioning is how the mind consciously chooses and focuses.

If we open up an internet browser, we are suddenly overwhelmed by choices and distractions. Having a strong executive functioning means only focusing on what you had an intention to do unless something of greater value comes into play. It means not buying the pack of cigarettes or the piece of cake or a new couch when it's not in accord with the overall health of your system. It means being more content with where you are, which is a challenge to a consumer system. Low executive functioning is good for the economy and devastating for the living relationships in personal life, the community, the cultures, and the ecological world.

I'm not sure who to attribute it to, but I have heard it said that the inner life is colonized by media and that silence is the antidote. Silence is the honing of the blade edge of executive functioning. It is our primal baseline. Silence is a portal to our primal psyche. It is how we perceive the call of the wild.

I suspect there is some confusion when many people in my culture use the word *wild*. Oftentimes, wild is a word that we use socially to indicate breaking cultural conditioning. We are wild and we do not obey the conditioning set upon us. This has great power in the sense of questioning systems and creating alternatives. We can be wild in our passions and wild in our ways of thinking. We can create new cultural norms through this embrace.

One challenge we have with this is equating the word *wild* with the unchecked ability to follow our own impulses. We equate wild with uninhibited: with low executive functioning.

The problem with this is that it does not exactly apply to the natural wild, the wilderness. The wilderness is an ongoing biotic emergence of response to non-negotiable conditions. In the wilderness, defiance means death. Literally, if a plant tries to defy the conditions of the soil or the weather by not accepting them and responding in accord, the plant will never yield seed and produce offspring.

The wild unyieldingly teaches the importance of impulse control and of directed and suspended attention. The most disciplined minds in the world are surrounding us: the song sparrow or the kokanee, the bigleaf maple or the cougar.

When we live with the Earth, we have to gather what food there is, what water there is. We have to accept where the shelter and the fire are. When a person spends time in the wilderness like this, she has to sit through states of hunger and tiredness. Often times, for those of us raised in the consumer society, this experience includes the detox of swearing at the sun for being too hot, demanding of the Earth some mercy, cursing the wind, crying, and enduring vast states of boredom. This is the birth of primal discipline. After time, the mind calms. Paradoxically, it is tamed by the wild. When the mind becomes tame to the wild, the mind perceives conditions as much as it can as they are. The mind cannot abide being taken by the defiant grasping toward the things as it wants them to be. The mind must accept the conditions as they are and become a disciple to learning how to work skillfully with them. The wild is the world's church or dhamma hall in this respect. The deer mouse knows this. The dandelion knows this. We, too, know this when we fast from our consumer world of resolving any impulse we choose. When we step into the wild, we are naked in this way. This may be a reason we fear it.

Working directly with the natural world means being tamed. We are tamed to the deep morality and ethics that bind us. We learn to act in accord. Only then are we wild.

The wilderness and the body also teach justice.

I was regularly accused, as a child, of having an overdeveloped sense of justice. Maybe you were too. I thought this was an unjust accusation, which becomes a real head trip as you think about it. Maybe I'm still reacting. Maybe it's my overdeveloped sense of justice demanding a lifetime place in my psyche. But I still don't think that that is a just accusation. I wonder if we have an underdeveloped sense of justice as a culture. Not that we lack the ability or the intermittent expression of powerful justice. I'm wondering about the baseline of our actions and our acceptance of outcomes. Maybe we stifle and distort our sense of justice because it would be too painful and too overwhelming for a culture of individuals believing in a baseline of individual responsibility to handle.

I suspect that many in individualistic cultures live with a lot of personal shame. We contribute to unjust systems and we don't know what else to do. We feel bad or we rationalize or we get angry. And we hold this hurt, this injustice, as a personal experience. What a hard thing to do. What a harsh thing to do. We are small. We are little lives swayed by an unfathomable living globe of force in an uncountable cosmos of globes.

Justice runs through a person, but is not personal. We hold justice as a spirit of living. We cultivate justice. We do this together. Not just human beings. All of us. The land teaches justice. The oceans. Justice is a spirit of the big mind.

What happens when the individual thinks as "we?" Does that mind stay individual? Has not the container expanded and connected into a larger mental network? How does it feel in your being to make one simple change in your approach to justice: change the "I" to "we?" If you choose, right now I suggest trying it. Center your mind and say your own true version of the following sentences in both ways: When (I) (we) contribute to injustice, (I) (we) feel bad. (I) (We) feel angry. (I) (We) rationalize.

We don't like injustice. It does not make us feel good. What if the "we" with which we think is also heard in the cry of the kestrel? What if we are the grass blade in the sidewalk crack or the pocked sandstone cliff? We still feel this way. We feel bad when we contribute to injustice. We see the shape and volume of injustice. And we have suddenly become much bigger with much more life force and creativity. We have the resources to respond to this.

We have endured ice ages. Floods and meteors. We have created living continents. Now, the holocene age has passed and we are changing. We change our ways to endure the coming era as we have done many times before. Our ways, now, will shift dramatically in the human species. We do this as one.

One of the ways that we embrace our power of the big mind is through practice. We, humans, now, practice remembering who we are. We re-mind ourselves. There is a Japanese adage: *For something to acquire religious significance, two conditions alone are necessary: it must be simple, and it must be repetitive.* As we, intentionally and repetitively put our minds into our bigger identity spread out through all our relationships, we become that bigger identity.

There is nowhere in the world to spit. We are one body and one mind as a congress. What a fascinating shape. What a wonder, this grand ever-movement of light and sound. Imagine it, if you will. Us, the whole world as one being.

There is nothing to take. Everything is granted. We are a passing through the one body.

We are calling. Right now, in your body, your blood and thoughts are all calling along with every other being. The call of Earth. Outward into the symphony of the universe.

Hear, as Earth, the calling is strange. The movements of each life form are their own entireties. Their own fully composed song. And in this strange orchestration, we inspire one another.

The cougar has the deer's medicine and the deer has the cougar's medicine.

I was recently huddled in the bushes next to a ten-week-old kitten who we had adopted. It was the middle of a sunny summer day in the Pacific Northwest. A raptor in the distance pierced the silence with its sharp call. The kitten huddled. The chickens just outside the bushes froze and turned their heads to the sky.

One question for the congress of us?

Why do we, the raptor, call?

What benefit could it have for we, the raptor, to call our presence to us, the prey?

When we call as the raptor, all of us, the prey, remember the presence of the raptor. We, the prey, huddle and prepare. We scurry under bushes, cease our chewing, prepare our bodies. We, the prey, remember that the predator is always out there, and we, the prey, develop our whole beings over time toward response.

We, the predator, call to push us, the prey, toward excellence.

We, the prey, then, push us, the predator, toward excellence.

This is the essence of non-violent competition. This is competition in ultimate collaboration. Competition means *to pray together for something better.* Martin Prechtel says that "violence is the absence of conflict." In non-violent competition the conflict is between two sides intentionally pushing each other toward excellence, knowing the long-term benefit of meeting another's increasing excellence. Violence happens when one side, out of fear of its own inadequacy, seeks the extermination of the other side. Suppression, repression, and oppression are all violent by nature.

This is difficult for an individuated consciousness to understand. An individual cooper's hawk seems to have violently exterminated a single mourning dove. What if, however, there is a greater network of information being exchanged? There are vibrant exchanges of species as a whole, of ecosystem, and of bios taking place in that moment. Are they not bigger minds at work? Literally, the body of the dove changes into the body of the cooper's hawk. Is it not an interaction of mind as well? Of hawkness and doveness? Of predatorness and preyness? The predator call is one part of a larger mind calling to another. A mind sharing one body, one being. Such a mind is the mind of us, all of bios. It is one mind. Our mind. The vast network of the primal psyche.

Now, I suggest pausing. Where is the silence around you?

Where are the spaces between the thoughts?

Who are you in that silence?

The Faculty of the Heart

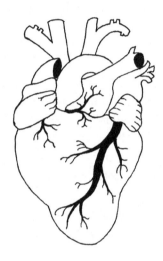

Dear darkening ground,
you've endured so patiently the walls we've built,
perhaps you'll give the cities one more hour
and grant the churches and cloisters two.
And those that labor—let their work
grip them another five hours, or seven,
before you become forest again, and water, and widening wilderness
in that hour of inconceivable terror
when you take back your name
from all things.
Just give me a little more time!
I want to love the things
as no one has thought to love them,
until they're worthy of you and real.

—Rainer Maria Rilke

Jake Swamp, a Mohawk leader and the founder of the Tree of Peace Society, graced the world by sharing a foundational personal and communal practice of the Haudenosaunee. This great gift to the world is the Thanksgiving Address. There is a traditional Thanksgiving Address that belongs particularly to the Haudenosaunee, yet elders have encouraged other people of other cultures to find their own form of a Thanksgiving Address. If you are curious about the traditional address, you can contact the Haudenosaunee Confederacy.

Thank you, Haudenosaunee Confederacy.

Personally, I suspect that giving a thanksgiving address regularly has been the single most transformative practice that I have learned out of any in this book.

I have learned, through practice, that we give thanks to remember who we are.

Here and now, in this guide to wonder, we can practice. Creatively. This is how a thanksgiving address came through a poet sitting on the browned grass near the Salish Sea at a dry summer's end. I welcome you to read this or pause and find your own way give thanks to the great web of being of which you are a part.

We begin by noticing our breath. How it breathes in and how it breathes out. How the world comes in and comes out. How we are breath.

We notice our Place. We listen. Smell. Touch. Taste the air.

We see how we are connected, sharing breath and ground and gravity. Breathing in and out.

We bring our minds together in this way. As one.

We pause and breathe as one.

With one mind, we give thanks.

We give thanks to the great rumbling Earth, who feeds us and eats us. You wonder-rock in the cosmic unraveling. You, the foundation of iron and bone, of feather and frond. The body. The home. The caregiver. The tender. The boundary. Thank you, Earth, for creating us.

We give thanks to water. The shift-shaping body of one water that coats the whole Earth, into the breath and ground, up the mountains and through the caverns. You ever-vasting expanse of life's source, gracing us with your flowing touch and feeding the world entire. Thank you, water, for creating us.

We give thanks to all of the beings living within the Earth. The crawling creeping creators with shelled claw and many legs. You silent sleepers chewing the world to fine loam. You that slither and tunnel drafts of life-giving breath through the ever-churning remains. Thank you for creating us, beings living within the Earth.

We give thanks to all of the beings living within the waters. Breathing life through the fluid body that birthed us all. Fin and follicle. Plankton and protozoa. Whale and worm. Thank you for your vibrant aliving together in the great song of creation. Thank you for creating us, beings living within the waters.

We give thanks to all of the fungus beings. From the creeping searching of mycelial thread through the decaying cedar stump to the quiet colony on the skin of an elder. To the curious pulse of consciousness you spread in, on, and around all of our bodies. Mushroom to mulch. Thank you, fungus beings, for creating us.

We give thanks to all of the animal beings. You shaking, creeping, pouncing, springing, winging, dartly movers. You who pierce skies and call to mountains. You who nibble the Earth anew. You fast-changing listeners who wrap the Earth in fur, feather, and skin. Thank you, animal beings, for creating us.

We give thanks to all of the human animals. With your strong-minded hands and your oblong songs you send out to the universe. You, who bring imagination to the world and grace us with the ever-changing oblique sweetness of your languaging. You who weep and praise and eat and drink and die us. Thank you, human animals, for creating us.

We give thanks to all of the plant beings. You eaters of starlight and transformers of color. You fooding and sheltering, poisoning and drinking, blooming and dancing. You reach your bodies above all toward the unedited absorption of light and you stretch the shape of life high. You dig to the darkest corner of the deepest rock. You connect heaven and Earth. Thank you, plant beings, for creating us.

We give thanks to the air. The one home of you, the invisible river of creation that we all share. You, the air that enters and exits us each from moment to moment. The unstoppable truth of sharing. You terror teaching winds. You whisker's touch of a hinting breeze. Thank you, air, for creating us.

We give thanks to the clouds. You rebirth of the waters. You sailors of the skies. You baby blanket that tucks us in around the globe, sheltering from the hardness of the star, keeping just enough heat in and keeping just enough out. You porous skin. You wrath wielders, people feeders, and land shifters. Thank you, clouds, for creating us.

We give thanks to the four directions. You, the aspect of our world that teaches us Place. You give birth to *where?* You teach us to be Place. To understand the dance of Place. To be people in Place. Thank you, four directions, for creating us.

We give thanks to the sky. You who hold us all in to be a community in space. You great cupped hands of protection. You holder of we. Thank you, sky, for creating us.

We give thanks to the moon. Our older sister who long ago split and circled us. Taking the brunt of the impact so that we may thrive. Steadying us. Pacing our oceans and minds with the education of swaying. Thank you, moon, for creating us.

We give thanks to the sun. You, our star. Our center. Our heat. Our light. You, the great warmer. You, the unerring and the great reliable. You, who we circle in love. Thank you, sun, for creating us.

We give thanks to the planets and stars and all the bodies in the cosmos. Every one of our cosmic relatives who are cycling and circling, burning and cooling, causing eddies of light in the blanket of the unfathomable. You who stretch beyond imagination. You who are bigger than possibility. Thank you, planets and stars, for creating us.

We give thanks to all beings. To our grand and unfettered whole. From the smallest to the biggest and to all of the through. To all in all directions. Thank you, all beings, for creating us.

We give thanks to the spirit of Love and Truth moving through us all.

Thank you for creating us.

Thank you for creating us.

Thank you for creating us.

This is one way of giving thanks. It is a practical re-minder.

You may have noticed that the mind, more-or-less, spirals outward in that address. From the center of the Earth to the great beyond. This is a way that the Haudenosaunee practice. We start at the center and we grow our identity outward from there. We re-member gracefully in this way.

I briefly mentioned attuning to other mammals through our limbic systems earlier in this book, and I suspect it is a good time to come back to it. This strange scientific phenomenon is called limbic resonance. It is where we notice actual physical changes in the brain when two or more people are in each other's presence. The two nervous systems seem to harmonize or resonate with each other. This is a mammalian phenomenon, so if you, right now, happen to have a cat or dog in the room or you're sitting under a tree next to a squirrel, you are resonating with each other. We bend each other's nervous systems, which bends each other's entire experience of living. Some research suggests that we do not even have to be conscious that the other person is near us. They can be hidden behind a screen and our nervous systems still resonate. Research suggests that when two nervous systems are in resonance, the more disregulated or disorganized system tends to resonate toward the more organized and regulated system. A person who is calm and centered calms and centers others.

When we give thanks, we set a more positive and resilient baseline for ourselves. Over time, this "sticks" to us. We become more thankful overall. The world and our relationships become more precious because we have practiced seeing their innate preciousness. We practice seeing our world in a positive, beautiful, and supportive light, and we become attuned to these attributes of our lives.

It is interesting to then consider what happens when we practice thanks together. If we are all together and giving thanks, and if our systems are made to bend toward the more organized and regulated systems, then what happens in a group? It seems that, with the intention of focusing on thankfulness, our systems will work in orchestra to tune each other up. The best parts of each of us will lift each other up. And we are directing all of this real energy toward all of the other beings and aspects of the world upon which we depend. What a powerful medicinal experience for each individual person. To experience positive, connected, love and thanks in their being to greater degree and with more stability than they could have managed alone.

How does this affect the world? If we are limbically resonating with other mammals, do they feel this in their systems?

Have you ever been to a monastery or place of peaceful and loving spiritual practice and noticed the way the wildlife interacts? If you have, I suspect I don't have to say anything more. It's very observable curiosity. I wonder if this is not just because of the behaviors of the residents but also because of the quality of those humans' minds resonating together.

On the behavioral level, when we are more and more thankful and we see the preciousness, this inherently changes the way we treat each other and the world. How could it not?

I have a friend who apprenticed under a curandero in Mexico. He told me that he spent a lot of time in the beginning as a janitor. His job was to clean rooms and live simply. This was, of course, its own education, and I'm sure he could say quite a bit about what he learned from doing this. When he had found a certain calm and had resigned himself to simply serving by cleaning, only then the curandero began to work directly with him.

His next job was singular in focus. He was asked to sit in the corner of the room while the curandero saw patients. His job was this: for the entire time, with each patient, he was to imagine that person in her or his greatest happiness. He was to see it in his mind's eye. To perceive the deep happiness within the person.

He shared that sometimes when he and the curandero were both sitting there doing this, not saying a word, the patient would break down in tears and release great sadnesses. It was all the medicine needed to dismantle the person's armor and allow for grieving and feeling again.

The mind is a force that bends the world. Please, may we never forget this.

We share the positive and we share the negative. In a way, the big traumas and the terrible wounds get distributed among people. Vicarious trauma is a well-known phenomenon for many health care providers. It is basically what happens when a health care provider, such as a counselor, hears the story and sits with someone as they express the pain and terror of their traumatic experience. The health care provider is in resonance with this person, and so the health care provider's own personal system is experiencing a degree of that trauma. It is up to the provider's own system to metabolize that experience. Sometimes it is too much, and then the provider also ends up holding onto trauma in her or his body. This may be a reason why it is good to have elders in the room with us. The elders are well-experienced with grief and trauma and pain, with accepting it and moving through it in a healthy way. Life over time inevitably teaches this. Being in resonance with an elder can help move trauma for every personal system in the room.

The scientific approach is discovering more and more about the way we share trauma. Transgenerational trauma is trauma that is passed down from generation to generation. This term began in the West when health care providers began noticing how many children of holocaust survivors were seeking help. How could we not pass on such trauma? If we are in the most intimate resonance with parents and we are formed in accord with them, how could the trauma escape us? That being the case, trauma is shared suffering and it passes through the world slowly over time. Humans move trauma through many different individual systems.

It may be terrifying to recognize that we all get born into other people's trauma, but isn't there also a beauty in it? Isn't it a little easier to know that it is not just yours? That, as Hafiz says, *out of great need, we are all holding hands and climbing*? That we move this wound through time and space in a slow way, and that one person does not have to resolve the terrible wounds and violence of such a thing as the holocaust? The wound gets distributed. Peter Levine, founder of Somatic Experiencing Trauma Institute, calls trauma "unintegrated resource." Meaning that beneath trauma is great power. Perhaps, if we step back and look, we can see that traumas experienced by multiple generations have most likely been the seeds for some of our greatest acts of humanitarianism and justice, our greatest spiritual realizations, our greatest art, our greatest insights, our greatest kindnesses.

What kind of ancestral trauma might we be holding as a people? What kind of losses have we incurred, lands have we been forced from, or atrocities have we committed?

What could we be holding as a species? What might we be holding for the destructions of our living biosphere? Francis Weller points to questions around this: what if the depression or anxiety that I am feeling is not my own? What if it is a deep part of my humanity missing some vital ingredient that makes me whole? What if I am feeling depressed because of the absence of bird song or lush vegetation in my life? What if, for 99% of human life on Earth, we have had a village or a tribe and we are made to be whole in the presence of an intimate relationship with the entire village? What if we are made to be whole in the presence of an intimate relationship with our landscape? What if the loneliness I feel is a longing for that birthright?

Trauma is unintegrated resource. As we accept traumatic content and we feel it, we can artfully experience this without going into overwhelm or blind reactivity. We bring the content to consciousness. It then moves and changes. It is no longer an invisible and allusive force creating strange vortices of suffering in our lives. The trauma, the impediment to our deep power and wisdom, moves and we experience a flow of generativity. We become the embodiment of greater wisdom and power.

Here is another story told to me by Tai Hazard. I am still chewing toward the marrow of this one and most likely will be until my own death:

Long ago, in feudal Japan, the way of the samurai was that of serving. The samurai served the lord and the samurai code. The desires of the personal ego of the samurai were largely an impediment. The value of an entire life was measured in the excellence of service.

During this time, there were countless wars and skirmishes, political intrigues and sabotage. Some samurais who had sworn to serve their lord found themselves lordless as the power games of men spread destruction across the land. There was a code for how to act upon the death of a samurai's lord. In this code, it dictated bringing a killer to justice if the lord was killed by ignoble means.

In a place where the mountains touched the valley and the distant arm of a great river was formed, a stubborn and well-defended lord suddenly took ill. He died shortly afterward. It was discovered that he had been poisoned, and all of his samurai now had one task of avenging his death by executing the murderer. The samurai code sought to protect the people as a whole from the illness of deceit and the panic of distrust. The code made sure to vanquish any spores of such illness, and to have honesty and order prevail. The code meant morality and ethics. Which formed the village. Which formed the people.

The code was greater than any one samurai. It was an ever-practice toward an ideal. Everyone fell short to some degree.

Some samurai gave up right away and became rampaging ronin, lordless brigands, on the land. Some made vein attempts while conjuring other work for themselves. Others took on the task. These spread in all four directions and dedicated their lives to the dictate of their code.

Some of these got distracted over time. Some got lost in the land. Some got lost in sake. Some were killed. Some kept roaming but forgot why.

One roamed, searched, and remembered season by season, year by year. Clothes long-tattered. Dirt lodged in the folds of his skin. But this one kept his practice up. Every day he remembered himself a samurai and every day he practiced toward his ideal. His mind was sharp. His spirit was sharp. His blade was sharp.

As this samurai searched, he slowly pieced together a story of intrigue and politics. Hint by hint, clue by clue, person by person he oriented his life closer and closer to the killer. He endured long bouts of failure. He maintained committed calm with each success. Finally, after years of searching, he learned, through ample evidence, who the killer of his lord was.

The killer was as ignoble as men may get. The only skill he seemed to have was some strange, dark talent for covertly murdering people. He went to bars nearly every night and lost himself in his appetites.

The samurai prepared himself through meditation and practice. He honed his mind and his intention. He honored the code.

He went to the man's house. Walked directly into the man's bedroom. Sat down on the floor and waited. Hours passed and night spilled over the land. The stars journeyed along the sky. In the latest hours, the samurai shifted. He heard the approach of the man. The slide of the shoji screen. The trample of drunken feet.

He witnessed the man's silhouette in the doorway and saw him stumble toward his bed. The samurai stood and faced him.

The man seemed to be peering through a thick aura of sake as he slowly perceived the samurai before him. The samurai could feel the ignobility radiating from the drunken murderer. He felt right in the code. He pulled out his sword and stated his purpose.

The murderer turned toward the door, but the samurai's blade flickered in front of him. The man screamed and cursed. He looked at the samurai, bloodshot eyes beaming hate. He insulted the samurai and his lord. The samurai remained focused with an inner calm. The murderer bared his teeth, then seemed to realize he had no escape. He was doomed. As his last act, he gathered as much saliva as he could in his mouth and spit on the Samurai's face.

The samurai's mouth twitched. A moment of red washed over his face. He took in a deep breath. He looked the murderer right in the eyes, sheathed his sword, and walked away.

Why did he walk away?

I remember Tai, with her kind, untamable eyes asking me this question. Her gaze, a fierce love-inferno where she held me. I, the bumpy roughly-shaping metal. That question was the anvil. My answers became the hammer blows that shaped me.

Why did he walk away? First, I feel compelled to say that this story itself does not carry a clean and clear pan-cultural ethic. The samurai sought justice by killing the man. This is a strange source of ethical and moral questioning in and of itself. Can we bring justice to a murder by killing the murderer? What is the difference between killing and murder? Real questions: hammer blows to shape the mind and the people. If I hold this story within cultural context and consider that the code was a way of justice and truth for that people at that time, then in this event, the samurai was about to commit a clear act of justice. Why, then, did he sheathe his sword?

After holding her fire-eyes on me for a time, then letting me work the question for a much longer time, Tai did share more thought. She said that, in that moment, the samurai felt anger. A value greater than even delivering justice overcame the samurai. He could not swing his sword in anger.

I have carried this story for years. It nestles itself somewhere between my heart and gut, and occasion by occasion I pause to spend concentrated time with it. I share it with others when it feels like the right moment.

At this time, let us consider anger. When we are angry, we are in a state of reaction. Some boundary has been crossed and our deep mind flares up in protection. Energy courses through our bodies directed at fighting the offender. Anger is personal. In anger, we re-act the trespass to stoke the fire. In the very moment of anger, to swing the sword, then, has nothing to do with justice. Our higher functions, our greater ideals are not accessible. In the very moment of anger, to swing the sword at another means injuring the world and oneself. We injure by carving anger and reactivity into the world and into our personal systems. We train the neural pathways that do not inhibit. We imprint the biochemistry that is blind and reactive. We literally damage our physical hearts when we are consistently angry over time. We kill another, and in doing so, we send an echo into the world, into the greater mind, of the power of anger. This invites more anger. This means less higher functions of the human mind. Less justice.

At the same time, it seems that there is nothing inherently wrong with anger. It is our deepest and simplest response to trespasses. Healthy people have anger because they care about themselves and what they perceive as an extension of themselves. Allowing ourselves to feel angry and healthfully express our anger can be deeply healing and empowering.

One powerful ethic and deep challenge that this story points to is not to hand anger the sword. It is powerful to accept the anger when it arises. To even thank the anger. But not to give up the "I" so that the anger can do whatever it wants. This is no easy task. Anger can be a hurricane in the body.

Overwhelm and reactivity, such as anger, happen when boundaries get crossed. The heart and the higher functions of the mind go away when anger is in charge of protecting the being. We lose the here and now in those moments we are reacting to what already happened. When we are healthiest, it seems, we can feel these experiences and then allow them to pass. Then, with the recognition of the boundary that was crossed, with compassion for the protective instincts that came rushing forth, we can be here now and truly act. We can then include the heart in our actions. The heart, in some ways, is a relational organ that is always in the present.

If you are willing, I suggest you try a mental exercise. You can call it a meditation or a practice or a wonder. Whichever boat leaks the least for you. A version of this was first taught to me by Glen Hartelius. Thank you, Glen.

Begin by centering yourself in the here and now. Find a comfortable position, standing or seated where you have a relatively straight back. The straight back isn't rigid or flaccid, but firm. Like the directed mind.

Here, find your own way to center yourself. Maybe paying attention to the breath. Maybe through increased sensory awareness. Do this until you actually feel yourself "land." Then just hang there for a few breaths.

Now, bring the attention to the eyes.

Relax the eyes.

Let the light in at the periphery of your vision.

Breathe and be here.

Feel the physical sensations of the eyes and then wonder where you are looking from. Where, in your body, do you experience the observer? For most of us, it will feel like we are looking literally from the eyeballs. Now, move the observer back into your head. Imagine you are observing your visual field from the center of your head. Do this until you actually experience a perceptual shift.

Stay with this and notice the world. Notice how it feels.

If you have success here, then move the observer further to the back of your head. Observe the visual field from the back of your head. If you find this difficult, then just play with it. Wonder how your being could let you experience it. Only proceed after you have had an actual perceptual shift and you can sit with it for a while.

Proceeding, drop the observer downward. Whatever pace works for you. Down the spine. Pause and observe at different places as you move down. For most of us, the mind might have a quick second of experience and we will call it good, then want to proceed. Slow that down and wonder what it takes to be able to hold that observer there. Wonder what it feels like to be observing from that place as your baseline.

Finally, move the observer all the way to the heart. Observe the whole visual field from the heart. What happens when you look from the heart?

It is possible, that for some of us reading this, this may seem like a self-indulgent imagination project. What I wonder about is the actual subjective experience that we have when we do this. If you did try it, and you did move the observer, you most likely found that your thought chatter largely or wholly subsided. You may have found that your body felt differently as well. You may have felt grounded and calm. If we have a change in subjective experience, there must be a change in neurology and in biochemistry. If it is self-regulated, low intensity, not harmful to self or others, and experienced as positive, it's pretty darn likely that it is good for us. If we are more grounded and calm, this must affect our actions in the world. Over time, this affects values and identity.

It is worth noting that for many cultures over time, the mind was considered to be located in the heart. Not the head. The current western mind is unusual in this respect. In the subjective experience, when we locate the mind in the head, it may radically change many of our actions and values in the world.

Courage

Courage. From the French word, *cour*, which is from the Latin, *cor*, which is from the proto-indo european root, *kerd*. All meaning «heart.»

The suffix -*age* can mean a bunch of different things. It can mean "the outcome of," "the fact of," or "the physical effect of." Examples would be the words *seepage, wreckage, or spoilage.* Courage could be then considered the outcome or effect of the heart. Digging a bit deeper into the suffix and considering the quality of the word, I wonder about the term *faculty*. Faculty means the inherent mental or physical power. It seems that courage might well be considered the faculty of the heart.

A couple years ago, a ten-year-old mentee, Jake, was struggling with conflicts he was having with an adult. He became afraid of interacting with this person. This came at the same time that he found himself having social anxieties and performance anxieties. We talked a lot about this, though it was hard for Jake to speak of it. He had a tendency to work such things out internally and independently. Yet, here, it was clearly causing suffering. We did manage to identify some supports that he has and some ways he might shift things around. One day, while we were talking, we really looked at fear itself. I asked Jake what he was actually physically afraid of. He said, "heights."

So, we went to the nearby cliff. I believe it is important to take a step back at this moment. This was not *me* bringing *Jake* to the cliff so much as it was two human beings in the world asking real questions. We went to consult the cliff. We went to learn from the Place that held wisdom.

When we got up the cliff and could see the view of the wave-pocked bay and the gentle slope of evergreens reaching to the water's edge, Jake began to feel the real, embodied experience of fear. It was subtle at first because he was far back. It was simply the idea of moving forward that brought the first tremors of fear. Here, we started by working with the experience. We went through a similar process detailed earlier in this book: using the breath, senses, and somatic experience to process the fear and grow. This was a beautiful process to witness with Jake. He moved closer little by little. As he did, from time to time, we would pause and he would feel into his other fears. We would pair the learning so that his deep body and mind could get a sense of agency in moving through them.

When Jake got to his edge. Not *the* edge, but his edge: the place where his system was not ready to grow, the place near the cliff's edge where he just knew he would not feel comfortable and could not self-regulate, we paused. He felt it in his body. I then held out my hand.

I offered it and I asked Jake to feel what it was like in his body when he took it. He did. He felt the shift of safety, regulation, and calm. He took a step forward of his own accord.

It is so important to learn how to find your own edges and teach yourself how to grow. It is so important to take a hand sometimes and receive help and guidance. The help and guidance take us places we could not have managed to go on our own. They embolden us, imbue us with courage, so that we can learn to get there without the hand if needs be. So that we can be the hand for others.

Let's listen again to Hafiz.

> *Out of a great need, we are all holding hands and climbing.*
> *Not loving is a letting go.*
> *Listen.*
> *The terrain around here is far too dangerous for that.*

One essential part of the cliff experience that I did not just mention is the wonder. When Jake got to his regulation edge, he went to his senses and then he got curious. He wondered at the scene. When he got to the next edge, while holding my hand, we wondered together.

Wonder is in the present. Wonder is courageous by nature because wonder includes the heart.

Parker Palmer writes of the ancient meaning of heart as "the place where intellect and emotion and spirit will converge in the human self." He shares that "the courage to teach is the courage to keep one's heart open in those very moments when the heart is asked to hold more than it is able so that the teacher and student and subject can be woven into the fabric of community that learning, and living, require."

Wonder and courage brings us to a story about Lonnie. Lonnie was part of the wilderness therapy program I worked for in Alaska. Lonnie, like many kids in our group had a lot of trauma and a lot of challenges mixed with some awe-inspiring beauty and power. Like most Alaskan village kids, when he got overwhelmed, he ran away. He went to be alone in nature. Lonnie had the power to be our most cohesive and caring force of community. He also had the power to rend the group into tatters. The first time he really ran away meant spending hours looking for him. The rest of the group stayed on the beach edge in a makeshift camp while others took turns walking in a particular pattern and calling his name. We had initiated further stages of searching, and we were concerned that we would have to go to more extreme measures soon.

This was a way that Lonnie came back to himself. He needed to go away and just be himself and the wild world. This coping strategy was unfortunately practically dissonant with what our program could provide. We were in the deep wilderness and we were responsible, before anything else, for the safety of each participant. Safety meant knowing where everyone was.

So, we searched and called. Lonnie did not come out. We called the office and began another stage of response. We searched and called.

Finally, everyone reconvened and we had food together. We set out a bowl for Lonnie and talked about the next stage of trying to find him. The group was a taut bow string and the archer was blind. We had no idea where the arrow of our near future would land.

Then we heard it: the gushing of a whale spout. A participant pointed to the surfacing whale nearby. Then another pointed to the left of it. He shouted, "Lonnie!"

We all saw Lonnie standing on a spit of crustaceous land looking out over the water toward the whale. Despite the distance, we could all see the smile. He looked back at us and excitedly pointed to the whales. As a little kid might. He smiled and watched them.

I got up and walked out to where he was. Some part of me was compelled to say nothing to him. I stood near him and we faced the whales together in wonder.

It was wonder that pulled him out. Wonder with the whales pulled him enough out of his sadness and anger to bring him to the water's edge. Wonder with the whales pulled him so far out that he forgot the sadness and anger and looked back toward his community, calling them to witness the wonder with him.

Wonder and the whales were medicinal in every sense of the word.

And next, Lonnie came back to the fold. He ate with us. He talked. He got cold. He got frustrated again. He took a crap. He laughed. He helped with chores. He got annoyed at others. He slipped on rocks. He set up his tarp and unrolled his damp sleeping bag. He closed his eyes expecting to be woken up in the same way he had been for weeks. He came back to what was, for us, the daily.

And this was medicinal too.

While peak experiences guide the direction of the "I" toward love and truth and create powerful imprints on our systems, the daily experience is what constructs our baseline. The daily work, the most often used neurology, largely defines who we are and how we experience. We are, experientially, what we do the most. We live, largely, as the mundane. We see that, while big highs and lows happen, it is the little everyday work that does most of the crafting.

In this mundane, we meet some subtler aspect of every emotion. We barely touch the edges of every single spiritual insight, every peak experience. It is all there, available. We simply have it toned down to a whisper.

That is a big part of being human. In many ways, we are simple and small. We are concerned with the next meal, the relationship we have with our neighbor or loved one, the state of our back yard or our neighborhood. The bigger things can't be addressed all the time. If we tried, we wouldn't be able to effectively get dressed or brush our teeth.

Just because the larger beauties and problems, the cosmic aspects of being, are toned down to a whisper, it doesn't mean they are not affecting us. The whisper is how we work with them effectively on the daily. The annoyance we have with a coworker is the way we handle deep movers in our psyche, great social forces, cosmic shifts, and world conditions. We are not just individuals. We parse out the big things amongst us, and we each tell individual stories in order to make sense of them and craft them into something workable. Like a giant colony of termites working one tree.

Lonnie's peak was to take off and leave us for hours. And on the daily, we worked with him finding ways to take some moments off to the side or to take some deep breaths. The magnificent moment with the whales pulled him out of his deep process, and so on the daily we worked with ways to find wonder in the tide pools or in a red columbine flower.

One of the big challenges we face now, as a community, is that often times our cultural connection to the larger processes is focused on the negative. We are terrorized by the news. Most likely, each person reading this can easily tap into a host of problems, potentially fatal, that the world is facing. I wonder if we can just as easily tap into a host of powers and beauties that the world is facing right now. What happens if you try that? Do you find your psyche balanced in this way? Have you been given a balance of news from your media sources? If it is imbalanced, what does that do to your psyche? To your empowerment?

Thomas Merton says, "to allow oneself to be carried away by a multitude of conflicting concerns, to surrender to too many demands, to commit oneself to too many projects, to want to help everyone in everything, is to succumb to the violence of our time."

We are too small as individual psyches to handle such force, especially if it is not balanced by resources.

When we do make ourselves face the big conditions, and when we focus on the problems and the pain, some of us become soldiers who never leave the battle field. We fight without stop. The world-saving soldierly of us feel frantic because they feel like most people aren't doing enough; they feel they must shoulder extra burden. The soldier fights the hundred-headed hydra of causality for the injustice and suffering in the world. And if he or she manages to lop off a head, two more spring up. What ends up dying is either the soldier or parts of the soldier's heart. The soldier who manages to retreat with a wounded heart crafts together the smaller life of post-burnout. The soldier learns that the war never ends as long as he or she is fighting it. It seems a hard lesson, does it not? To have such noble and true intentions and strong efforts and to feel the inevitable defeat in the face of such large forces.

The opportunity, for the most courageous of the soldiers who have fought this way, is to heal the heart and to change. Not to give up, but to change. To recognize the noble intentions, and to find a new way toward them. The soldier may then leave the whole identity of soldiering. The person might learn that she or he is bigger than ever believed, is not alone, and that courage can lead us to learn how to transform the most terrible things in the most mysterious of ways.

And even after finding a more powerful and inherently regenerative way to help heal the suffering, most of us must face the fact that we must eat and find housing in a way that contributes to the system that seems to be causing most of the suffering. This is a deep grief that many of us can't afford to let ourselves feel fully or often. Is there a vein of shame running through us, often buried deep below the skin of our personas? Do we feel it sometimes when we fill up the gas tank or purchase a cheaper item that was made by sweat shops out of wood from the rainforest? What do we do with this situation? If we were to feel it fully, do we fear that it would lead inevitably to despair?

Some of us, it seems, swing the opposite direction. With great force of mind and with what seems to be a volatile ingredient of anger, we force our contributions to life-destructive actions into the realm of legitimate and just. We make our worlds smaller, into nations or cities or races or dogmas and we force ourselves into a position of righteousness. We must cling to these positions because if they falter, then the whole fabric of meaning, the entire armor against shame and despair will be destroyed. We will feel it all. And that would crush us. It would not be fair because we are feeling pain and suffering for things we were born into and that are so far out of our control that we are basically helpless to change them. So, we refuse to believe that they are sources of suffering. We buy bigger cars, attack the planet-sympathizers, refute the inherent rights and values of the natural world, and dehumanize vast expanses of humanity. Many of us are in situations where we are effectively stuck trying to get a "normal" job to pay the bills, take care of our basic needs and those of our loved ones. How can we hold being "bad" and "wrong" for the very actions that sustain us and our family? Such a terrible thing to hold as an individual. When we really look at what a difficult situation we are in, and how hard it could be on a human heart, how could we not be compassionate for this position? Do we not all do some version of this at different times in our lives?

When we choose to reason the harm out of our harmful actions we, unfortunately, face another hundred-headed hydra. We can never fully erase the knowing once we have known. We have to try to defeat it again and again and again. We have to chop off head after head of someone or something showing us that the jobs that are sustaining us are also damaging the integrity of our entire planet, or that they are harming people and the future generations, or that the natural places we grew up with are in peril.

I wonder if, when we battle the hydra from either position, we are truly battling the experience of feeling. What if we just don't want to feel the pain? What if we are afraid of the pain because we are terrified of the despair?

Fighting these feelings means armoring ourselves from all feeling. The armor is what protects us from a truth that the deep feeling animal of our body is constantly aware of. As our lives continue and the body experiences increasing pain, our dependency on this belief armor increases as well. Any threat to the belief is a threat to the entire reasoning structure that has made it possible to live without consciously feeling the terrible dissonance. Over time, we develop a certain numbness or inability to feel anything but the most intense and gross sensations in the body. We have cut off so much that we need greater extremes of sex, violence, and intoxicants to feel anything. It is entirely possible that the most fanatical of our human brothers and sisters actually began as the most sensitive, connected, and caring. Through life traumas or overwhelming influences, our brothers and sisters did not have the support, capacity, or tools to live with this pain of also being complicit with the destruction of so much of our world. If we step back and see some of the depth reasons for such fanatical reinforcement of destructive systems, how can we not feel compassionate?

The end game of this reaction pattern is to cling to the belief armor until the destructive behavior has annihilated us and all that we love: the great Armageddon drive that promises a final release from having to keep holding that structure. Like doing all the drugs in order to stop doing drugs. Or eating the whole box of cookies in order to not eat any more sweets. I suspect we can all see, and have experienced to some degree, the flaw in such behaviors.

Alternately, we soften and we feel. We feel the pain. We accept the conditions of the present as they are, not as we would like them to be.

Feeling the pain of harming what we love means facing our own smallness and the limits of our personal power to change our actions. We face that we cannot completely extract ourselves from the global economy and, though we do have the power to shift toward less harmful actions, we will continue to commit harm to our world purchase by purchase. This is a very hard way and it leads each one of us to toward that chasm of despair. All of us would rather avoid this on many levels. However, it is through the courage to feel and the inner power to navigate the chasm that we begin to release our smaller identity and our corresponding assumptions and demands of the world. We realize that others feel the same way. We drop this hyper-individualistic and atomistic project because we know at our core that we just can't hold it anymore. We become part of a larger movement of the larger life community.

Feeling in this way and transforming our identity into being part of something bigger is not revolutionary. Revolution means "to turn again." Turning again means having the same basic mindset while changing the superficial conditions. As Madame Blavatsky said, this is "like putting new wine in old bottles." Revolution is akin to the whole populace going into overwhelm. We lose our collective temper and break things and hope that it fixes things. This is a strange pattern that rarely works on the individual level. When we experience such an extreme of throwing a tantrum, there is a pleasurable feeling that usually follows in our personal systems. The body and mind finally release and they feel like they have let go of mounting tension. One problem is that we often do things in these experiences that produce shame once we become level-headed again. Our higher functions are not in charge, and we are reacting at a very base level. Another problem is the overall pattern. If this is the way we resolve tension, we teach ourselves, at the deepest embodied level, that, in order to feel good, we have to feel bad first. We learn a pattern that says we have to have the tensions mount and get completely fed up so that we can go into overwhelm so that we can then experience a release of tensions. The only part of a temper tantrum that is effective is that it communicates to the other the depth of the trespass and the intensity of how we are willing to respond. The depth and intensity can be communicated effectively without losing our heads. Without swinging the sword in anger.

A better word is evolutionary. Evolution means "to turn out." Like a spiral growing. Something new. Not passive. Growing and responding. Powerful.

Now, I suggest a pause as a part of the practice. The mind might want to keep going. If so, ask it why? Why not pause?

What are you actually feeling when you hold this content?

What happens when you connect to your living Place right here and right now? Do you feel a shift? Try it.

What happens if you move the observer from the eyes to the heart? Does it change your capacity to hold this content?

What happens when you give thanks?

This is the chapter of courage. Here, we ask ourselves how we can face the deep and frightening without shrinking or reacting or armoring. Can we look at great darkness and stay awake and engaged? What follows is dark, yes, and it is one perspective. The intention is not to feed more negativity. The intention is not to say that all the perspectives are fully correct. It is to look at darkness from one perspective just enough to glean wisdom from the looking, to metabolize it, and then to respond with vitality. What else should we do with darkness?

We'll start with a question: how do we evolve from conditions where media and political investments are flooding our systems with in-formation about the world? In my practice, working with youth, I have noticed a consistent trend for parents to justify showing their children violence on the screen because "it is a violent world" and they don't want to shelter their kids from it. Is it actually accurate to say that it is a violent world? If we keep getting told that it is a violent world and that we are on the brink of disaster, how does that influence the way we act in the world? The way we act in the world creates the world. Is it not true, then, that the story we tell about the world is what shapes it? Violence is an aspect of the world, yes. People do unspeakable things, yes. And how much of your daily actual experience, away from the media and entertainment, is filled with violence? Violence seems to be most prevalent in places where power-holders, who influence the media, have created war, poverty, or injustice. Even in many of these places, a majority of daily life, while it may contain fear and threat, is not actually violent.

In my experience, and I bet in yours, a vastly overwhelming majority of the people I have met across the world do not prefer a violent environment. When we say "it is a violent world" is that speaking from direct experience? Or is that an expression of a skillfully in-formed nervous system? Or maybe a traumatized nervous system that does not know how to handle negative content that happened in the past? This point is asking us for real discernment. What is the truth here? What would happen if we actually committed ourselves to recording every time we directly witnessed, committed, or were recipient of some form of violence in our daily experience while recording every time we experience some form of benevolence? What would the accurate statement about the world then be?

When we begin to believe that it is a violent world, that radically shifts our nervous systems. A nervous system is made to react to the perception of violence with sympathetic arousal, fight or flight. Our systems amp up in an effort to protect us. This takes energy away from the parts of our nervous systems that are associated with socially positive and connective behaviors as well as those that serve to help the body rest, digest, and regenerate. Over time, we become less and less physically healthy and we have less ability to be positively socially engaged. This means a deterioration of our personal lives and of the fabric of society.

When a system is conditioned to go into fight or flight, it wants to identify the threat. But the threat placed in our systems by media is an abstraction; it is often not physically present. The primal animal of our being needs to identify the threat in the physical world, because then it has the power to do something in response and to resolve the situation. If a deer hears a twig snap in the woods, it will remain aroused until it can identify that there is either a threat or there is not a threat. The deer's senses orient toward this identification. If twigs keep snapping and the deer can't see the threat, the deer will get nervous and, eventually, it will resolve the situation by fleeing to a place where it feels safe. A nervous system goes into arousal so that it can get to a place where it feels safe. We need a baseline of feeling safe.

Consistent media input of a threat is, for our animal, exactly like hearing the potential threat of twigs snapping all around us and, no matter what we do, not being able to find a place where we can get away from them. We can't find them and fight them. If we run, they are still there. If we can't resolve the situation, we go into a state of learned helplessness, which, for humans, usually creates some experiential cocktail of anxiety, depression, or other disorders. Our simple animal, out of a need to resolve the arousal and take care of the personal system, will often resort to some form of displacement. If we cannot physically respond to all the threat and negativity we have experienced through media, the mind will find something that we do have the power to respond to. It will find a new recipient to hold the charge of that threat: the mind's best guess at an immediate explanation for why the being feels the way it does. It is a brilliant last-ditch self-protective function of the nervous system. Unfortunately, it is not favorable toward creating well-functioning people in a happy and healthy community. We have almost no direct contact and no control over potential nuclear war, the destruction of the biosphere, institutionalized oppressions, or the workings of the economy, so our personal systems will give us something that we can at least react to and resolve. We will often identify other people as a threat. The enemy. Maybe our minds will choose race or political affiliation or gender or some other label as the threat. We will fight or flee from that. We will fight or flee from each other.

The other general nervous system option in response to a threat, which is very much different from fight or flight is to freeze. When we are facing the continuous conditioning of feeling threatened and our nervous system keeps choosing to freeze, this can create a baseline experience of becoming disassociated with others, the physical world, and the sense of self. We tend to have higher suggestibility, which means we are more prone to accept and act on others' suggestions. We also lose empathy. We lose feeling. We lose essential functions of our being that are associated with our core humanity.

It is important to remember that fight, flight, or freeze are not cognitive choices. They are primal choices of the nervous system, of our deep animal, and our entire waking consciousness plays catch-up to this choice, giving us a viable story to explain the experience.

When we, the people, are conditioned into a state of being scared and we can't resolve our arousal, we are, at the core mammalian level, primed to cling to some suggested avenue for resolution. It is the way that each individual works to protect himself or herself. Our higher functioning and our social bonds wane. We become divided and suggestible. We vote for war to find peace. We destroy our lands to create abundance. We build walls to keep us free. We are not, in these times, remotely at our best. We don't choose our best leaders. We are not well-equipped to tend to each other and to our shared planetary home.

We need medicine. We need to take in less poison. This starts with clearer and clearer identification of what the poison is. We need to be conscious of it. The reason for this section of the book is not to say that this is the absolute truth of the situation. Rather, this is a plea for us to come together and look at these things even more and to figure out what is actually true. We need to see the conditions clearly as they are and to be able to see clearly how they are affecting us. Then we can make informed and wise choices. Little by little, most likely.

If we are working toward the truth and we are honest in how we feel, we can figure out what works for us and our relationships and what does not.

With the truth of who we are and how we work, we can see when and how to take our medicine. One part of this is accepting and loving our basic mammalian nervous system that needs to fundamentally resolve threats.

One simple way that we are made to do this is to pay attention. Here and now. The reality as it is.

The senses teach us, primally, that there is no threat present. If we are conditioned into sustained arousal, it will most likely take repeated time and effort to teach our systems that there actually is no physical threat hear and now. The mind often revolts, insisting that there actually is a threat of war or ecocide or economic demise or some other problem. But these are conditioned thoughts, deeply entrenched neural networks with a lot of attractive force. They are not operating on the same channel as the physically immediate here and now. If we know that we are teaching our minds to resolve threat, and we know that we are doing this so that we are better equipped to respond well to such bigger challenges, then we keep taking the simple medicine of coming to our senses.

Accepting and speaking the truth is medicine. If we practice coming closer to the root of our fears and we communicate them, then we are no longer using displacement to resolve our arousal. If we accept that we are sad or angry because of the state of the Earth or our society and we have the courage to speak that to others, our minds won't have to find some other source of the problem. We won't transfer all of our anger and fear onto a mission against a tangible enemy. This truth-telling process can be frightening, vulnerable, and painful, but such a deep relief.

What truths do we bury and carry? What are we afraid to admit to ourselves and others?

Have you ever had thoughts about how the impending doom of a dying biosphere makes planning for the future idiotic? Have you ever looked at a retirement fund or thirty-year investment and thought you might be lying to yourself about ever getting to see it? Have you stopped and watched cars and people rushing by you, tied to clocks and to do lists, not daring to look up or gaze at the wind in the trees and thought that we might all be participating in a desperate web of collusion? Is it a terrifying and strange thought, and do you let it pass quickly so that you may continue your work in the web, buying groceries for your family or putting money in your checking account? Does human life feel futile sometimes? Does this spear your gut when you look at a child you love playing so innocently with life?

If so, thank you for your courage.

What if it is true? What if the biosphere is dying?

The wolf did come for the boy who cried wolf.

How do we live into this possibility?

Have you ever clung to the idea of fleeing?

Many are actually working very hard on the dream of fleeing and colonizing other planets. Our technical skill points to it as an actual possibility within an honestly slim set of very particular conditions and a lot of unknowns. What I wonder about is the deep mental and spiritual aspects of this endeavor. This intellect-driven dream could be the product of a heart in flight from painful conditions. A heart that does not want to face the suffering of the planet and the results of our behavior. A heart that wants a new environment where that suffering is not present. It is good to remember that wherever we go, we take ourselves with us.

Have you ever fled a relationship because you could not get over just one aspect of it? Most of it was good, but there was one nagging element that you experienced as a cause of suffering, so, instead of attending to the positive and doing the personal work with the negative, you severed the whole thing. It was easier to leave because you didn't have to change. If you have experienced this, and I bet most of us have in some way, have you experienced realizing after the fact just how much you threw away?

I suspect that we cannot fathom what it would mean to throw away our relationship with our planet. We cannot fathom what the wind and the chickadees and the clouds and the scruffy plants in the sidewalk cracks and the cycles of seasons and the sounds of weather shifting and the unseen and unknown waves of energy that surround us are actually doing to consistently create our humanity. I suspect that to leave the Earth means to leave humanity. I suspect that this may not be possible for our systems, as resilient as we may be. I suspect that it is a very foolish thing to put any time and energy into.

There is nowhere to spit. And, in context of our planet, there is nowhere to run.

Have you clung to fighting?

We can use tech-fixes to try the old man versus nature approach. We are seeing our biosphere struggle with the fruits of the idea that technology can replace nature right now. Is it honestly possible to replace the trees and the oceans and the atmosphere with technological creations? Even if it were, which, honestly it is not, how could we be remotely human afterward? Humanity would not survive.

There is no way to fight.

Have you clung to freezing?

The inertia of our actions and our ways will keep going if we dissociate. We cannot separate our minds from our bodies or our bodies from the Earth. We cannot close our eyes and make problems go away.

There is nowhere to freeze and hide.

How do we simply accept that we have these experiences and that they are tied to feelings. Start with the truth as a foundation. Not to even do anything about them. We feel despair. We want to run. We fight. We flee. We freeze. We are not alone in the experience. We don't have to think it alone. We don't have to solve it alone. We don't have to feel it alone.

I am just one voice. When you are calm and here and your heart is willing to feel, what does your voice say?

We are not alone. We are not just individuals. We are also the biosphere. As so much of this book points to, we are an unfathomably powerful and responsive planetary web of generativity.

This is not a book about keeping comfort and luxury, as this chapter particularly illustrates. It is not about wilderness survival. The "man versus nature" idea of wilderness survival is a lie. Humanity cannot be versus nature any more than a finger can be versus a body. No trees means no breath. No wild oceans means no humans. This book is not even about the survival of the wilderness itself. This is a book about Living. Living happens only in the now. There are no guarantees. Everything changes and us, the wilderness, the planet itself, and even the sun will at some point transform completely and be no more.

With no guarantees and with no absolute knowledge, we have a choice to step into living and to explore being the fullness of our human experience, of ourselves as people and planet. Humans, in our fullness, have the celestiality of the jellyfish, the opaque mystery-mind of the raven, the myth-deep wobble-song of the woodthrush. We are wilderness and, together, we thrive. We are temporary but we have also all made it through ice ages. What else might we do in this grand story? How might we manage to tell it toward far future generations?

In the face of such grand and ubiquitous impermanence, how do we choose to live?

Do we wallow in darkness and fade quickly?

Do we exhaust the darkness by tending to the light?

How do we choose to live?

I had a teacher who spent a good portion of his life as a devout Buddhist. He transformed, as all things do, and now walks a different path. He told me a story from his days as a Buddhist practitioner.

His teacher was a rinpoche who had gone through a year meditating alone in a cave in Tibet. His teacher's teacher would come on occasion and would speak to him through a hole in the wall of the cave, offering guidance when needed. The rinpoche, then a student, shared that while he was meditating he went through weeks of torment. He was working on a meditation to craft a detailed image of the Buddha in his mind's eye. When he got to the point of completing the image in his mind, suddenly a demon would pop up from behind the Buddha. The demon would be far bigger than the Buddha and would be wielding a giant sword. The demon would pull back his sword, swing, and chop off the Buddha's head.

The student struggled to focus on the Buddha and keep the demon from appearing, but he found no success. Time after time, unbidden and unwanted, the demon came and chopped off the head of the Buddha.

Finally, he shared this with his teacher and asked for guidance. His teacher listened and paused for a long time. Then he spoke through the hole in the wall, "when the demon comes again to chop off the head of the Buddha, picture an even bigger Buddha."

The rinpoche shared that this, strangely, was the path that worked for him. The demon came and chopped off the head of the Buddha, but behind the demon and the little headless Buddha was an even bigger Buddha. And if another demon came, then an even bigger Buddha was behind him.

This story is childishly simple. There is no satisfaction of having the mind control to keep the demon from coming. Yet, I suspect it is one of the more profound and wise stories I have heard. We cannot keep the demons from coming. Violence and pain are a part of this world. Always here. Because they are present, they don't have to be so big that they cut off the head of what is beautiful, healthy, and empowering in this world. We grow what we pay attention to. We cannot smite all evil and suffering. We can choose to cultivate powers that are greater. We can exhaust the darkness by tending to the light.

Wonder is a bigger Buddha. Tiny demons become manageable next to a giant Buddha of wonder. Wonder is a positive, generative engagement with the present. When we are in wonder, we lose our small selves. We are something mysterious witnessing something mysterious. Wonder, as it is, is bigger than all of the suffering detailed in this book.

Wonder is a feeling state of connection. We *feel* wonder. We become what we feel. It is possible that the most courageous act we can take in this life is to feel. Feeling is consciousness of what is taking place within our own bodies. When we feel another, we become conscious of them within ourselves- the most intimate relationship possible. We become not one, not two. Feeling always comes with pleasure and with pain. To let something impermanent and always changing inside of us means to accept the pain that will go with it. It means to accept the conditions of loving. To love is to invite grief into our home. Grieving is a face of love.

With feeling and with courageously engaging the heart, we open the channel for wisdom.

There is no metric for wisdom. We don't own it. There is nothing to own. Wisdom simply is.

Wisdom is a cosmic force we learn to carry through us.

The Tiger's Eyelash

Here is a story.

It is inspired from a traditional story, and it has transformed through many mouths and many cultures into a unique incarnation that is here now on this page.

It is a story for you.

Once, long ago in a village in southeast Asia, the people were living in a time of war. The forces of hatred had gripped the hearts of certain people and those people used their power to do violence.

This is the recipe for war.

So, war was in the land and in the human hearts, and those with the power to do so had conscripted people from the villages and the fields. They put weapons in their hands, put sufficient hate and fear in their hearts to make them kill, and then sent them into the field to slaughter one another.

In one small village, a husband and wife had been living a very happy life. They loved and appreciated one another and they were daily thankful for what they had been given. The land provided enough and they supported and admired each other throughout the days.

Then the husband was called to war. And those in power forced him to leave his happy life and his loving partner.

He lived war for one full year.

Those in the village, including his wife, grieved the loss of their sons and husbands, and prayed for their protection and survival and that they would come back so they could live a life that was never again touched by such hatred and violence.

This grieving and praying happened on both sides. Which is one of the tragedies of war.

So, after a year of waiting, the village was notified that those who survived would be returning home. The wife lined up with all the other family members and gripped and rubbed her hands as she waited for the men to approach. They looked pale and skinny and the lights in their eyes had retreated so deeply that to look at them was to stare into a hollow darkness. But, one by one, the families and the men found each other. In those moments of connection, one by one, they seemed to remember their light, and the tears came, and the hearts broke open.

But for the wife and others, no such moment came. Some loved ones did not return. And the hearts wailed and skin grew cold and the world seemed to tremble and fall apart. And for these families, the walk home was long and dark and empty.

The wife, alone, made her way to her house, and as she set her hand on the railing of the porch where she and her husband used to sit and laugh together, she could barely feel her own touch. She was a shell of something that used to feel.

She knew she needed to lie down, and, barely conscious of herself, she opened the door to the house. As she did, she heard a rustling in the bushes. It was a strange rustling. The world seemed to shift and it became momentarily crisp. She became alert and felt a strange heat in her heart. She heard the noise again. She turned and looked into the bamboo and waited.

From the darkness emerged two hands, parting the bamboo to reveal a gaunt face with hollow eyes staring at her. A wave of heat rushed through her chest, causing her whole body to jolt. She looked as deeply as she could at the face, and the features began to bend into a deep familiarity. It was her husband. She screamed, "husband!" and almost fell over for her lack of breath.

His eyes widened with fear.

She called, "Husband, it's you! Oh thank God!" and she ran toward him.

Terror washed over his face, and he turned and ran.

Her joy collided with a wall of rejection and, overwhelmed by confusion, she screamed "No! Come back!" She ran into the bamboo after him, but he fled with the power and speed of the sambar deer fleeing the tiger. He was gone. She stood there in shock. Tears came. She stood there until her legs almost collapsed. Then, almost without any of her own will, her body lead her back to the house and into her bed.

The next morning, she woke and wondered if it was a spirit or a hallucination.

She scrambled up, opened the door, and looked toward the bamboo.

The figure of her husband, huddled by the edge of the bamboo, jumped up, wild terror in his eyes, and fled again into the bamboo. She ran after him, but soon realized that there was no way she could catch him.

And so it happened. Later that day, the same thing. That evening, the same. The next day, the same.

By the third day, she had become desperate to find some way to catch her husband. No matter how fast she was, no matter what she said, she had failed. The desperation made her soften, and in that softening, a deep and wise part of her emerged. She knew that she needed help.

So, she ate some food, put on fresh clothes, packed a lunch, and made her way to the wise woman who lived up in the foothills.

The forest seemed to grow around and through the wise woman's hut. The hut seemed as much a part of the land as a glacial boulder or an old fern-covered stump. She knocked on the door and waited.

As the door opened, it brought a spicy and musty array of smells. The wise woman had skin like sand dunes and in her eyes was the sparkle of Venus on a clear night.

"Yes, dear? How may I help you?" An old and almost forgotten way of kindness in her presence.

After the woman had explained, and the wise woman had done her wise listening, they stood in silence. Only the sounds of the birds and the wind in the forest. The wise woman nodded slowly. "Yes. Yes. I can help you. Come in and sit down."

The woman watched as the wise woman set about her craft. She brought a small pot to near simmer. From her shelves, she gathered six small glass bottles filled with curious plants and other objects. She hummed a loamy tune as she did her work. She put a pinch of the contents of each bottle in the simmering liquid until she came to the sixth.

She opened up the bottle, turned it upside down, and gasped. "Oh no…" she droned. She shook her head. "Oh no…"

The woman jumped up. "What? What happened?"

"Oh dear, I am very sorry."

The woman walked up to the wise woman, her heart a rapidly beating drum. She needed to catch her husband, and she could not handle another rejection. "Sorry? Sorry for what? Can't you do it?"

The wise woman shook her head. "My dear, I am sorry but I am missing the most important ingredient in your husband's medicine. Without this, you will never heal your husband."

The woman felt a surge of energy course through her. She loved her husband, and in that moment, the love turned to something fierce and unconquerable. Her eyes fixed firmly on the wise woman. "What is the ingredient? I'll go get. Just tell me what you need." She took one solid breath. "I will get my husband back whatever it takes."

The wise woman's eyebrows raised, and the sparkle in her eye became something so big and so old that you must fear it. "My dear, what propose is no easy task. The ingredient I am missing is an eyelash from the great tiger of Makai."

The woman felt dread. But the love was stronger and it pushed the dread aside. "The great tiger that lives at the top of Makai mountain?" The wise woman nodded. The woman took a breath and felt the love give her strength. "I will have my husband back," is all she said.

The wise woman nodded. "Very well. If you choose this task, then listen closely. This is what you must do…"

The woman returned to her hut and again saw her husband flee at her sight. Though her heart wept and called her to run after him, she kept her focus. She called into the bamboo, "I will return to you, husband. And I will see you well again." She then went into her home and gathered everything she needed.

She went into the village and bought some supplies.

She set foot on the path that eventually lead to Makai mountain. The path was rarely trodden and the stormy season had left it full of rocks and mud.

The path ended at the base of the mountain. The tales of the great tiger of Makai mountain had long since scared away any curious explorers. To get to the top meant to enter the wilderness. To follow the meandering paths of the deer and the pig. To walk as the land and water carves you to walk. The woman entered. The forest received her as a lake receives a flower petal.

The way was not easy. In fact, the way was a terrible and confusing mission to find any way at all. The plants were mighty and the ditches deep. The rocks denying. The forest so thick it blinded her of the four directions. At times, she cried. She sat and pounded the faceless landscape with her fist. She prayed for courage. She felt as if she had been swallowed by a beast and there was no way out. She wondered at the cruelty of life. And each time, that deep love and that deep commitment pulled her up, and she walked on.

At last, the vegetation thinned, and the air took on the light and sweet taste of the high sky. She saw the knoll that held the ancient cave which the tiger had made his lair. She slowed her walk and opened up her senses, alert to the danger she was stepping toward.

The cave was at the base of where the rocky knoll jutted skyward. A long open slope spread out in front. The woman stared at the dark entrance. The entrance to the lair was a black mark on the land. A reminder to all of the presence of death. The woman imagined the great tiger sitting just inside the line of shadow, staring at her. Hungering for tang of blood.

She unrolled her pack and walked to the farthest edge of the open slope. There she set a chunk of delicious deer meat. She then returned to her pack, which was positioned far enough away from the meat for her to barely see it, unrolled her ground blanket, and sat. She waited.

The silent sun barraged her skin. The flies pecked holes in her flesh. She waited.

At dusk, she saw the tiger.

His body was a terrible greatness. Larger than any words. The choppy sea of his muscles made her body seize with fear. He walked toward the meat with the ease and arrogance of a king.

When he got to the meat, he paused and sniffed the air. He turned and looked directly at the woman. Held his gaze on her. She clenched. Her body screamed to run. But the love of her husband worked its secret force within her, and she found the strength to stay.

The tiger turned back to the meat, grabbed it, and walked back into the cave.

The next morning, the woman woke. She did not remember how or when she fell asleep. She took another piece of meat and walked the slope. This time she set the meat halfway closer to the lair. She then grabbed her pack and blanket and set herself halfway closer to the meat.

Again she waited. Again: the sun; the flies. Dusk. The tiger. Her fear. His stride. The pause before the meat. His massive head turning. His eye gaze playing a song of doom within her body. She remembered the love. She sat and waited. The tiger grabbed the meat and returned to the cave.

And so it went. The woman cutting distance in half each time the tiger took the meat. The meat closer to the lair. Her closer to the meat. Her body weakening. Her mind pleading for reprieve from this terrible task. The love fueling her.

Finally, the day came when the woman set the meat directly in front of the lair. She set herself directly in front of the meat. Her weak and weary body felt like a hollow thing. Her mind and spirit were strong, though, and she sat with the confidence of a boulder.

She waited. The blackness of the cave directly before her. The scattered bones. The smell of death. As she stilled, she became aware of a strange sound. Like waves of a distant ocean. From just inside the cave. It was the tiger's breath. On the edge of shadow, the edge of her vision, the edge of imagination, she thought she might just barely see the image of the tiger's great head.

She sat. The waves of fear came like squalls. The love steadied her. She remained.

Then a movement from within the darkness. The tiger's head emerged. The eyes of the greatest predator did not look at the meat. The woman sat. Some deep spark within her knew it was time.

The tiger stepped closer until his head was right before her face and right above the meat. The woman had her first thought in days. In her head, she asked the tiger directly: "please." No other words. The rest of the request was in a far older language than human tongues. She felt every atom of the air. She waited.

Then, a softness moving through her body. She pulled in her breath. The tiger bowed his head toward the meat and waited, not taking it. The woman could barely feel her arm as she extended it outward. She pinched an eyelash. Breathed out. Breathed in. And pulled.

The roar of the greatest beast of death consumed her entire being. Her vision went white. Her body consumed by the tunnel of sound and hot breath. The great teeth inches from her face and wider than her head. She became no thing in the face of her own annihilation.

Then a rush of warmth again. And she felt her familiar body. And she saw the tiger grab the meat. Turn and walk back into the cave.

Only shadow and rock and bones before her. The hot sun. The empty air.

The woman remembered. She looked down at her fingers and saw the eyelash. Her hand started to tremble, and she quickly reached in her pocket with her free hand, pulling out a small container. She placed the eyelash in it. Wrapped it. Tied the wrap to her body. Gathered her things. Walked away, willing herself not to run.

She had the eyelash. Her heart wanted nothing more than to be able to teleport directly back to the wise woman's hut.

But she could not. She had to now go down the mountain.

The way was not easy. The plants were mighty and the ditches deep. The rocks denying. The forest so thick it blinded her of the four directions. At times, she cried. She wondered at the cruelty of life. The deep love and the deep commitment pulled her up, and she walked on.

The path as the base of Makai mountain was full of mud and rocks from the stormy season.

The woman was dark with dust and sweat. Pocked with welts from flies. Thin with hunger. But her heart was as fierce as any great tiger.

She came, at last, to the wise woman's hut.

The wise woman answered and stood in the doorway staring at the woman, holding her in the Venuslight of her ancient gaze. "I see that you have done it."

When the wise woman spoke, the woman's resolve softened. She felt the pain. She remembered who she was. She remembered her husband and her longing. She felt the urge to cry, but would not pause to do so. She pulled out the container with the eyelash and shakily handed it to the wise woman. "Please," was all she said.

The wise woman grunted and nodded. "Follow me." The wise woman grabbed the same pot with the medicine she had begun and warmed it up over the fire. "You have succeeded. You have found the medicine that will heal your husband." A hint of a smile passed over the wise woman's face. She opened the container and held the eyelash over the concoction. She made as if to drop it in, then looked at the woman with a gaze as terrifying as the tiger's. She pursed her lips and blew the eyelash away.

The woman's heart dropped to the bottom of the Earth. Her body convulsed. She could not breathe. When her breath recovered, she screamed, "what have you done?"

The wise woman's gaze switched. Her eyes became endless pools of love. "My dear," her voice a lullaby and a blanket. The woman paused, held in a strange stasis. The wise woman smiled. "The eyelash is not the medicine you've returned with." She took a deep sweet breath. "The way you treated that tiger... go home and treat your husband the same way."

The Fifth Need: A Great Need

What if we treated our bodies the same way? What if we treated ourselves the same way? Each other the same way? Our Place the same way? The world the same way?

What if we all need a gentleness that only love can conjure and sustain?

To be fully human, we have five needs: shelter, water, fire, food, and love.

In that infamously cruel experiment of Frederick II's we clearly see the necessity of love. The caregivers never touched any of the babies. The babies all died.

They received no touch. They received no love. And they died. So too with our world. Each human holds the world entire. So, primarily, the love that is needed is love within each and every one of us. We court loving ourselves in our deepest nature. Inwardly courted love, by nature, radiates.

Courage is the faculty of the heart. And we cannot talk about the faculties of the heart without talking about love. The fifth need of survival is love. We cannot live without it.

The natural world teaches us how to love. Again and again we witness unceasing changes and we suffer the pangs of loss. The redcedar that we loved is felled by the storm. The doe in our back yard loses her fawn to a speeding car. The chicken that let us hold her in our arms develops a limp and one day never leaves the hen house. The douglas squirrel that we so pleasurably witnessed busily gathering maple leaves for his wintery home one day disappears, leaving only a tuft of fur behind. The glaciers recede on the mountains in the distance until one year they don't return. The polar bear drowns in a sea of water, eyes searching to the last for that absent glint of floating ice. Each pang of loss strikes the mindfulness bell within us, resonating through our being with the question, "will you love what you can't keep forever?"

"Will you be with me still?"

"When I die, will you notice what I have left behind? And will you have the courage to love that?"

We learn to love our partners, our children, our mothers and fathers, our community, and ourselves as we do a wild thing.

The undomesticated world coaxes the heart into a state of vulnerability. And that state is the only state where we can be present. That is the only state where we can actually feel the uncontrollable gravity of love and let ourselves be drawn into orbits we do not understand. As we develop our relationship with the greater being of our Place, we find ourselves, without voluntary effort, feeling those draws with other people. We learn that the commitment of partnership has very little to do with control. We learn patience and listening and true responsiveness. We learn how to weather storms and to let them awaken the aliveness in us and in our relationships. We learn to be still with another. We learn to let ourselves rest in that most vulnerable state of admiration. We learn to simply observe the frightened bird calls of the mind, to let them pass, and to witness what happens next. We have the power to do this with our relationships intact and growing still.

Listen.

The winds around you are calling, asking you to feel them with your fine fur.

Listen.

The creeks are shifting the world of your loving stone by stone.

Listen.

Out there.

A calling.

Place is the university of Love.

Breaking the Heart Open

Lead

Here is a story
to break your heart.
Are you willing?
This winter
the loons came to our harbor
and died, one by one,
of nothing we could see.
A friend told me
of one on the shore
that lifted its head and opened
the elegant beak and cried out
in the long, sweet savoring of its life
which, if you have heard it,

you know is a sacred thing.,
and for which, if you have not heard it,
you had better hurry to where
they still sing.
And, believe me, tell no one
just where that is.
The next morning
this loon, speckled
and iridescent and with a plan
to fly home
to some hidden lake,
was dead on the shore.
I tell you this
to break your heart,
by which I mean only
that it break open and never close again
to the rest of the world.

–Mary Oliver

"They moved away, and the next year they came to the same place to get salmon. When the salmon came again and ran up, a shining one was on top. Then he told them not to spear it, but it was the very one they tried to spear. By and by he made a spear for himself and speared it. When he pulled it ashore, and the salmon died, he too had died. He did not know that it was his own soul."

–Haida chief of Those Born at House Point, Tom Stevens.
As recorded by J.R. Swanton

When I was in high school, our school was blessed with a visit from Coretta Scott King. She spoke with great courage and clarity of the way of peace and justice amongst people in the face of so much violence and injustice. I can't remember exactly what she said, but I do believe that I will never forget what happened when she finished speaking. I hope that this memory will be an intimate companion as I take my final roll toward the grave. Everyone clapped. As I placed my hands together, a sudden force far greater than I swept through me, a primal strength that shot through my legs and without my own will I was lifted up. I stood there clapping. I was the only one in my school standing. I could not sit and I felt the deep surge of love and truth fill me with a buoyancy that would never be sunk. Not ever. I stood there for what may have been a full minute, and then that power began to leave me. I became self-conscious and I looked around for a moment, seeing that I was the only one standing. My legs became weak and I small and I began to sit down. There, at that precise moment, I experienced the true power and wonder of what some might call God. Right as I was falling, all the people in the row to the left of me and to the right of me spontaneously stood up as if catching me, catching us. My faltering legs paused, and the strength of the people took hold of them, raised me back up as one simple part of a great, great many. The whole auditorium stood.

May that day teach me for the rest of my life.

This is the final chapter: the chapter of spaces. Spaces for each of us to live into. Questions upon which wonder will lean. And in this way, we will author the great story of our world, of ourselves.

In an interview with Krista Tippett, Brené Brown asks the question, "what if our capacity for whole-heartedness can never be greater than our willingness to be broken-hearted?"

What strange container becomes whole as it breaks? How does this odd, courageous bender of time and space that we each hold at the center of our being break with each relationship it says yes to? How does this mystery organ become stronger as it becomes more vulnerable?

What happens when your heart breaks?

We will lose everything we love. And so the heart, in loving, will break. For all of the Place connection we have journeyed through in this book, our Place itself will die. Inevitably, the universe will lose and never recover or remember this crumbly, wet planet. This chaos ball of connections, vibrating into itself will change into oblivion, and there will never be a knowing of human hands beating drums and cacophony of coyote calls; no shade of the stretching oak tree or towers of crumbling basalt cliffs; no ornery camels gnawing spiky desert plants; no fire like Earth fire; no food like Earth food; no strange one shape of the water of Earth; no dens or houses; no sticks; no breaking bones; no ring of bird song; no wonder like a human in wander; no mind like Our Mind; no heart like Our Heart. How can a container made to love and to connect to every one of these things hold their passing?

Is the heart that breaks open the personal heart?

In opening, does it connect to other beings, and, if so, what does it become?

Whose heart is it?

Right now, wherever you are, can you fathom what you will actually miss? Can you feel where your heart is protected for fear of loving what you will lose? Can you feel how it wants to break open exactly there? What if these were your last breaths? How does this heart want to live? Can you pause and imagine just how big this globe is? How far the sky around you stretches. The story of the breath that enters you, becomes you, and exits you. Can you feel your ancestry so alive in your bones, vibrating with what was won from so many willing hearts? Can you imagine who you would be without willing hearts to have guided you, to have loved others and the world? Do you feel a calling to join this lineage? To be courageous and to love? To break as so many before you have done, and to let your broken-open heart be the soil for next generations?

If you have a moment to step outside, what happens if you do so and remember where you are? This big temporary wonder spiraling through expanding beyond. What work does love have to do in the world through you?

Widening now. Breaking. Who are you?

Are you the tiger or the woman or the man in bushes? Are you the wise woman or the mountain? The stormy season? The eyelash falling to the floor? How, as wide and varied as you are, can you teach how to love in the face of terrible loss? How do you teach the world to sheathe the sword but live justice? What wounded men are in the bushes spreading violence and hate through the planet, waiting for some deep cosmic wisdom in you to heal them? Are you the courage that faces the tiger? The wrathful roar? Where does the shape of your love, your broken-open heart, begin and end when all things are changing?

How do you, as the world, bring justice without simply putting new wine in old bottles? In your broken-open courageousness, how will you teach us the way to disarm the aspects of people and the systems that are harming? To change when some parts of you do not want to change? To seek the truth as it is, not as you would like it to be? What does love look like as justice through you?

Naomi Klein asks, "what if part of the reason so many of us have failed to act is not because we are too selfish to care about an abstract or far off problem, but because we are utterly overwhelmed by how much we do care? And what if we stay silent, not out of acquiescence, but in part because we lack the collective space in which to confront the raw terror of ecocide?"

What happens when we break the walls, let the fear drop, and allow the heart to open? Let the heart break open. Let all our hearts break open.

This book is the story told by just one heart. There are billions of human hearts.

When the heart breaks, the fears that had been holding it crumble forth. This heart fears speaking of all of the connections that have not been made in this book. Fears the mistakes and inconsistencies. Fears that writing about social justice, ecocide, racial injustice, war, the economy, and oppression will harden the hearts of those I love toward me.

This heart is terribly afraid that the world is dying. This heart is afraid of not being able to change that. Afraid of being so small that I cannot understand how love and truth will go on after that. This heart is pre-emptively grieving the absence of a human smile in the universe, the touch of my lover, the warmth of a child against my chest, the smell of the Salish Sea, the bloom of a tiger lily, the taste of a peach, the feel of warm grass underfoot. This heart does not want these things to pass, and I don't know how one human heart can possibly hold all of this love and all of this grief.

When the fears have crumbled and cascaded forth, what follows is a strange and inexhaustible force far greater than the heart had ever previously experienced. There is a resilient force in us all that can face the most terrible of forces. Since that day with Coretta Scott King, I know that when legs falter, others can stand. We pull each other up. Since that day with the raccoons I know that if the sense of self shifts to include more than the little I, my race, my tribe, or even my species, we will join a greater, supportive power. The job is to stand when we can, to keep loving, and to orient to truth.

We are standing together, now, at the edge of time.
Everything will go.
What does your heart say when it breaks?

In my time at Naropa University, we practiced facing heart breaking challenges. Our hearts broke open again and again. Again and again we found that as those little containers broke, there was a larger container holding them. Like Russian dolls. Like bigger Buddhas. Like an ever-widening "I".

Rabbi Reb Zalman told us once that, "in this time of human history the sangha is the guru." The sangha is a Buddhist term for the community. A guru is a teacher or guide, especially in the spiritual sense. The teacher is the community. We will do this together. No one leader can hold this.

Are we hospice workers for a dying biosphere? Are we midwives for a new era?

I suspect that, right now, the biotic congress is in session and we are all voting. The members of the Earth congress vote with their actions. Every action affects each other being. We are a relationship. The answer will only be perceived in hindsight. So we must simply Live.

In effect, in facing ecocide or other devastations, we are in no different a personal situation than any other human who has ever existed. We are facing the exact same dilemma: "how do I love and live fully when I know that everything I love, and I myself, will die and be forgotten?"

How do you hold this question?
Who do you need to be to have the capacity to hold this?

I had a kung fu teacher, Danny, who was one of the most intense human beings I have ever met in my life. He lived with a semi-feral pack of half-wolves in a ramshackle cabin at the end of an obscure dirt road on the edge of the Deerfield River in Massachusetts. He and his dogs fasted one day a week, he practiced a form of bodywork a few days a week for income, and throughout it all he literally lived and breathed kung fu. I love that man, and a reason I do is because he struck me as so ruggedly honest. He did not waste his valuable life's story trying to project his goodness to others. Rather, there was always this sense that his scrutiny was turned inward and he was not convinced by his own fabrications of self-image. Like he was holding his core being to the fire with a love and ferocity and asking *who are you* and *how do you really act?*

We would practice outdoors and the beginning of the practice was each person, on their own, walking in a circle. We would turn and turn and turn with each person's focus on their own circle's center and on the shape and caliber of their being as they turned. As we would turn, Danny would walk amongst us and chant, almost to himself, "change, change, change."

This book, as you know, is a naturalist's book. Nature teaches that, though we may want it to be otherwise, there is no panacea. Everything changes and we are bound to a universal law of relativity. What is offered here surely has some medicine for every person who reads it. But what and how it is taken, how much and when is up to each individual. We all have our own circles, our own centers, and the only thing we have really have a degree of control of is the shape and caliber of our beings as we turn.

The change is scary, yes, but the work and the result is more beauty and truth.

As we turn now, as a world, what will we change into?

How do we want to live?

I propose a truth to the congress of life: we are tired of consumerism. We are not happy because of it. We are tired of the strain of constant war. Our hearts are tired of the pain of working to feed our families and live a good life while knowing that the base values of our economy are violent and destructive. We are tired of this.

What if the job of humanity is not to defeat the demons? Not to conquer the unknown? What if it is to arrange the unknown in such a way that it makes a meaning that can orient us toward love and truth? To craft story.

Stories bend with the world to create meaning in the ephemeral tide. Humans are a story people. We live and die through story. We fight wars, we eat, we give birth, and we heal the heaviest wounds through our stories.

This entire book is made of shapes that have no meaning but the one's we have attributed to them. The story has all been crafted in your mind.

We, the human family, are the authors of story.

We are standing at the base of the great and devastating tidal wave of impermanence. And that wave is filled with beauty if we dare look. That wave teaches us who we are if we dare look.

We are individuals. We are animals. We are minds and bodies. We are mysteries. We are much more.

We are the Earth. The deepest taproot. No empire can break us. No fantasy can destroy us.

We are riding the tidal wave of change through the course of our entire story. In each of our short terms of being, we can enjoy the bigness of who we are. We are the blood on the sharp-shinned hawk's beak. We are the deep intelligence of the microbes around a beach pea's roots. We are a whole planet. And every single last one of us deserves the truth.

The truth.

We are the story. Authoring ever.

Pause now.

Listen.

Inside.

Do you feel a strange tingling like an entire cosmos in your heart? Do you feel the spaces between? All the places where you are breaking open.

The wonder that you don't own any of it.

You simply give it.

Pause now.

Wherever you are.

Listen.

Do you hear it?

The calling?

The wind... the bugs... the distant stars...

It is all You.

Index of Practices

Index of Passed On Stories

About the Author

Matthew Fogarty is a curious mammal living on the edge of the Salish Sea. He has been graced with many guides, counselors, mentors and coaches to whom he cannot possibly express enough gratitude. Matthew is a Washington State Certified Counselor. He has an M.A. in Transpersonal Psychology with a focus on ecopsychology from Naropa University and a B.A. in English and Nature Studies from Hampshire College. He has worked as a university instructor and a therapeutic behavioral health clinical associate for an Alaska-based wilderness therapy program. He has spent 20 years studying and teaching Chinese martial arts as a transformation of violence. Matthew invested 5 years apprenticing and coaching as a structural rehabilitation therapist, a body-based therapy focused on decompressing the skeleton and promoting courage, integrity, and pain-free strength. He is an active practitioner of Somatic Experiencing© trauma therapy. Matt co-created a long-term, outdoor youth mentoring program based on exploration, service, and connection. He is a graduate of the Kamana Naturalist Training program and is trained as a rite of passage guide with various organizations. He is a co-winner of Whatcom Dispute Resolution Center's Peacebuilder Award.

www.squareonecounsel.com

Made in the USA
Las Vegas, NV
17 May 2022

48994345R00167